Mastering Breadth Indicators: Your Essential Analysis Companion

Victoria Q. Hayes

Challenges are inevitable, but how you respond to them defines your character and resilience.

Engage with voice-activated assistants; they're simplifying tasks and offering hands-free device interactions.

Always have a clear business plan; it provides direction and clarity.

Every setback is an opportunity in disguise; approach it with curiosity and a growth mindset.

Introduction

This is your ultimate resource for understanding and utilizing market breadth indicators in technical analysis. Dive into the world of technical indicators and grasp the significance of breadth relationships to make informed decisions in the market.

In the initial sections, "Technical Analysis" and "Technical Indicators," you'll gain a foundational understanding of the role of technical analysis and how indicators play a pivotal role in market assessment. Explore a familiar breadth indicator and learn about the intricate dance of market breadth.

"Necessary Breadth Information" equips you with essential knowledge about breadth components and their significance in relation to price movements. Understand the advantages and disadvantages of using breadth indicators and familiarize yourself with the necessary terminology.

The heart of the guide, "Breadth Indicators," presents a comprehensive breakdown of various breadth indicators in a user-friendly format. Gain insights into the intricacies of advance-decline difference indicators, advance-decline ratio indicators, and new high-new low indicators. Understand up volume-down volume indicators and composite indicators that provide a holistic view of market breadth.

The McClellan Indicators receive special attention, with in-depth analysis and a look at "Common Only" A-D data. Explore the McClellan Oscillator and Summation Index, along with the concept of the neutral point. Discover how the McClellan Summation Index can provide valuable buy signals in the market.

This book empowers you to navigate the market with confidence, utilizing the wealth of information provided by breadth indicators. Whether you're a novice or seasoned investor, this guide serves as an indispensable reference to make sound decisions based on market breadth data. Master the art of interpreting market signals and gain an edge in your investment strategies with this comprehensive guide.

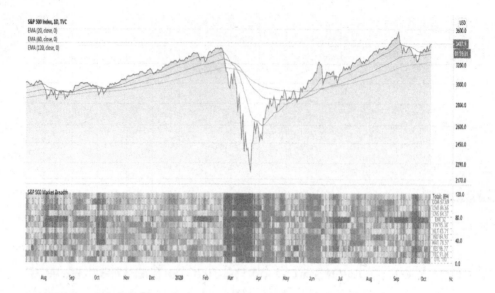

Contents

CH 1 - INTRODUCTION

"The noblest pleasure is the joy of understanding." Leonardo da Vinci

How can you even begin to predict or forecast the market if you are not using the correct tools to determine its present state? If you do not fully grasp the present state of the market, your prediction, whether real or anticipated, will be off by an amount equivalent to at least the error of your current analysis. And your error will be compounded based upon the timeframe of your prediction or forecast. Breadth analysis is like quantum mechanics, it does not predict a single definite result, instead it predicts a number of different possible outcomes, and tells us how likely each one will be. Breadth directly represents the market, no matter what the indices are doing. It is the footprint of the market and the best measure of the market's liquidity.

Market breadth indicators are those indicators that are sometimes referred to as broad market indicators. Probably the simplest way to think of them is to realize they generally do not refer to, or use information relating to an individual issue. Breadth will treat all stocks in an index equally. The stock with the largest capitalization and the smallest are both equal in breadth analysis. Most breadth analysis is total market related in that it deals with the complete market. A rising tide raises all ships is the more picturesque way to grasp its meaning.

Market breadth uses market data such as advancing and declining issues, new highs and new lows, up and down volume, etc. This is an area of market analysis that deals only with the stock market and does so in a generic way. It cannot be used on individual stocks, mutual funds, or futures. It is a broad approach to overall market analysis that helps investors and traders realize the underlying strength or weakness associated with a market move. The analysis normally is done on the New York market, the American stock exchange market, and the Nasdaq market, but can be applied to any exchange or index of securities for which breadth data is available.

Actually, breadth calculations can be accomplished on any sector of the market or industry group as long as you have a method of determining the components mentioned above. I'm quite certain that with the explosive use of computers for analysis, this is just around the corner, if not already being done in some places.

Technical Analysis

"I know of no way of judging the future but by the past." Patrick Henry

The subject of market breadth indicators falls squarely into the field of technical analysis. What is technical analysis? Books are filled with definitions and interpretations on technical analysis. A significant part of technical analysis is the art of studying the past, attempting to identify a pattern or event that seems to represent or reflect the market being studied, and then believing that it will work with some certainty in the foreseeable future.

My definition for technical analysis and my adherence to using it comes from a belief that everyone needs something to believe in or rely upon. I believe in technical analysis because of its close relationship to the supply and demand of the market. Fundamental analysis, which is by far a more popular method of analysis, is generally flawed in that it does not address the issue of 'when.' When should I buy or when should I sell? Researching the hundreds of different fundamental ratios is the full time job of thousands of securities analysts. However, think about this simple fact. Almost all fundamental ratios involve price. So why not analyze price? Most forms of technical analysis do just that.

Is technical analysis the same as market timing? Sometimes it is, sometimes it isn't. Market timing has received a bad rap, especially by those who believe it is a process by some who blindly follow some over-optimized mechanical system without utilizing money management or an asset commitment plan. In that regard, its bad rap is appropriate. The analysis of risk and reward is not market timing in the sense that many think of when using that often misused term. Determining when the market has too much risk is not market timing, but prudent and discretionary investing. Next time you hear a brokerage firm analyst mention that no one can time the market, or that technical analysis does not work, ask to see his record during the bear market of 2000 – 2002 or 2007 - 2008.

Another challenge to technical analysis is that of whether it is an art or a science. I cannot believe anyone would seriously ask this, and suspect the question comes almost totally from the non-scientific or the innumerate among us. I do believe that scientists, engineers, and mathematically-inclined investors migrate toward technical analysis over time because of its ability to look back in history and see how supply and demand played out. It is certainly a more analytical approach to market analysis.

Those who get excited and experience a warm feeling about the overused adjectives of quality, strong, healthy, etc. when wall street talks about investing in specific companies are surely the ones who think technical analysis is witchcraft. Years ago when I used to be entertained by watching Wall Street Week, and was humored by the fundamental analysts who would talk endlessly about how they liked to pick good quality companies and hold onto them. They then quickly point out the Ibbotson study that shows that equities have performed at about a 9% annual rate for the last one hundred years. Hogwash! While the study is true, it is totally irrelevant as one does not have a one-hundred-year investment horizon, and is therefore not applicable to humans. Most investors have a good fifteen to twenty-year period in which to make their serious investments. There were many, many fifteen to twenty year periods in the last one hundred years that resulted in negative returns. The most egregious example is if you had bought in 1929, you did not break even until 1954; twenty-five years later. And guess what, getting even is not what investing is all about.

A good detective will tell you that some of the least reliable information comes from eye witnesses. When people observe an event, it seems their background, education, and other influences unrelated to the observed event, color their perception of what occurred. Most will also be influenced by what they hear from others. This is also amplified by a number of individual studies done by behavior psychologists. In a nutshell, they all agree that groups of people will tend to amplify the consensus view rather than challenge it. A group's ability to focus on common knowledge and uncover anything new is commonplace. Plus, the fact that if someone in the group is acknowledged as an expert, their opinion can totally dominate the thinking for the group and can lead to what is known as the "herd" mentality. Talk radio is a perfect example of this.

One should remember that things are quite often not what they seem. It is absolutely amazing to me how much people believe that which is not true. Some believe water runs out of a bath tub faster as it gets toward the end. Assuming the tub's sides are straight, the pressure is constant, it only appears to drain faster because you observe it starting to swirl toward the end, something you could not observe when the tub was full. How many think that George Washington cut down a cherry tree? George Washington did not cut down a cherry tree. That was a story told so that adults could teach their children that it was bad to tell lies - even our founding father didn't tell lies. Parson Mason Locke Weems, the author who wrote about it, was trying to humanize Washington. Question: Did

Washington throw a silver dollar across the Potomac River? Hint: The Potomac River is almost a mile wide at Mount Vernon and silver dollars did not exist at that time. What about the Battle of Bunker Hill? It was fought at Breed's Hill in Charleston, Massachusetts. Here's one of the best: Dogs sweat through their tongues. Guess what? Dogs don't sweat. Their tongues have large salivary glands that keep them wet. Okay, one more! He drinks like a fish, but fish don't drink. Hopefully, you are getting my point. In the last few years the internet has been the source and exploitation of much hype and false information. How many times have you received an email from a friend (who probably did not originate it), and believed it to be true but did not bother to check it out, but forwarded it anyhow? You should start verifying them because many of them are a hoax. Believable misinformation flourishes.

I don't want to turn this into a science book, but I am adamant about correcting the proliferation of bad or incorrect information that exists in the financial markets and by showing you similar misconceptions that you may have believed before is the best way to get your attention. If you believed one or more of the above misconceptions, then how many market-related ones do you also believe?

Technical analysis will let you deal with reality and keep you from falling victim every time the evening news offers their expert opinion on why the markets did today what they did. As I write this the Indonesian earthquake tidal waves have killed thousands of people, but you cannot begin to know how many. Most news sources are stating guesses anywhere from 15,000 to well over 150,000. Many news sources cannot even keep the number consistent within their own articles. Do you think they can also tell you why the markets did what they did on a daily basis? Stick to technical analysis, it will increase your understanding of the markets, if only by the fact that you are uncovering information about market behavior.

Here are some comments on technical analysis that I read over 30 years ago in "The Commodities Futures Game" by Richard Teweles, and believe to be just as valid today. Almost all methods of technical analysis generate useful information, which if used for nothing more than uncovering and organizing facts about market behavior will increase the investor's understanding of the markets. The investor is made painfully aware that technical competence does not ensure competent investing. Speculators who lose money do so not always because of bad analysis, but because of the inability to transform their analysis into sound practice. Bridging the gap between analysis and action requires overcoming the threat of greed, hope, and fear.

Technical analysis is the art of analysis that will keep your emotions from being a part of your investment decision-making. While not fallible, it certainly gives you the tools to do so. It will also assist you in overcoming the human traits of ignorance and bliss. Ignorance is an intellectual state and appears to be chronic in many people as regards to the stock market. Bliss is an emotional state and it characterizes many investors as long as the market is going up. Deluded by emotions, one cannot begin to be successful in the investing arena without some means of controlling greed, fear, and hope. This is what technical analysis does.

Technical Indicators

"Those who cannot remember the past are condemned to repeat it."
George Santayanna

An indicator is defined by Webster as a pointer or directing device, an instrument for measuring or recording. What then is a technical indicator? Technical indicators are mathematical manipulations of data so that specific values or levels can reflect the market or security being indicated upon (analyzed). There are other types of market indicators that are commonly used, such as: economic time series, interest rates, etc. Stock market indicators utilize open, high, low, close, volume, and open interest which are the basic components of stock and futures data. Here, we will use market breadth indicators.

"He who does not know the supreme certainty of mathematics is wallowing in confusion." Leonardo da Vinci

I hope that the mention of mathematics doesn't scare anyone. You don't always have to understand mathematics to know that it will work. Most people believe that Leonardo da Vinci was a mathematician, when he was actually far from it. He had a close friendship with Luca Pacioli, who inspired Leonardo. Leonardo did, however, create a number of mathematical instruments and measuring devices, but his knowledge of mathematics was not exceptional; his friendship with one, whose mathematical knowledge was exception, was where the confusion may lie. One word of caution here, do not confuse mathematics with numerology.

A simple mathematical series of numbers can sometimes get misinterpreted (promoted) to be something magical. Personally, I see no value in the actual numbers that make up the Fibonacci series; a series developed by an Italian mathematician (Fibonacci) in the thirteenth century to help understand the propagation of rabbits. First I must say that I do value the ratio of the numbers that are expanded in a Fibonacci-like series (1,1,2,3,5,8,13,21,34,55,89,…). That ratio is 0.618 (and its reciprocal 1.618), often called the golden ratio because of its wide occurrence in nature. Here is a fact: the actual numbers in the Fibonacci series have little to do with the ratio. Any two numbers expanded in the same manner will produce the same 'golden' ratio. Here is a test: Try it with 2 and 19. Add them together, and then add the total to the previous number just like in the Fibonacci series (2+19=21, 19+21=40, 21+40=61, etc.). Expand this until you get to some four digit numbers so that the accuracy will be acceptable (2, 19, 21, 40, 61, 101, 162, 263, 425, 688, 1113, 1801, 2914, 4716, …).   The last two numbers in this sequence are the two numbers that I will use for this example: 2914 and 4716. Now divide the first number by the second number and you will get 0.618. This is exactly the same as with the one obtained using the Fibonacci series of numbers. So why did I pick 2 and 19 for this example? Hint: the second letter in the alphabet is B. Think about it. What is the nineteenth letter? And that is what numerology is all about. One last thing, the Fibonacci series also failed at understanding or predicting the propagation of rabbits. It is the ratio that is important, not the actual numbers in the series. So, when you hear someone say they are going to use a 34 day moving average because 34 is a Fibonacci number, you can immediately begin to doubt the rest of their analysis.

Most breadth indicators are at best, coincident indicators, and usually somewhat lagging. Any of the indicators that are smoothed with moving averages are certainly lagging. Lagging means that the indicator is only telling you what is happening after it has happened. Lagging is not a problem, once you realize that picking exact tops and bottoms in the market is better left to gamblers. The confirmation of lagging indicators, however, is very important. Some breadth indicators, especially some of the ratios, can offer leading indications based upon the identification and use of previous levels or thresholds that are consistent with similar market action. An oscillator that reached a threshold level, either positive or negative, with consistency relative to market tops and bottoms is such an indicator. Many breadth indicators work in this manner.

No indicator is right all of the time; fortunately, you don't have to be right all of the time. You just need to ensure that you do not hold onto losers and keep your emotions out of the game. Choose some good reliable indicators and stick with them. Learn how they respond during different market environments and master the interpretation of them. And remember, when your favorite indicator fails you, avoid thinking that this time is different, it probably is not.

Drawing Trendlines on Charts

Almost all references on supply and demand are directly tied to price. This involves the pricing of goods and services, as well as securities. It seems that some analysts have not understood this concept and draw trendlines all over a chart without any real understanding as to what it is they are trying to accomplish, unless, of course, it is to support (sic) their hypotheses.

Can you use support and resistance for oscillators, ratios, and accumulated values like you do with price-based issues? I believe this is carrying the supply and demand analysis a little too far, yet many analysts are doing it. Can an oscillator made up of internal breadth components have a support line or a resistance line? No, but it can reach certain levels on a consistent basis and if that is what is being represented, then so be it, but it is not support or resistance. Similarly, I see some who will draw trendlines across moving average peaks or troughs. This is irrelevant analysis and does not represent any type of support or resistance. Like most things, there are exceptions to all this. An analyst may point out that the 200 day moving average offers support for the issue being analyzed. This may well hold out to be true, only because of that particular moving average's popularity. It probably would not hold true if an average that is less familiar or a totally random average were picked, say 163 periods.

Also, and in fairness to these analysts, drawing trendlines on some indicators such as the advance decline line is not done to identify support and resistance, but to assist the analyst in identifying divergence with price. This example should put it in perspective. You cannot relate rates of change linearly. Sun City is 20 miles from Keith's home in Pratt. He drives 60 mph going to a meeting in Sun

City but coming home he drives 30 mph. What is his average speed for the time he is on the road? Going to Sun City took 1/3 of an hour. Coming home took 2/3 of an hour. So the total 40 miles took one hour. Therefore, the average speed is 40 mph. Many will believe it was 45 mph ((60 + 30) / 2). You cannot average rates of change like you can constants and linear relationships. Distance is rate multiplied by time (d=rt). We are dealing with the harmonic mean here and not average rates. This is one reason drawing trendlines on rates of change oscillators is not support and resistance identification.

A Familiar Breadth Indicator

Most investors are familiar with the long-running Friday night show, Wall Street Week, on Public Broadcasting hosted by Louis Rukeyser, who, every week would comment on his elves (his term for technical analysts) and the Wall Street Week Index. What you may not have known is that this index was a composite of ten indicators, three of which were breadth-based. Robert Nurock, long-time panelist and Chief Elf, created it. Robert Nurock was the editor of the Astute Investor, a technical newsletter for many years.

The Arms Index was one of the indicators in the Wall Street Week Index. A 10 day moving average was used with bullish signals given when it was about 1.2 and bearish when it was below 0.8. The advances minus the declines were used over a 10-day period and bullish signals were from the point where the index exceeds 1000 to a peak and down to a point 1000 below the peak. Bearish signals were just the opposite. The third breadth indicator used was the new highs compared to the new lows. For bullish signals an expansion of the 10-day average of new highs from less than 10 up to 10-day average of new lows. Similarly, bearish signals were an expansion of 10-day average of new lows from less than 10 until it exceeds the 10-day average of new highs.

Breadth Relationships

In the chapters on Breadth Indicators (Chapters 4-11), you will see these market components used in almost every conceivable method and mathematical combination, by themselves, or in combination with other breadth components. After they are mathematically arranged, they are then again smoothed, averaged, summed, and normalized.

There are some basic tenants that have been created over the years; each one has its place in analysis history and here we will not attempt to say which is better or worse. Here is a list of various advance decline relationships and the analyst(s) that is(are) credited with initially using them. Many times they were the first to write about them. A student of the market will recognize many of these names.

The primary breadth components for this example are: Advances = A, Declines = D, Unchanged = U. A component between | | means absolute value. For example, the absolute value of 3 is 3 and the absolute value of -3 is also 3.

Breadth Relationship	Analyst
$A - D$	McClellan, Miekka, Haurlan, Eakle, Fugler, Arms
$\lvert A - D \rvert$	Fosback, McGinley
A / D	Nicoski, Zweig, Arms
$(A - D) / (A + D)$	Swenlin, Miekka, McClellan, Tabell
$(A - D) / (A + D + U)$	Hughes
$\lvert A - D \rvert / (A + D + U)$	Fosback
$A / (A + D)$	Appel, Zweig
$A / (A + D + U)$	Schulz
$(A - D) / U$	Merrill
$\lvert A - D \rvert / U$	Bolton

Similar types of relationships can be made using new highs, new lows, up volume, and down volume, but the advance decline relationship is used the most.

In the Beginning …

Who was the first to use breadth for market analysis? And when?

General Leonard P. Ayers, of Cleveland Trust Company, is generally credited with being the first to count the advancing issues and declining issues. In 1926, he produced his first work, which he called "making the count of the market." However, twenty-five years earlier, Charles H. Dow, of Dow Theory fame, commented in his June 23, 1900 editorial in the Wall Street Journal about the number of advances and declines thusly, "Of these 174 stocks, 107 advanced, 47 declined, and 20 stood still." However, it is widely accepted that General Ayers and his associate, James F. Hughes popularized the concept that is widely used today.

My good friend George Schade, lawyer, researcher extraordinaire, and confidant has given me permission along with the Market Technician's Association (MTA) to reproduce an article George wrote in 2013. You can also view it on the MTA's library in Issue 67, page 46 of the Journal of Technical Analysis. The link is http://docs.mta.org/journal-ta/jota67_2013.pdf.

How the Advance-Decline Indicators Came About from Observation, Logic, and Perseverance by George A. Schade, Jr., CMT

Abstract

In September 1927, the Cleveland Trust Company published the first Advance-Decline Line originated by Leonard P. Ayres and his assistant James F. Hughes. For the next three decades, Hughes applied and expanded the count of the market while adding the

Advance-Decline Ratio to the group of market breadth indicators. After 1958, Richard Russell popularized the innovative work of Ayres and Hughes. Today, these indicators have wide following.

I. Introduction

In September 1927, the following chart appeared on the last page of the Cleveland Trust Company's

Business Bulletin:

Figure 1 – The First Published Advance-Decline Line, 1927

STOCK PRICE CHANGES, SHARES TRADED, AND ISSUES DEALT IN, DAILY IN 1927

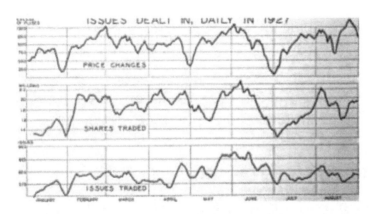

The Bulletin explained that the line in the top section "does not show the average prices of a group of stocks, but rather for each day the preponderance of advances over declines, or of declines over advances, among all the issues dealt in during that market session. It shows the changing daily trend of the market as a whole." (Business Bulletin, 1927) The chart showed the trend between January and August 1927. The other two lines, correctly named, were a "six-day centered moving average" of the number of shares and issues traded. (Business Bulletin, 1927)

The chart was the first depiction of an advance-decline line. The writer was Leonard Porter Ayres who is correctly credited with originating the Advance-Decline Line indicator. Twenty-four years later, his assistant James F. Hughes recalled "the first count of the market" which Ayres had compiled and shown him "one morning in January 1926," on a sheet of paper from a yellow pad. Hughes became Ayres' assistant in 1923.

When Ayres showed Hughes the "first count of the market" Hughes had seen, Ayres told him, "I think this will make an interesting stock market statistic." (Hughes, 1951) The phrase "count of the market" has been attributed to Ayres, but Hughes wrote that the term was what Hughes called the "routine daily reporting" of advances, declines, and unchanged. (Hughes, 1951)

This is the story of how the foremost statistician of his time conceived a technical concept which his assistant applied and expanded building the foundation of today's advance-decline indicators, a story that lasted nearly forty years. Seventy-five years later, advance-decline indicators are relied upon by technicians everywhere.

II. Leonard Porter Ayres (1879-1946)

Ayres has been referred to as Colonel Ayres, and he was a United States Army Colonel in 1920 when he began working at the Cleveland Trust Company. However, in 1940 he was recalled to active duty with the rank of Brigadier General. Thereafter, the press referred to him as General Ayres.

Figure 2 – Leonard Porter Ayres

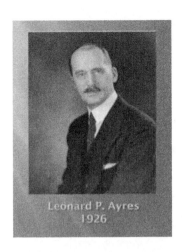
Leonard P. Ayres
1926

Portrait is by permission of www.asapresidentialpapers.info hosted by National Opinion Research Center, University of Chicago, for the American Statistical Association (www.amstat.org).

Ayres was born in Niantic, Connecticut, on September 15, 1879.2 He attended public schools in Newton, Massachusetts, and in 1902 graduated from Boston University. He taught English in Puerto Rico; in 1906 he became the superintendent of the island's school system. In 1910, Ayres received a Ph.D. degree from Boston University.

Statistical analysis was his professional career. Between 1908, when he was appointed Director of the Department of Education and Statistics at the Russell Sage Foundation, and 1917, he applied statistical methods to educational practices. Ayres wrote numerous monographs documenting the application of statistics to learning programs.

As a preview of his economic statistical career, in 1915, Ayres published an innovative scale for measuring ability in spelling. The scale (republished in 1985) has been called "one of the most elegant and carefully standardized tests available in the domain of literacy."(www.arlingtoncemetery.net)

During World War I, Lieutenant and then Major Ayres organized the military's Division of Statistics. He was the chief statistical officer of the American commission to negotiate peace.

Between 1940 and 1942, Ayres served in the United States Army. He was awarded the Distinguished Service Medal, the highest non-valorous military decoration given for exceptionally meritorious service to the Nation.

After suffering a heart attack he died at home on October 29, 1946. Announcing his passing away, The New York Times remembered that: He was one of the few economists who made persistently pessimistic predictions on the eve of the 1929 crash. He declined to agree that the crash was only a sixty-day period of 'business correction' and insisted it was one of the major depressions in American history. (Leonard Ayres, 67, Economist is Dead, 1946)

The American Statistical Association, of which Ayres was president in 1926, wrote in memorial appreciation: Few have nurtured so well the art of statistics....He was always seeking new methods – new ways of manipulating figures - new chart forms....He was never lost, however, in his statistical

techniques nor was he overly impressed by them. He made them tools to squeeze the meaning out of the data. He will be remembered as a master of the presentation of statistics. But his mastery was based on patient analysis and reflection which reduced problems to their simplest elements. (Burgess, 1947)

A.   The Business Bulletin

In 1920, Ayres began working at the Cleveland Trust Company (established in 1894; shown in Figure 3) where he was a vice president, economist, and member of the executive committee. For 25 years, he edited and almost entirely wrote the trust company's Business Bulletin which became a highly regarded four-page publication released on the 15th of every month. Today, KeyCorp is the successor to the Cleveland Trust Company.

Figure 3 – The Cleveland Trust Company

In 1920 and 1921, the Bulletin covered the automobile, pig iron, and coal industries as well as building construction, employment, and agriculture. Thereafter, Ayres began analyzing interest rates, bond yields, dividend stocks, and business cycles (a subject in which his work has been influential). Stock market movements and volume began garnering attention. The bull market that had begun in August 1921 likely prompted the increasing analysis of stock market statistics.

In November 1922, the Bulletin reported the number of stocks, out of the 678 issues traded on the New York Stock Exchange ("NYSE") that had reached their highest and lowest prices in each month of that year through October. Ayres concluded that while stock prices tend to move in one direction, all stocks do not move together. The stock market is selective as the market averages and some stock prices diverge in trend.

In January 1924, he wrote that while the stock market in 1923 had risen rapidly until March, fallen to July, recovered to September, fallen to November, and then risen until the end of the year "many individual stocks did not follow this general trend." (Business

Bulletin, Jan. 15, 1924) Figure 4 recreates the table published in the Bulletin. Figure 4 shows that among the 629 NYSE issues tabulated, 203 reached their highest prices in the first quarter and their lowest prices in the fourth quarter. In the fourth quarter, 26 stocks made their highs and also their lows for the year.

Figure 4 – Stocks Making Their Highs and Lows, Quarterly, 1923

1923		Stocks making their lows in each quarter of the year			
		1st	2nd	3rd	4th
Stocks reaching high in each quarter	1st	19	62	143	203
	2nd	13	19	24	29
	3rd	3	2	8	7
	4th	24	18	29	26

B. The Advance-Decline Line

From studying highs and lows, it is a short step to tabulating advances and declines to see if the divergence of market averages and stock prices is clearer. In January 1926, Ayres showed Hughes the first "count of the market." Ayres' comments published in September 1926, show that both men had been tabulating the daily advancing, declining, and unchanged stocks: On the first of September the stock market had been open for trading in securities 200 days this year. On 105 of these days a majority of the stocks that were dealt in, and had any net change in market quotation, advanced in price; on the remaining 95 days a majority of them declined. Neither the days of advance nor those of decline came in long consecutive sequences. (Business Bulletin, Sept. 15, 1924)

The Bulletin does not indicate why Ayres and Hughes were studying these statistics. In 1951, Hughes explained that the "primary purpose was to discover a technical method that would time more accurately major turning points in the stock market after various fundamental relationships had indicated that a turn in the major trend was a virtual certainty within a few months." (Hughes, 1951) Ayres was interested in timing major turning points.

Ayres studied economic relationships in business activity. He found that the relationships can show that a major turning point in the stock market is ahead, but cannot time when the reversal will occur. According to Hughes (1951): After a year or so of trying to combine various economic series so that they would exactly indicate months of major highs and lows in the stock market, General Ayres reluctantly conceded that this was expecting too much. He finally decided that economic relationships were of primary importance in indicating the probability that the market was approaching a major turning point but that it was more logical to use technical evidence based on the action of the market itself to time more closely actual reversals in major trends of stock prices.

Current interest rates, which Ayres considered to be "the dominant factor in determining the course of stock [and bond] prices," were included in the analysis, but although extremely helpful, the rates were not fully satisfactory for timing major turning points. (Hughes, 1951).

Ayres and Hughes considered several popular technical methods, but those told that a turning point had occurred. According to Hughes, "what we wanted was something that told us a turning point was imminent at a time when our fundamental relationships told us that it was going to be a major turning point." (Hughes,1951) These were the objectives that prompted studying the daily advances, declines, and unchanged statistics.

In the chart published in September 1927, Ayres and Hughes observed that the three lines showed a tendency toward a similar direction of movement, but the agreement was not close. They concluded that "it does not appear that there exists a sufficiently close agreement to be of much use in judging the probable future course of the market." (Business Bulletin, Sept. 15, 1924) It is unknown if this conclusion paused their further studies of the count of the market.

It does not appear that the Bulletin, at least through 1937, published a subsequent chart of an advance- decline indicator. In 1938, the Cowles Commission compiled a list of all stock market indexes published from 1871 through 1937. The Commission reported that the Cleveland Trust Company had in September 1927, published an index of "Daily, Jan.-Aug., 1927, all issues traded on [the] New York Stock Exchange, excess of number of stocks advancing over those declining." (Cowles, 1938) No other similar indexes published by the Cleveland Trust Company were described. This absence indicates that the Business Bulletin through 1937 did not publish further charts of an advance-decline indicator.

However, in October 1929, the Bulletin published a chart that may be the first description of a cumulation of advances and declines. The chart shows the percentage of stocks traded on the NYSE that sold higher or lower at the end than at the beginning of the month. The chart shows that in "five of the nine months the advancing stock issues have been more numerous than the declining ones, while in the remaining four months of February, March, May, and September the declining issues have outnumbered the advancing ones," and "despite the fact that more issues have advanced than have declined in a majority of the months the total of all the percentages of advance is 333, while the sum of the declines is 434." (Business Bulletin, Oct. 15, 1929)

The chart's information is redesigned and recreated in Figure 5 as follows.

Figure 5 – Percent of Stocks Traded that Moved Up or Down Each Month January to September 1929

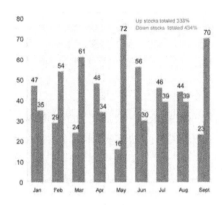

Adding the percentages of advances and declines revealed a deterioration that the individual percentages did not show. During most of 1929 a "creeping bear market" had been hidden by certain stocks advancing so much they carried the stock market averages up to new levels prior to the October Crash. In spite of new high records for volume and the market averages (the Dow Industrials closed at its then highest of 381.17 on September 3, 1929), a bear market had been in progress.

I have not found documents showing that in those early years Ayres and Hughes either cumulated advances and declines or used ratios. The earliest reference to a cumulative advance-decline line I have found is 1948. (Mindell, 1948) Ratios came later as a result of Hughes' innovation. They used daily data. Their analysis covered the broad market traded on the NYSE.

C. Charles H. Dow (1851-1902)

Dow Theory scholar late Professor George W. Bishop, Jr. noted that Charles H. Dow penned a Wall Street Journal editorial on January 23, 1900, in which Dow observed, "Take last week for instance: There were dealings in 174 stocks…. Of these 174 stocks, 107 advanced, 47 declined, and 20 stood still." (Bishop, 1964)

Bishop did not give any other reference Dow made to advances, declines, and unchanged. Bishop was noting that Dow discussed stock market "techniques credited to others at a much later date." He cautioned that by quoting from this editorial "we do not mean to imply that General Ayres did not arrive at the 'count of the market' independently." (Bishop, 1964)

My opinion is Dow made a commenter's observation but cannot be credited with originating the advance and decline indicators.

III. James F. Hughes

Little is known about the early years of James F. Hughes, Ayres' creative and diligent assistant who achieved his own fame. According to financial analyst A. Hamilton Bolton, writing in 1960, Hughes was one of the market technicians who "left an indelible mark on Wall Street in the present generation." (Prechter,1994)

In 1923, Hughes became Ayres's assistant at the Cleveland Trust Company. By 1930, he was with the Wall Street firm of Otis & Company. By April 1934, he was an analyst for Charles D. Barney and Company which later became Smith Barney & Company. It appears Hughes remained there until March 1946, when The New York Times announced that Hughes was a market analyst and economist with Auchincloss, Parker & Redpath. (Financial Notes, 1946)

In 1940-41, Hughes served as Vice President of the New York Society of Security Analysts. He wrote at least three articles for The Analysts Journal, predecessor of the Financial Analysts Journal. Hughes cited Ayres's research in the three articles. Between January 15, 1950, and June 15, 1953, Hughes wrote the "Stock Market Outlook" column for Forbes magazine.

A. American Statistical Association

The American Statistical Association ("ASA") is the professional organization for statisticians and related professionals. ASA is the second oldest professional group in the United States having been founded in Boston in 1839. Florence Nightingale, Alexander Graham Bell, and Andrew Carnegie were members.

Ayres and Hughes shared a connection to the ASA. Ayres served as the ASA's 21st President. Hughes was a member at least from 1930 to 1936, and he spoke at several of the famed ASA dinner meetings held in New York City. The meetings were highly regarded educational events presenting the leading business and financial people.

Hughes spoke at the following meetings:

May 9, 1929

April 24, 1934 - The other two speakers were Harold M. Gartley and Robert W. Schabacker. The summary shows Hughes stated that "the best method of forecasting [stock market] movements is to use indications from the market itself." (American Statistical Association, 1934)

January 26, 1937 - Two of the other speakers were Gartley and Charles J. Collins of Elliott

Wave fame. Five hundred people attended.

December 30, 1949.

Figure 6 – The Giants of Technical Analysis at Work

B. The Advance-Decline Ratio

Hughes developed the Advance-Decline Ratio which is the difference between advances and declines divided by total issues traded. After seeing Ayres' count of the market in January 1926, Hughes wrote that "one of the first things I thought about this new 'statistic' was that the total number of issues traded would provide an exact measurement each day of the breadth of trading on the NYSE." (Hughes, 1951) The number of daily total issues traded is the denominator of Hughes's indicator.

Hughes's non-cumulative advance-decline ratio had its beginnings in what Hughes termed the "Climax- Breadth Method of Recognizing Market Turning Points." His interest in temporary selling climaxes, spurred by the February-March 1926 stock market break, led to his search for an indicator that could time a selling climax. Hughes was doing this research prior to 1948.

A selling climax is a burst of liquidation when investors frantically sell their holdings. Hughes noted that a selling climax was the result of an abnormally large concentration of declines in stocks for several days prior to a sharp rebound. The question became what "technical developments" could be considered to be abnormal in the action of a breadth index or in the relation of breadth to a market price index. Hughes (1951) observed that: After several years it became obvious that one important abnormal development was the failure of the breadth index and the industrial average to keep in close alignment. Fundamentally they had so much in common that it was highly abnormal for them to show any protracted divergence in trend.

Hughes noted that the abnormality of an important divergence between breadth and price resulted in a reversal of the market trend that had produced the divergence. Ayres had observed that in a selective stock market, the prevailing current of prices did not carry all stocks; some diverged. Hughes concluded that an important divergence between breadth and price was abnormal and led to a major trend reversal.

In a 1959 interview with Burton Crane, a leading financial writer for The New York Times, Hughes explained why an important divergence between the breadth index and the market averages warns of a reversal. (Crane,1959) There are many stocks on the NYSE whose prices are influenced by interest rates. As rates rise, these stocks tend to fall while the more volatile growth stocks that populate market averages continue to soar. A trend reversal corrects this abnormality.

While at Auchincloss, Parker & Redpath, Hughes edited a market letter based on the Advance-Decline Ratio. Hughes cautioned that these concepts are not easy to grasp. Referring to the climax-breadth method, he wrote, "Knowing that it took me from 1926 to 1949 to acquire confidence in this technical method, I am not amazed that people do not understand it at first sight." (Hughes, 1952)

IV. Richard Russell

In 1977, noted Dow Theory exponent Richard Russell wrote that: The Advance-Decline Ratio was conceived by James Hughes of NYC working jointly with Colonel Leonard Ayres of the Cleveland Trust Co. They did much of their original work back in the 1920's and before. During the 1950's and 60's Hughes wrote a market letter (based on A-D Ratio action) at Auchincloss, Parker, Redpath. I used to read this report religiously, and on occasion I would talk to Hughes about some point or other that I did not understand. As I got to know more about the A-D Ratio (with Hughes' help), I introduced it in Dow Theory Letters.

It seems hard to believe now, but in the early 1960's the A-D Ratio was relatively unknown on Wall Street. In the introduction to the chart books, I termed the A-D Ratio 'the single most valuable aid to technical analysis,' after (of course) the Averages themselves. I still hold that opinion.

As the A-D Ratio became more familiar to Wall Streeters, variations and sundry sophisticated formulas were introduced. Some of these were excellent, most were not. Hughes himself insisted that only the daily A-D line was significant, and he had little use for the combined weekly and even monthly A-D Ratio computations. I tend to agree with him….

Hughes always used the A-D Ratio in conjunction with the Dow Industrial Average, observing whether the movements of the two were progressing in harmony or whether divergences were occurring. History demonstrates that the Dow and the A-D tend to move in harmony, and where divergences (dis-harmony occurs), the market will usually erase the entire movement which caused the dis-harmony." (Russell, 1977; Emphases in original)

Russell had been studying the relationship - "a critical one" - between the Dow Industrials ("DJIA") and the Advance-Decline Ratio for over twenty years by himself and "with the help of James Hughes." According to Russell, it "was Hughes who first called my attention to the fact that extended periods in which the Dow makes new highs, unconfirmed by new highs in the A-D ratio, lead to trouble. This is not always true, but it is true in the great majority of cases." (Russell, 1976; Emphasis in original.)

Since the mid-1960s, Russell has published a chart book of the DJIA and Advance-Decline Ratio which are shown back to 1931. He wanted "to provide market students with an overall view and feel for this valuable indicator." (Russell, 1977)

V. Conclusion

Russell took the work of Ayres and Hughes to the front stage. Russell is the closing actor in this wonderful story.

Leonard P. Ayres and James F. Hughes originated the Advance-Decline Line and published its first chart in September 1927. Ayres had noted that the stock market is selective as market averages can trend in one direction while the movement of some stocks will diverge. Not all stocks move together.

This observation led to the innovation that a technical indicator based on advances, declines, and unchanged could more accurately time major turning points. Economic relationships in business activities can tell us a reversal is ahead, but the Advance-Decline Line can tell us when the reversal will occur.

For the next three decades, Hughes continuously applied and expanded the use of advances, declines, and unchanged while developing the Advance-Decline Ratio. Hughes believed that a breadth and price index have so much in common that it is highly abnormal for them to show a protracted divergence in trend. An important divergence between breadth and price results in a reversal of the market trend that created the abnormal divergence.

These are the concepts underpinning the Advance-Decline Line and Advance-Decline Ratio that Ayres and Hughes originated. Derived from statistics of market action, with their logic grounded on observations of market behavior, these indicators continue to excel.

References

American Statistical Association, 1934, Technical Methods of Forecasting Stock Prices, Journal of the

American Statistical Association, vol. 29, 187:325.

Bishop, Jr., George W., 1964, Who Was the First American Financial Analyst?, Financial Analysts Journal, vol. 20, 2:28. Dow's editorial was published in The Wall Street Journal, Jan. 23, 1900, vol. 11, 16: 1.

Burgess, W. Randolph, 1947, Leonard P. Ayres: An Appreciation, Journal of the American Statistical

Association, vol. 42, 237: 128.

Business Bulletin, Jan. 15, 1924. Cleveland Trust Co.

Business Bulletin, Sept. 15, 1924. Cleveland Trust Co.

Business Bulletin, Sept. 15, 1927. Cleveland Trust Co.

Business Bulletin, Oct. 15, 1929. Cleveland Trust Co.

Colby, Robert W., 2003, The Encyclopedia of Technical Market Indicators Second Edition. New York: McGraw-Hill.

Cowles 3rd, Alfred and Associates, 1938, Common-Stock Indexes, 1871-1937. Bloomington, IN: Principia Press, Inc., p. 439.

Crane, Burton, Stock Indicator Shows No Danger, The New York Times digital archives, Mar. 15, 1959.

Dickson, Richard A. and Tracy L. Knudsen, 2012, Mastering Market Timing. Saddle River, NJ: FT Press.

Financial Notes, The New York Times digital archives, Mar. 14, 1946.

Gartley, Harold M., 1935 (1st ed.) repub. 1981, Profits in the Stock Market. Pomeroy, WA: Lambert-Gann Pub. Co.

Hughes, James F., 1951, The Birth of the Climax-Breadth Method, The Analysts Journal (today Financial Analysts Journal), vol. 7, 3 (3rd Qtr).

Hughes, James F., Mar. 1, 1952, Stock Market Outlook, Forbes Magazine, p. 34.

Leonard Ayres, 67, Economist, is Dead, The New York Times digital archives, Oct. 30, 1946.

Mindell, Joseph, 1948, The Stock Market Basic Guide for Investors. New York: B. C. Forbes & Sons Pub. Co.

Morris, Gregory L., 2006, The Complete Guide to Market Breadth Indicators. New York: McGraw-Hill.

Prechter, Jr., Robert R. ed., 1994, The Complete Elliott Wave Writings of A. Hamilton Bolton. GA: New Classics Library, p. 117.

Russell, Richard, Dow Theory Letters, Letter 668, June 30, 1976, p. 2.

Russell, Richard, Dow Theory Letters, Letter 686, Jan. 14, 1977, p. 2. I have not found documents showing that Ayres or Hughes worked on market breadth before 1920, but it is improbable.

The Encyclopedia of Cleveland History. http://ech.cwru.edu (visited on Nov. 6, 2011).

www.arlingtoncemetery.net (visited on Nov. 6, 2011).

George A. Schade, Jr., CMT, has extensively researched the history of technical indicators and written about their origins and development. He has sought to answer long standing questions of attribution and continuity. Before his retirement, he was a trial court judicial officer.

The Breadth Dance

Here is an attempt (possibly lame) to help you understand the longer term bullish and bearish moves in the market and how the various breadth components play their part. And yes, I do not dance well.

The big dance is about to begin (bullish up move). Some of those that showed up are the advances, the declines, the unchanged, the new highs, new lows, and the ever present volume twins (up and down). The dance partners are always the volume pair. As the music begins to play there are only a few dancers on the floor – mainly the advances and primarily with the up volume. The number of dancers is good but more show up as the evening continues. As the evening gets underway more and more advances start to dance, and almost always with the up volume. The declines, kind of a nerdy group, only dance at certain times, usually only when it is an unpopular song (short corrections).

As the evening moves on, a few of the new highs start to dance. They did not dance earlier because there have not been too many dances of late. The usual small group of the unchanged are dancing but most are without dates and just watch from the side. As the night continues the advances, who have been dancing most of the night, begin to sit out a dance here and there. They are worn out.

Because of that, the unchanged are starting to dance more while the declines still are not doing much dancing.

With the beginning of the last music set (topping action in the market), the sound is high, everyone is at the dance. The advances have been totally worn out and only dance now and then when a really popular song is played (short up moves). The unchanged are doing a lot of dancing even though there just aren't that many of them, and the declines, realizing the night is coming to an end, begin to dance more. In fact, as the last few songs are played, the declines get a second wind and are doing most of the dancing. Most of the advances have gone home with the new highs. The new lows are still on the sidelines, but some of the declines are taking a second look at them. As the last couple of songs are played, the only ones dancing are the declines and the new lows, both of whom are dancing with the down volume; in fact, some of the unchanged are also dancing with the new lows. The music stops and the dance is over. On the way home (established down move) the declines do most of the driving, initially by themselves, then more and more with the down volumes, and as they get closer to home (market bottom), the declines are accompanied by the new lows. As they all approach home, the declines and the down volume are almost the only ones who are not there yet. They talk about the next dance.

The three charts below show the period from early 1982 to the summer of 1984. This was a period where a bearish market was followed by the beginning of a big bull market (August, 1982), and then by a slow rolling top formation into mid-1984. You can follow along with the breadth dance and verify the information on the next three charts. The raw breadth data is the lighter of the two lines. The darker line is a 10-day exponential average of the raw data. Chart 1-1 shows the advances, declines, and unchanged, all as a percentage of the total issues.

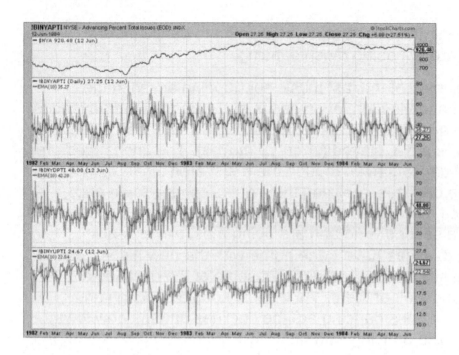

Chart 1-1

Chart 1-2 shows the new highs and new lows as a percentage of total issues.

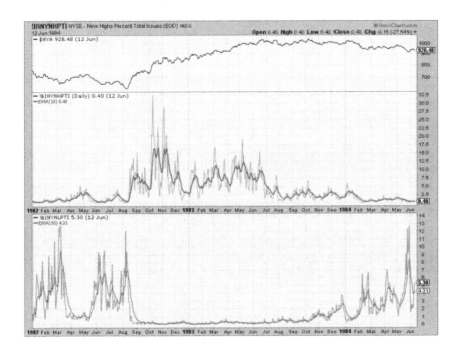

Chart 1-2

Chart 1-3 shows the up volume and the down volume as a percentage of total volume.

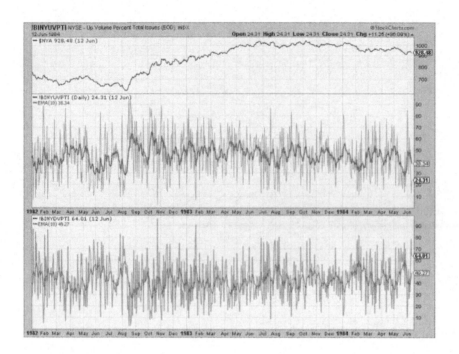

Chart 1-3

References:

Bramly, Serge. <u>Leonardo</u>, <u>the Artist and the Man</u>. New York: Penguin Books, 1994.

"Understanding breadth gives market insight that can't be obtained any other way. Breadth works. You need to understand it and use it. From the many in this book choose a few indicators that are in sync with your portfolio objectives and enjoy a lasting relationship with them as they help you through the market's many ups and downs."

Sherman McClellan

Publisher, McClellan Financial Publications, Inc.

CH 2 - NECESSARY BREADTH INFORMATION

In this chapter a lot of basic information will be provided to assist you in understanding the remainder of this book. There are definitions, mathematical formulae, explanations of anomalies, indicator formulae, historical events that affect the data, differing methods of calculation, and a host of other important information normally found in an appendix. It is of such importance to understand this material that it belongs prior to the discussion of breadth indicators.

Breadth Components

Breadth components are readily available from newspapers, online sources, etc. and consist of daily and weekly statistics. They are: Advances, Declines, Unchanged, Total Issues, Up Volume, Down Volume, Total Volume (V), New Highs, and New Lows.

From one day to the next, any issue can advance in price, decline in price, or remain unchanged. Also any issue can make a new high or a new low. Here are more specific definitions:

Advancing Issues or Advances (A) – Stocks that have increased in price from one day to the next, even if only by one cent, are considered as advancing issues or advances.

Declining Issues or Declines (D) – Stocks that have decreased in price from one day to the next are considered declining issues or declines.

Unchanged Issues or Unchanged (U) – Stocks that do not change in price from one day to the next are considered unchanged issues or unchanged.

Note: Prior to July, 1997, stock prices were measured in eighths of a point, or about 12.5 cents as the minimum trading unit. In July, 1997 the NYSE went from using eighths to sixteenths. This made the minimum trading unit about 6.25 cents. On January 2, 2002 they went to a decimalization pricing that made the minimum trading price equal to one cent (a penny). This is dealt with in more detail in the unchanged issues section.

Total Issues (TI) – This is the total of all issues available for trading on a particular exchange. If you added the advances, declines, and unchanged issues together it would equal the total issues.

Advancing Volume or Up Volume (UV) – This is the volume traded on a day for each of the stocks that are advancing issues. It is the total volume of all the advances.

Declining Volume or Down Volume (DV) – This is the total volume for all the declines for a particular day.

Total Volume (V) – This is the total volume of all trading for a particular day. Total volume is the sum of Up Volume, Down Volume, and Unchanged Volume. To find Unchanged Volume subtract the sum of Up Volume and Down Volume from the Total Volume. Total volume is not generally considered a breadth component, but is many times used in a ratio with the up or down volume to alleviate the increase in trading activity over long periods of time.

New High (H) – Whenever a stock's price reaches a new high price for the last 52 weeks it is termed a new high.

New Low (L) – Whenever a stock's price reaches a new low price for the last 52 weeks it is termed a new low.

Note: The NYSE new highs and new lows are now computed on a fixed 52 week moving time window starting on January 1, 1978.

Before that, the new highs and new lows were computed on a variable time window of anywhere from two and a half months to 14 and a half months. This rendered the new high new low data prior to 1978 almost useless, and certainly confusing to use.

Breadth versus Price

Breadth does not consider the amount or magnitude of price change. It also does not consider the number of shares traded (volume). And it does not consider the shares outstanding for individual stocks. Most stock market indices, such as the New York Stock Exchange Composite Index, the Nasdaq Composite Index, S&P 500 Index, the Nasdaq 100, etc. weigh each stock based upon its price and number of outstanding shares. This makes their contribution to the index based upon their value and are sometimes called market-value weighted indices or capitalization weighted indices. Because of this (at this writing), Microsoft, Qualcomm, Intel, Cisco, eBay, Nextel, Dell, Amgen, Comcast, and Oracle account for over 40% of the Nasdaq 100 Index and its ETF, QQQQ. Ten percent of the components account for 40% of the price movement of the index. This can lead to an incorrect analysis of the markets, especially if some of these large cap stocks experience price moving events. Many times the reference to the large caps issues is that of the generals, while the small caps are referred to as the soldiers. As you will find out, the generals are not always the leaders.

Breadth treats each stock the same. An advance of one cent in Microsoft is equally represented in breadth analysis as the advance of thirty cents of the smallest, least capitalized stock. Breadth is truly the best way to accurately measure the liquidity of the market.

The Difference between Daily and Weekly Breadth Data.

You just cannot add up daily breadth data for the week to get the weekly data. Here is a scenario that will explain why.

Stock: XYZ Corp.	Day	Price	Daily A – D	Weekly A - D
	Friday	12.00		
	Monday	13.00	+1	
	Tuesday	14.00	+1	
	Wednesday	15.00	+1	
	Thursday	16.00	+1	
	Friday	11.00	-1	-1
Total			+3	-1

Here's the narrative: An advance or decline for the week should be based upon its price change from the previous Friday close to the close of the current week. It has absolutely nothing to do with the daily data. Take a single stock; its previous Friday close price was $12.00. On Monday it was up $1.00 to $13.00. It went up a dollar each day for the first four days of the week and closed on Thursday at $16.00. However, on Friday it dropped $5.00 to $11.00. For the week it was down $1.00, which would be one decline for the week. However, on a daily basis, it accounted for four advances and one decline, or a net three advances.

John McGinley, past editor of Technical Trends, and sidekick of Arthur Merrill's, sent this note: "I strongly believe that in creating weekly figures for the advance declines, one does not use the published weekly data for they disguise and hide what really went on during the week. For instance, imagine a week with 1500 net advances one day and the other four days even. The weekly data would hide the devastation which occurred that dramatic day."

Advantages and Disadvantages of using Breadth

Breadth data seems to not be consistent among the data providers. If you think about it, if a stock is up it is an advance for the day, so why is there a disparity? Some data services will not include all stocks on the exchange. They will eliminate preferred issues, warrants, rights, etc. This is fine as long as they tell you that is what they are doing.

In the last few years, the number of interest sensitive issues on the New York Stock Exchange has increased so that they account for more than half of all the issues. These issues are preferred stocks, closed-end bond funds, electric utility stocks, to mention a few.

Many analysts such as Sherman and Tom McClellan, Carl Swenlin, and Larry McMillan use common stocks only breadth indicators. Richard Russell refers to it as an operating company only index. Using stocks that have listed options available is another good way to avoid the interest sensitive issues, since most stocks that have listed options are common stocks.

Indicators and Terminology You Should Be Familiar With

There are basically four different indicator types: differences, ratios, percentage, and cumulative. Differences are most common and should be adjusted for time independent scaling. As the number of issues increase over time, the scaling will get expanded and thresholds that worked in the past will need to be adjusted. One way to do this is to normalize the indicator so the scaling is always between zero and one hundred.

Absolute Value – In mathematical script this is denoted with | | around the value in which you want to have its absolute value. Absolute value calculations ignore the sign (positive or negative) of the number. In regard to breadth data, absolute value ignores market direction and only deals with market activity. The absolute value of +3 is 3, and the absolute value of -3 is also 3.

umulated / Summed ($\sum$) (also see cumulative below) - This is the term used to add up a series of numbers. For example, the advance decline line is an accumulation of the difference between the advances and the declines. That difference is summed with each new day's difference added to the previous value. Also used with the term cumulate. In many formulae in this book it is shown either as Previous Value + Today's Value or $\sum$.

Arithmetic / Simple Moving Averages – To take an average of just about anything numerical, you add up the numbers and divide by the number of items. For example, if you have 4 + 6 + 2, the sum is 12, and the average is 12 / 3 = 4. A moving average does exactly this but as a new number is added, the oldest number is removed. In the example above, let's say that 8 was the new number, so the sequence would be 6 + 2 + 8. The first 4 was removed because we are averaging only 3 numbers (3 period moving average). In this case the new average would be 16 / 3 = 5.33. So by adding an 8 and removing a 4, we increased the average by 1.33 in this example. For those so inclined: 8 – 4 = 4, and 4 / 3 = 1.33.

In technical analysis the simple or arithmetic average is used extensively. One thing that you should keep in mind, is that with the simple average each component is weighted exactly the same. This tends to make the simple average stale if using it for large amounts of data. For example, the popular 200-day average means that the price 200 days ago is carrying the same weight, or having the same effect on the average as the most recent price. It, therefore, is also much slower to change direction.

Cumulative - Cumulative indicators can be differences, ratios, or percentage. You are adding the daily results to the previous total. The advance decline line is a good example of a cumulative indicator. It is sometimes referred to as accumulate or summed.

Detrend – a term to denote when you subtract the price from a moving average of the price. This will amplify the price relative to its smoothed value (moving average). To visualize this, pretend you had the ability to take both ends of the moving average line and pull it taut so that the price line falls into its same relative position to the now straight moving average line. Doing this allows you to see cycles of a length greater than that of the number of periods used in the moving average.

Divergence – this is when an indicator and price do not confirm each other. At market tops, many times the price will continue to make new highs, while an indicator will reverse and not make a new high. This is a negative divergence.

Exponential Moving Averages – This method of averaging was developed by scientists, such as Pete Haurlan, in an attempt to assist and improve the tracking of missile guidance systems. More weight is given to the most recent data and it is therefore much faster to change direction. It is sometimes represented as a percentage (trend %) instead of by the more familiar periods. Here is a formula that will help you convert between the two:

$K = 2 / (N + 1)$ where K = the smoothing constant (trend %) and N = periods. Algebraically solving for N: $N = (2 / K) – 1$.

For example, if you wanted to know the smoothing constant of a 19 period exponential average, you could do the math, $K = 2 / (19 + 1) = 2 / 20 = 0.10$ (smoothing constant) or 10% (trend) as it is many times expressed.

Here is something very important in regard to exponential moving averages; by the nature of their formula they will always change direction when they move through the price that is used to calculate them. This means that during an uptrend in prices and their exponential average, when the prices drop below the average, the average will immediately begin to decline. A simple or arithmetic average will not do this.

Momentum – see Rate of Change.

Normalize – This is a mathematical procedure to reduce the scaling of unlike data so it can be more easily compared. To normalize a series of data one usually wants the resultant data to fall in a range from zero to one hundred. The easiest way to do this is by the following formula:

(Current Value – Lowest Value in the Series)

- -

(Highest Value in the Series - Lowest Value in the Series) * 100.

Some of you might notice that this is similar to the formula for George Lane's %K Stochastic indicator, with the exception that for stochastics, the highest and lowest values are set by the number of periods you want to use. Many indicators are served well by looking at their normalized values for a predetermined number of periods. For example, if there was a good identifiable cycle in the market being analyzed, the number of periods of that cycle length might be a good number to use for normalization. A number of the breadth indicators in this book are normalized in that manner.

Oscillator – A term used to explain a number of technical indicators such as rate of change, momentum, stochastics, RSI, etc. These are all indicators that oscillate above and below a common value, many times which is zero. Other times they oscillate between zero and one hundred.

Overbought / Oversold – These terms have got to be the most over-used terms when talking about the markets. Overbought refers to the time in which the prices have risen to a level that seems as if they cannot go any higher. Oversold is the opposite, prices have dropped to a point it seems as they cannot go any lower. While this sounds simple enough, the term is usually based upon someone's personal observation of price levels and not on sound analysis.

Overlay – this refers to the act of putting an indicator on top of another one. A simple example would be displaying a moving average of an indicator on the same plot. In this case the indicator and its moving average would utilize the same scaling. Many times an unrelated indicator can be overlaid on another using totally independent price scaling.

Percentage - Percentage is generally better than a ratio because you are making the item relative to its related base. For example, the number of new highs by itself can be meaningful in the short term, but over long periods of time and with more and more issues traded, the relationship cannot remain consistent. If you took the number of new highs as a percentage of the total issues traded, then the scaling will always be from zero to one hundred and large amounts of data can be viewed with some consistency.

Rate of Change – Used interchangeably with momentum, rate of change is looking at a piece of data relative to a like piece of data at an earlier time. For example, with stock data, a 10-day rate of change would take today's price and subtract or divide by the stock's price 10 days ago. If one takes the difference in price and then divides by the older price you will see percentage changes. Generally, it is not the value of the rate of change that is important, but the direction and pattern associated with it. However, some oscillators have consistent levels that can be used as overbought and oversold. Rate of Change seems to more often than not be in reference to the difference in values, whereas momentum is more often the ratio of values. The line shape will be the same, only the numbers that make up the line will be different.

Ratio - A ratio is when you divide one data component by another. This keeps them in perspective and will alleviate many of the problems associated with using just the difference. Sometimes the numerator and denominator are not balanced and you get a non-symmetrical problem similar to what you get with the Arms Index. This is really not a problem as long as you are aware that it exists. Finally, a ratio of positive numbers (or similar signs) is always going to be greater than zero.

Smoothing – this is in reference to averaging data either by a simple or exponential moving average. It is a better adverb to use than always trying to explain that you take the moving average of it or take the exponential moving average of it; just say you are "smoothing" it. It is also used as a verb in as if you can "smooth" it.

Support and Resistance – First the definitions of support and resistance, then an explanation as to what they are. More elaborate definitions are available in almost any text on technical analysis. In fact, one of the best discussions of it is in Steven Achelis' book, "Technical Analysis from A to Z," where he ties it to supply and demand. Support is the price at which an issue has trouble dropping below. Resistance is the price level that it has trouble rising above.

About the Charts in this Book

Most breadth indicators are mathematical equations that utilize breadth data such as advances, declines, up volume, down, volume, new highs, new lows, etc. Usually the indicator can be displayed as a line plot, and in this book will almost always be displayed below the New York Composite Index. The New York Composite Index is a capitalization-weighted index of all stocks listed on the New York Stock Exchange. This plot of the index is also scaled logarithmically on the price axis. Semi-log scaling (logarithmically on only one axis) is best for long term charts where the distance between each price point depends on its value. The distance between 10 and 20 is the same as the distance between 30 and 60; both are 100% increases.

The time frame for the chart was chosen to best reflect the value of the indicator. Some indicators are shown over the full 40-year period, while others are shown only over a few years. Many times the shorter time frames were chosen because of the frequent fluctuations (noise) of the indicator. Chart annotations were intentionally avoided to allow the chart to remain clean and uncluttered. This way you can take a straightedge and align the data to see the details of the indicators.

Some breadth indicators are combinations of various conditions that must be met in order for a buy or a sell signal to be generated. These are displayed as plots that have upward and downward spikes and sometimes steps. The upward spikes are generally for "buy" signals and the downward spikes are for sell signals. Some of the plots have spikes of different lengths. This is an indication that the process of reaching a signal is a multi-step process and all of the steps are displayed. In most cases, the longest spike is the final or best signal to act upon. A few indicators step higher and higher to their maximum then reverse and step downward in a similar manner. These are usually the ones that have multiple buy and sell parameters that must be met. Each upward step means one more buy parameter has been met over a sell parameter, and the opposite on the downside. Always read the associated discussion near the chart to ensure you are interpreting the information correctly.

Multicollinearity

If you find a group of indicators that are essentially telling you the same thing and with consistency, you need to pick one of them to use and then drop the others. If they are all saying the same thing they are not assisting you in your analysis. This is known as multicollinearity and is a trap you need to avoid. Ensure that you are using indicators that measure the markets differently, and are diversified. While breadth indicators are different than most price-based indicators, there are many breadth indicators that are essentially revealing the same thing.

Many times, investors think that they are more correct in their analysis if many indicators are telling them the same thing. They are supportive of your analysis only if the indicators are not collinear. If they are collinear, then the support the investor feels from having a lot of indications agree is misleading and dangerous. The support for their analysis gives them a false confidence.

CH 3 - BREADTH INDICATORS

This is the first chapter that will highlight the process of presenting details on all known indicators of market breadth. It will attempt to identify the creator of the indicator or methodology, the source of the information, and as much research on the indicator as possible. The formula will be disclosed in most cases, along with a number of different charts to assist you in understanding and interpreting these indicators. Finally, an opinion from the author on the indicator and its interpretation is given.

Individual Breadth Indicator Format

A textbook layout is usually appreciated, especially when a book is also to be used as a reference manual. All indicators in this book are presented using the format below. If you see that an item below is not included with the coverage of an indicator, it is because there was no information available for that particular item.

Also Known As: Many times an indicator is known by multiple names. A good example of this is the Arms Index, which is also known as TRIN and MKDS. This will also be where you can get information about very similar indicators located elsewhere in this book.

Author/Creator: Most indicators were created by someone. I have attempted to give credit when the information is available.

Data components required: These are the components of breadth data that are required to calculate the indicator.

Description: This is a brief description of the indicator which will also try to clear up any problems with any interpretation of the math.

Interpretation: Here is the generally accepted industry interpretation of the indicator, using value levels, zones, smoothing values, etc. A number of different analysts' various techniques are also mentioned here.

Chart: Here is a chart that best displays the indicator. Enough data is used in the chart so that only "hand-picked" areas are avoided. There are some indicators or breadth-based systems that were beyond the capabilities for creating a chart and they will be so noted. Many times there will be a number of charts showing different interpretations or uses of the indicator from various analysts.

Author Comments: Here the author tries to offer a personal interpretation, opinion, and use of the indicator. Because the author does not use all of them, he still offers this interpretation, including some modifications and ideas for further analysis. In some instances, he will also offer a modification that he believes will enhance the indicator. A few indicators were designed for buy signals or sell signals, but not both. On these he attempted to create the complementary indicator.

Formula: This is intended as an algebraic formula for the indicator. There are some math symbols that will assist you:

$\sum$ means the formula after it is accumulated or summed.

$\sqrt{}$ means the square root of the formula.

There are a number of formulae that are just too complex for this section. If I felt that was the case, I attempted to write a descriptive narrative on the formula. And in a few instances, the indicator was purely designed to be a visual display and no formulae would assist your understanding.

StockCharts.com's Symbol: This is the symbol to use when using StockCharts.com's website. Not all charts in the book have a symbol because they were already available in StochCharts.com's symbol catalog. Many only required a ratio or difference of components so were created without needing a special symbol.

References: This is a bibliography where you can find additional information on the indicator and/or its creator. This method was preferred over a formal bibliography and at times, there are notes about a particular book or magazine article included here. Displaying them here is a much more useful location for references in my opinion.

Chapter Format

Because of the large number of breadth indicators, the chapters on the breadth indicators are divided into different categories based upon the mathematical relationship between the breadth pairs. An indicator pair relates to the advances and declines, the new highs and new lows, and the up volume and down volume. Pairs can be mathematically related in a number of ways. The difference between the two and the division of the two are the two primary ways these pairs have been used to create breadth indicators.

Indicator Categories

A – D	AD Difference
A / D	AD Ratio
AD	AD Miscellaneous
H – L	HL Difference
H / L	HL Ratio
HL	HL Miscellaneous
UV DV	Volume
A D H L UV DV	Composite

When necessary, the numerator controls in which category the indicator will be. If A-D is in the numerator it is in the AD Difference category. A number of indicators could be in either the difference or the ratio category. For example, the ratio used by Tom McClellan and Carl Swenlin has $(A - D)$ in the numerator and $(A + D)$ in the denominator $(A-D) / (A+D)$. The numerator will usually control the direction of an indicator so that is what was used to determine the category the indicator will be in.

General Advance and Decline Information

Advancing issues (advances) are those whose price increased from the previous closing price. Declining issues (declines) are those whose price decreased from the previous closing price. A bullish market will take many, if not most, issues with it. As the market rises, the number of advances will remain fairly high with the usual oscillations as traders move in and out of the market. Most often the advancing issues will start to decline in number well before the price action reflects a market starting to peak. This is because fewer and fewer issues are continuing to rise. The prices continue to rise because most market averages are capitalization weighted and the generals continue to lead the charge. It is when the declines begin to rise that the topping formation is reaching its final stages.

If you are analyzing data over a long term (greater than 1 year), it is highly recommended to adjust any raw forms of the data by using a ratio of it to a more universal component. For example, viewing the advancing issues as a percentage of total issues is better than just looking at advancing issues. The same goes for the declining issues and the unchanged issues. Chart 3-1 shows the raw advance and decline data. Chart 3-2 shows the advance and decline data as a percentage of the total issues.

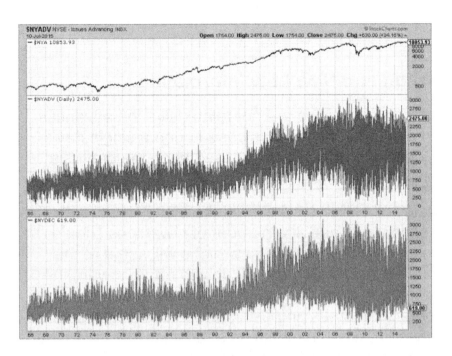

Chart 3-1

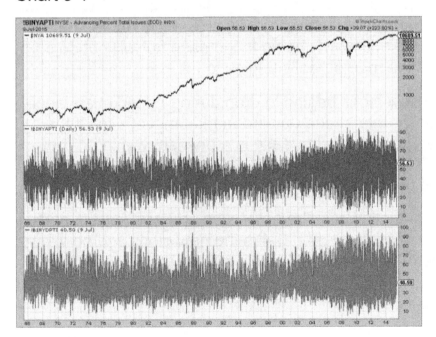

Chart 3-2

General New High and New Low Information

The new highs and the new lows are not related like the advances and declines. An advance or decline is based upon a single day's price change. A new high or new low is based upon the previous year's price changes.

As previously stated, a bullish market will take many issues with it. As the market continues to rise, the number of new highs should continue to increase. Many times the new highs will surge at the beginning of a bull market, then drop off, only to return toward the end of a long bullish advance. This is because stocks that have broken out of congestion areas and rising above their resistance levels have unlimited upward potential on a technical basis. As the market's upward move starts to falter, the first thing that happens is the number of new highs stops increasing. Then the number of new highs will begin to decline. As the topping process matures, the number of new lows will slowly begin to increase but will not do so dramatically until the market really begins to fall.

If the number of new highs begins to drop during a market advance, this is quite bearish. In a strong upward market move, even if the new highs do not continue to increase is a bearish warning. They do not have to drop in number, just the fact that they are no longer increasing is not good for the upward movement.

The two charts that follow use the new highs and new lows. Chart 3-3 is the raw numbers and chart 3-4 is the new highs and new lows as a percentage of total issues.

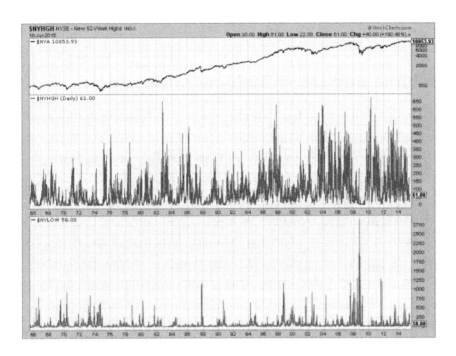

Chart 3-3

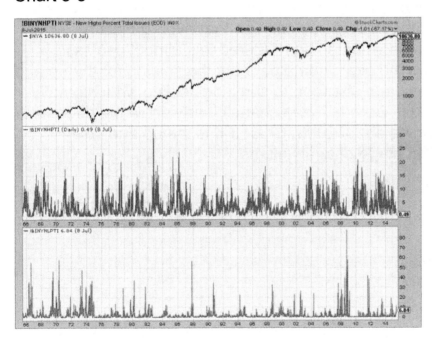

Chart 3-4

General Up Volume and Down Volume Information

Up Volume refers to the volume for the day of the advancing issues. Down volume is that volume for the declining issues. Stocks can still advance and the amount of volume will be the first indication of a weakening advance. As an up move begins to falter, the up volume will be one of the first hints that all is not well. It is generally not the case that the declining volume will lead the declining issues when the market is in a maturing top formation. Markets can drop merely from a lack of up volume; they do not need a large increase in down volume. As a market declines, the down volume will come back into play and can be used to help identify the beginning of a bottom. The down volume will quickly dry up and the up volume will rise quickly at a market bottom.

The next three charts use the up volume and down volume. Chart 3-5 is the raw numbers and you can see that over the last fifty years the giant increase in volume has rendered this almost useless. Chart 3-5b shows the exact same data but the scaling for the up and down volume has been changed to semi-log scaling; which greatly enhances the chart. Both of these charts clearly show the decrease in volume beginning about 2008. Chart 3-6 is the up and down volume as a percentage of total volume.

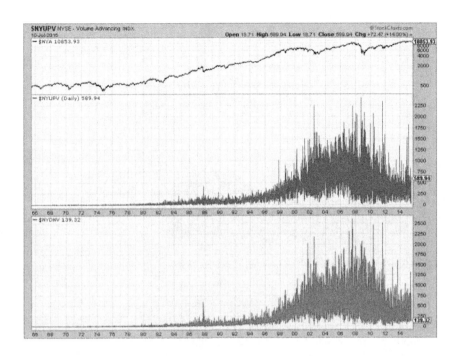

Chart 3-5

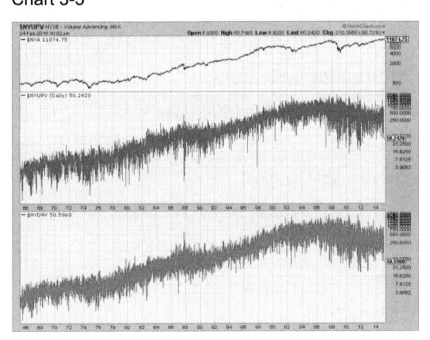

Chart 3-5b

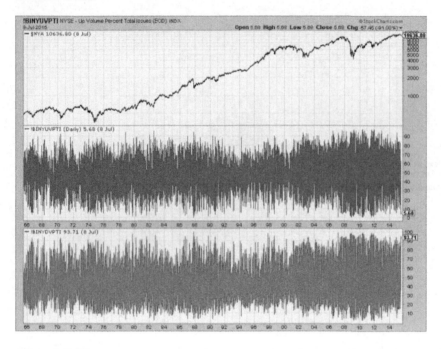

Chart 3-6

Complete List of Breadth Indicators

Chapter 4 – Advance Decline Difference

Advances – Declines

Advance Decline Overbought Oversold

Plurality Index

Advance Decline – Fugler

Advance Decline Line

Advance Decline Line – 1%

Advance Decline Line – Eakle

Advance Decline Line – Normalized

Advance Decline Line – Bolton

Advance Decline Line – Adjusted Total Issues

Big Movers Only

Advance Decline Line Oscillator

Absolute Breadth Index

Absolute Breadth Index – Adjusted

Advance Decline Power

Coppock Breadth Indicator

Haurlan Index

McClellan Oscillator

McClellan Summation Index

Merriman Breadth Model

Swenlin IT Breadth Momentum Oscillator

Swenlin Trading Oscillator – Breadth

Zahorchak Method

Zahorchak Method Alternate

Chapter 5 – Advance Decline Ratio

Advance / Decline Ratio

Breadth Thrust

Breadth Thrust Continuation

Duarte Market Thrust Indicator

Eliades Sign of the Bear

Hughes Breadth Momentum Oscillator

Panic Thrust

STIX – Short Term Trading Index

Chapter 6 – Advance Decline Miscellaneous

Advances / Issues Traded

Advance Decline Divergence Oscillator

Advance Decline Diffusion Index

Breadth Climax

Declining Issues TRIX

Disparity Index

Dynamic Synthesis

Unchanged Issues

Velocity Index

Chapter 7 – New Highs New Lows Indicators

High Low Difference

New Highs – New Lows

New High New Low Line

New Highs & New Lows Oscillator

New Highs & New Lows Derivations

High Low Ratio

New Highs / New Lows Ratio

High Low Miscellaneous

New Highs & New Lows

New Highs % Total Issues

New Lows % Total Issues

High Low Logic Index

High Low Validation

Chapter 8 – Up Volume Down Volume Indicators

Up Volume

Down Volume

Changed Volume

Up & Down Volume

McClellan Oscillator – Volume

McClellan Summation Index – Volume

Merriman's Volume Model

Swenlin IT Volume Momentum Oscillator

Swenlin Trading Oscillator – Volume

Up Volume Down Volume Line

Cumulative Volume Ratio

Up Down On Balance Volume (OBV)

Volume Percentage Ratio

Upside – Downside Volume

Upside / Downside Volume Ratio

Zweig Up Volume Indicator

Chapter 9 – Composite Indicators

Arms Index

Arms Open Index

Advance Decline New High New Low

Bretz TRIN-5

Cash Flow Index

Composite Tape Index

Dysart Positive Negative Volume

Eliades New TRIN

Haller Theory

Hindenburg Omen

Market Thrust

McClellan Oscillator with Volume

McClellan Summation Index with Volume

Meyers Systems

Moving Balance Indicator

Technical Index

Titanic Syndrome

Trend Exhaustion Index

Chapter 11 – Non-Internal Breadth Indicators

Stocks Above 200 day Simple and Exponential Average

Stocks Above 50 day Simple and Exponential Average

Bullish Percent

Participation Index, both Up and Down

Common Stock Only Indicators

Advance Decline Line

McClellan Oscillator

McClellan Summation

CH 4 - *Advance Decline Difference Indicators*

Advances - Declines

The breadth indicators in this chapter all utilize the difference between the advances and the declines as their primary relationship.

Advance Decline Difference Indicators

Advances – Declines

Advance Decline Overbought Oversold

Plurality Index

Advance Decline – Fugler

Advance Decline Line

Advance Decline Line – 1%

Advance Decline Line – Eakle

Advance Decline Line – Normalized

Advance Decline Line – Bolton

Advance Decline Line – Adjusted Total Issues

Big Movers Only

Advance Decline Line Oscillator

Absolute Breadth Index

Absolute Breadth Index – Adjusted

Advance Decline Power

Coppock Breadth Indicator

Haurlan Index

McClellan Oscillator

McClellan Summation Index

Merriman Breadth Model

Swenlin IT Breadth Momentum Oscillator

Swenlin Trading Oscillator – Breadth

Zahorchak Method

Advances - Declines

Also Known As: Overbought Oversold

Data components required: Advances (A), Declines (D).

Description: This is the difference between the advancing issues and the declining issues (Advances minus Declines).

Interpretation: Anytime you deal with the difference or the ratio of two items, it is always best to smooth the data because the raw information will be too erratic to be useful. Chart 4-1 is the 21 day moving average of the advance decline difference. You can see that it is generally above the zero line during up moves and below it during down moves. The arithmetic smoothing has a couple of anomalies with it; it unfortunately delays the crossings of the zero line, but then avoids a large number of whipsaws (short term crossing that reverse direction quickly). Using shorter term periods would help the timing of the crossings but increase the whipsaws.

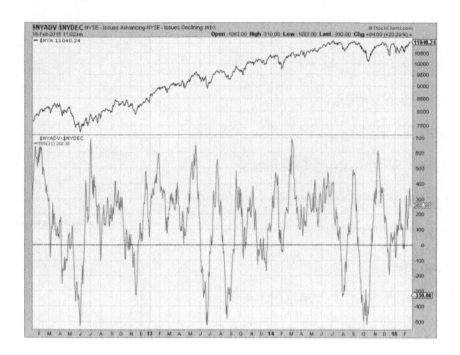

Chart 4-1

Author Comments: Gerald Appel has stated that he looks at this difference in Advances and Declines by smoothing it with a 3-day exponential average. He said in a 1994 interview that when this indicator went above 500, it could be the start of a good rally. Also, if it goes below -600, standby for a good down move. Soon after the interview with Gerald Appel, the volume and number of issues on the New York Stock Exchanges began to increase significantly. Chart 4-2 shows this advance decline indicator with the zones changed to +1000 and -1000. These seem to keep his concept alive and up-to-date.

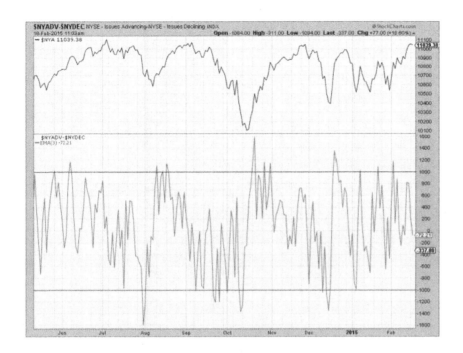

Chart 4-2

Justin Mamis, who, with Stan Weinstein started the Professional
Tape Reader newsletter, likes to look at the 10-day average of the
Advance Decline difference plotted with the 30-day average of the
difference. The digital (squared corners) line in chart 4-3 is showing
the times when the 10-day average is above the 30-day average.
Whenever it is above the zero line, the 10 day is above the 30 day
and it is bullish. If you are familiar with a moving average crossover
system, this is very similar; instead of using price this indicator uses
the difference between advances and declines.

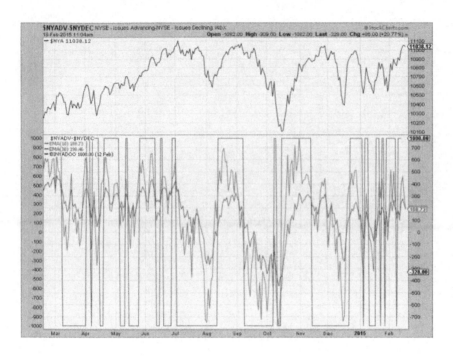

Chart 4-3

Formula: A - D

StockCharts.com Symbol: $NYADV-$NYDEC, digital: !BINYADOOD

References:

Appel, Gerald, "Gerald Appel, with Systems and Forecasts." <u>Stocks & Commodities</u>, Volume 12, March 1994, pp 98-105.

Mamis, Justin, "Justin Mamis and the Meaning of Life." <u>Stocks & Commodities</u>, Volume 13, August 1995 pp 359-365.

Advance Decline Overbought Oversold

Also See: Advances - Declines

Data components required: Advances (A), Declines (D)

Description: There are many derivatives on the relationship of the Advances and Declines and this is just one of them. This is a smoothed version of the advances minus the declines. This is actually a continuation of the previous section because there are some analysts who refer to this as the overbought oversold indicator.

Interpretation: Taking the difference between the Advances and the Declines produces an oscillator that moves above and below a zero line. Smoothing that line will reduce the daily fluctuations and provide a better tool for determining overbought and oversold. While it seems to show overbought and oversold areas well, it does not do so with the consistency one would desire to utilize this indicator. Steve Achelis claims that a range between +200 and -200 will yield good overbought and oversold signals. Chart 4-4 shows the overbought oversold indicator using a ten-day exponential smoothing.

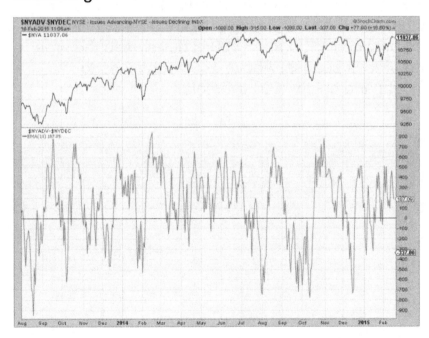

Chart 4-4

Author Comments: This is a good example of an indicator that has two definitions from two respected market technicians. Norman Fosback uses the ratio of Advances to Declines for the overbought/oversold indicator. Steven Achelis uses the difference of Advances and Declines for the overbought/oversold indicator. Either case can be easily justified; it just becomes confusing to newcomers. They both accomplish essentially the same goal, and that is a relationship between the advances and the declines.

I have generally gotten away from the somewhat standard 10 period smoothing and prefer to use a 21-day smoothing for most work. In an oscillator such as this, it greatly reduces the noise and sharpens the interpretation of the indicator. You can see from chart 4-5 that the area between the zero line and +400 is when the market is bullish. Similarly, the area between the zero line and -400 points out down markets well. One way to further improve this is to broaden the area around the zero line to define the neutral areas. For example, the area between +150 and +400 is bullish and the area between -150 and -400 is bearish. Above +400 continues to represent overbought and below -400 oversold.

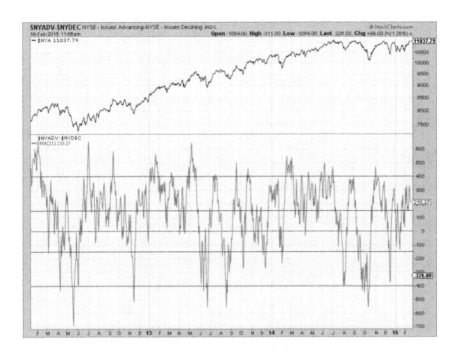

Chart 4-5

George Lindsay used an unsmoothed version of the difference between Advances and Declines. He looked for a triple zigzag pattern in the plot of raw advances minus declines. Three successively higher peaks in the Dow Jones Industrial Average along with three successively lower peaks in the advance decline difference, would be his sell signal. This is typical negative divergence and used by many today and is also difficult to quantify and totally subjective. Chart 4-6 shows a couple of examples of Lindsay's technique.

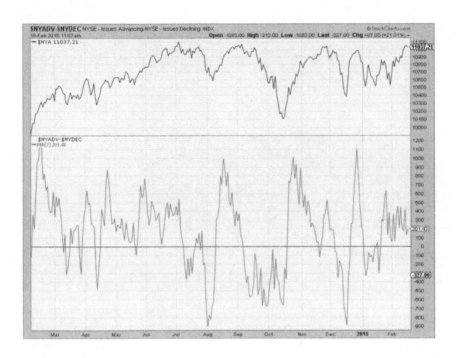

Chart 4-6

Robert Nurock, who created the Wall Street Week Index, also used an advance decline component. He used a 10-day sum of the difference. A bullish signal was generated when from a point where the index exceeds 1000 to a peak and then down to a point 1000 below the peak. A bearish signal was from the point where the index drops below -1000 to a trough and then up to a point 1000 above the trough. The concept here was to give the indicator an opportunity to reverse and not try to pick the actual top or bottom.

Robert Kinsman used a 7 period exponential average and called it the Kinsman smoothed A-D. His concept was to identify the general high low range for this oscillator and then look for spikes outside that range. He further states that large spikes outside the range are more revealing than just trading opportunities, but are a precursor to significant trend changes in the market. Chart 4-7 shows lines at

+600 and -600. You can see that the spikes outside those bands generally identified turning points in the market.

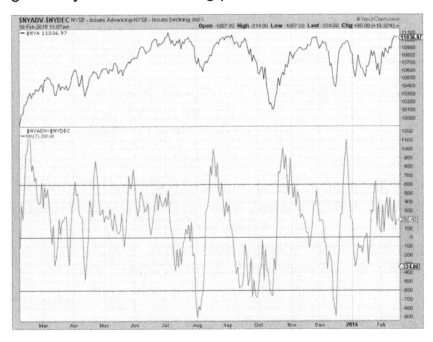

Chart 4-7

Formula: 21day Moving Average (A – D)

StockCharts.com Symbol: $NYADV-$NYDEC

References:

Achelis, Steven, "Forecasting the market with the overbought/oversold indicator." Stocks and Commodities, July, 1987, pp 231-232.

Favors, Jerry, "The Lindsay A-D Indicator." Stocks and Commodities, Volume 10, February 1992, pp 75-76.

Kinsman, Robert, "Advance – Decline Line Redux." Stocks and Commodities," Volume 14, January 1996, 29-33.

Plurality Index

Author/Creator: Paul Dysart wrote about it in 1937, Ralph Rotnem used it, and Alan Shaw named it.

Data components required: Advances (A), Declines (D).

Description: This is a moving total of the absolute difference between advances and declines over a 25-day period. According to James Alphier, this was part of Paul Dysart's broader "Theory of Equalization."

Interpretation: Alan Shaw used benchmarks of 6,000 and 12,000. If the indicator drops below 6,000, a sell warning is signaled. He then waits until the index turns back up, at which point the signal becomes a definite sell. If the indicator rises above 12,000, it gives a buy alert, at which point he waits until it starts to drop, when it gives a definite buy signal. Chart 4-8 shows this technique.

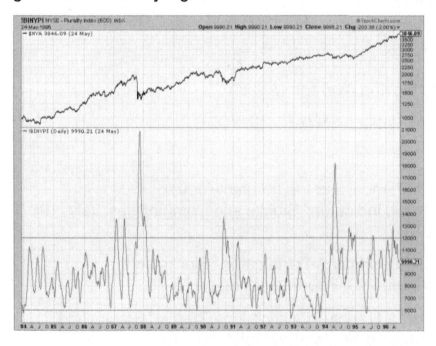

Chart 4-8

The reasoning behind this indicator is that there is usually complacency at the top and panic at the bottom. John McGinley, of Technical Trends, says that a bull market dies of exhaustion. While at market bottoms, everyone is rushing in to buy.

Author Comments: I have seen the Plurality Index calculated using a moving average, instead of a sum. They look similar, but the zones need to be reset.

Since 1994 this indicator has had an upward bias that makes Alan Shaw's zones in need of adjustment. It would appear that 23,000 can replace Shaw's 12,000 zone, and that 14,000 can replace the 6,000 zone. Incidentally, I'm quite sure Alan Shaw knows this or at least uses different zones than when Art Merrill wrote about it in 1990. Art Merrill claims that this must be a daily indicator and not one that uses weekly data. Alan Shaw says that this indicator doesn't always give a signal, but when it does, it should be noted. Chart 4-9 shows zones at 23,000, 14000, and 12,000.

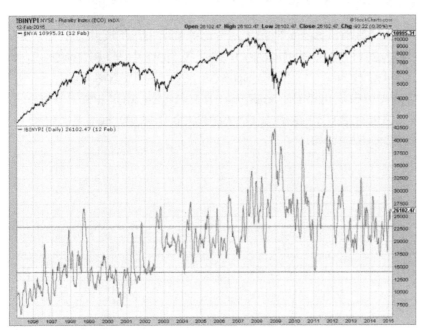

Chart 4-9

Formula: $\sum |A - D|$ over 25 days.

StockCharts.com Symbol: !BINYPI

References:

Merrill, Arthur A., "Plurality." Stocks & Commodities, Volume 8, April 1990, pp 137-138.

Advance Decline - Fugler

Author/Creator: George Fugler

Data components required: Advances (A), Declines (D).

Description: George Fugler called this his "quick and dirty" indicator. If value of Advances minus Declines is positive on three successive trading days, an up (buy) signal in generated. If they are negative on three successive days, a down (sell) signal is generated.

Interpretation: Arthur Merrill said that his indicator is afflicted with whipsaws, but it stays in gear during a trend. Chart 4-10 shows each signal for up and down. The up spikes represent the buy signals and the downward spikes represent the sell signals. There are usually a few similar signals in a row before a reversal, so one should ignore multiple signals.

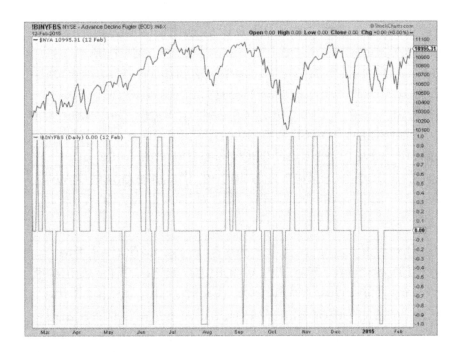

Chart 4-10

Author Comments: Arthur Merrill is correct when he said this has lots of whipsaws. He was never one to mince words.

Formula: (A – D)

StockCharts.com Symbol: !BINYFBS

References:

Merrill, Arthur, "More Trend Detection." <u>Stocks & Commodities</u>, Volume 6, Sept, 1988, pp. 219.

Advance Decline Line

Author/Creator: Colonel Leonard P. Ayers

Data components required: Advances (A), Declines (D)

Description: The Advance Decline Line is one of the most popular ways to measure the breadth of the market. The number of declining stocks is subtracted from the number of advancing stocks each day. If the advances outnumber the declines, the net total is added to the previous total. If the declines outnumber advances, the net difference is subtracted from the previous total. In a nutshell, when there are more advances than declines, the line goes up. When there are more declines than advances, the line goes down. The Advance Decline Line can be used with either daily or weekly data.

For example, if 800 stocks advance for the day, and 450 fall, the advance decline difference for the day would be +350. This value is then added to the previous day's advance decline line value. If the number of declines was greater than the number of advances and the difference between the two was -200, then that amount would be subtracted from the Advance Decline Line's previous value. Here is another example:

Day	Advances (A)	Declines (D)	A - D	Cumulative A-D
Monday	800	1200	-400	-400
Tuesday	1000	950	50	-350
Wednesday	800	1150	-350	-700
Thursday	950	1300	-350	-1050
Friday	1600	700	900	-150

Interpretation: The Advance Decline Line is usually compared to one of the popular market price indices, preferably the index that is also related to the advances and declines that are being used. For example, the New York Composite Index should be used with the New York Stock Exchange advances and declines. They should trend in the same direction. When the Advance Decline Line begins to diverge from the index, an early indication is given of a possible trend reversal.

During a strong advance, the Advance Decline Line normally will move more than the S&P 500 or Dow Industrials. If the market averages reach a new high and the Advance Decline Line fails to follow suit; that can be an early indication of non-confirmation. Chart 4-11 shows the advance decline line for the last 40 years. The numbers on the scale to the right of the chart are essentially meaningless since they reflect the summed difference from the first date on the chart. The numbers will change based upon when you start the calculation.

Chart 4-11

Author Comments: The material in this section (Advance Decline Line) was reviewed by Tom McClellan along with some added material from him with my sincere appreciation. You'll learn more about Tom and his family in later sections.

If there was one breadth indicator that has been analyzed, modified, adjusted, and discussed more than any other, the Advance Decline

Line is probably the winner. Like many of the other versions of this popular breadth indicator, it seems best at determining the ends of longer term up moves in the market. It seems that the Advance Decline Line gives a lot of false signals at tops, but is much better at market bottoms. It is not the absolute numerical value of the advance decline line that matters, but is its acceleration (up and down) or lack thereof that is important.

A common misconception of analysts is to compare the rate of change of the Advance Decline Line with a market index. One is based upon movement and the other is based on price. Because the units are different, such comparisons are difficult to make in a consistent way. The one analogy that seems to fit this best is that the smart money always leaves the market first, usually quite a bit of time ahead of the masses. The smart money is also the first to get into the market after a decline. Chart 4-12 shows the divergence that occurred in 1987 that helped identify the drop in the markets that started in August of that year, but is usually only remembered by the October 13th plunge. A close examination of the Advance Decline Line shows it was dropping significantly before that day.

Chart 4-12

Chart 4-13 shows the topping divergence in the advance decline line in 1998; a time when everyone believed the markets were never going to stop rising. This very early warning panned out as the markets rallied again in late 1998 through much of 1999, then began one of the biggest bear markets most will see in their lifetime.

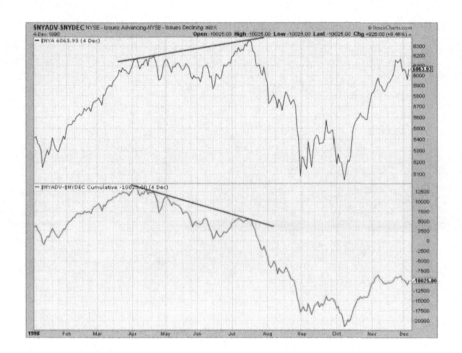

Chart 4-13

Chart 4-14 shows five divergent patters over the last 20 years. Three of them are identifying market tops in 1987, 1990, and 1999, while the other two are identifying market bottoms in early 2003 and mid-2004.

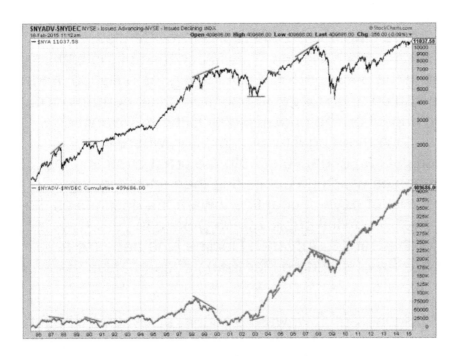

Chart 4-14

The chief value of looking at the Advance Decline Line comes from its relationship to liquidity. When there is a lot of money coming into the market, it tends to spread itself out into a majority of issues which shows up in the breadth statistics with more advances than declines. It is impossible to get a majority of stocks to go up unless there is sufficient liquidity to spread around. Conversely, when liquidity is tight, then the dwindling supply of money tends to go into only the highest quality issues, resulting in more declines than advances. It is possible for the major price indices to remain aloft while the Advance Decline Line starts declining, provided that the limited amount of liquidity is channeled into the right stocks to keep the price indices up. But this is a very weak condition for the market, and it usually resolves itself with an eventual negative outcome for the price indices. The 1998-2001 period, was a great example of this.

The Advance-Decline Line has an inherent downward bias, especially compared to price indices. This is because of the of the survivorship bias in the price indices. Only the big, established, and successful large-cap companies get to see their stock performance have much of an impact on the price indices. But the Advance-Decline Line is a much more egalitarian indicator, where every single listed stock gets an equal vote, both the great ones and the lousy ones. Companies which go public and then end up going bankrupt will see a lot of days of counting toward the declines as the price goes from the IPO (initial public offering) price to zero. This is especially true for the Nasdaq Advance Decline Line because the Nasdaq market has lower standards for listing of companies than the NYSE.

It is because of this inherent downward bias that analysts are better served by focusing on the upward or downward acceleration taking place in the Advance Decline Line rather than on the raw position of it.

One problem with the standard Advance Decline Line is that the changing number of issues traded on the exchange affects the amplitudes of the Advance Decline Line's movements. Many analysts adjust for this by dividing the advance decline difference by the total number of issues traded, or more simply by the total of advances plus declines:

$(A-D) / (A+D)$

The daily values are then summed as with the original version.

In addition to using daily advance decline data to construct an Advance Decline Line, one can also use weekly data. Chart 4-15 shows the weekly advance decline line. Remember that this uses weekly data for the advances and declines and is not a derivation of the daily data.

Chart 4-15

Formula: $\sum (A - D)$

StockCharts.com Symbol: Daily $NYADV-$NYDEC, Weekly $NYADVW-$NYDECW

References:

McClellan, Sherman and Tom, "The McClellan Market Letter."

Just about any technical analysis book that covers technical market indicators will have information on the advance decline line.

Advance Decline Line – 1%

Also known as: Momentum Index by Stan Weinstein

Author/Creator: Carl Swenlin and Stan Weinstein

Data components required: Advances (A), Declines (D).

Description: This is the Advance Decline Line with a long term smoothing of 200 days. Carl Swenlin prefers using an exponential moving average and Stan Weinstein prefers a simple / arithmetic moving average.

Interpretation: Stan Weinstein suggests that it gives buy and sell signals when it crosses the zero line. From below to above the zero line was bullish and from above to below was bearish. He further refines it to say that the longer it remained on one side of the zero line before crossing it, the better the signal. Also, the further into positive (above zero) or negative (below zero) territory that it had been would add to the value when it did cross the zero line. His most meaningful bearish signal is when the indicator has been in positive territory for quite a while and moved to an extreme. Chart 4-16 shows Weinstein's Momentum Index.

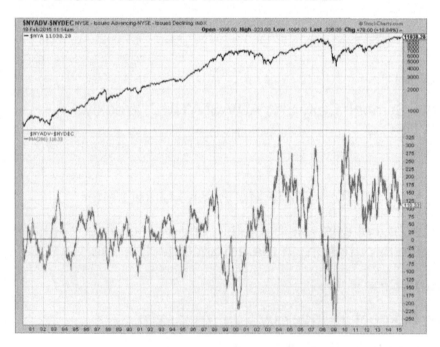

Chart 4-16

Author Comments: I found Weinstein's comment that this was more helpful at spotting tops than bottoms to be interesting. This is not usually the case when it comes to technical indicators. I believe the fact that he used a simple moving average might be the reason. Remember, with a simple average, the data from 200 days ago is carrying the same weight as the most recent data. To really make this point, the data from six to eight months ago (60+ days) is carrying the same weight as the data in the last three months. Most market tops are long spread out affairs of distribution and take a while to be put in place. This would somewhat explain that, and also why Weinstein thought it was not that good at bottoms, as most bottoms are sharp and decisive.

I have always preferred to use exponential smoothing when using large time periods. In this case the Swenlin version seems better at keeping you in most of the move, either up or down. Additionally, Carl uses the ratio of the difference between advances and declines divided by the sum of advances and declines. Here is what Carl Swenlin says about it: "I find it much more useful to watch where this indicator forms tops and bottoms. For example, in 1990, when the Dow made two successive new highs, the 1% Advance Decline Line was topping below the zero line. The 1990 bear market followed immediately after the second top. Again in late 1994, as the Dow was putting in a double top, this indicator was topping below the zero line. The market subsequently went to its final low prior to the monster rally of 1995, which leads to the significance of bottoms on this indicator. When you see it bottoming in the area of -100 to -150, chances are that the market is putting in a major low. This happened in late 1994, late 1990, late 1987, and mid-1984. The bottom in 1981 did not lead to a major rally, but it was followed in 1982 by two higher indicator bottoms corresponding with two lower market lows, the final low being in August, 1982." Chart 4-17 shows Carl Swenlin's exponential version of the momentum index, which he calls 1% EMA (exponential moving average) of Advance

Declines. While it offers more whipsaws, it is also considerably more timely than the Weinstein version.

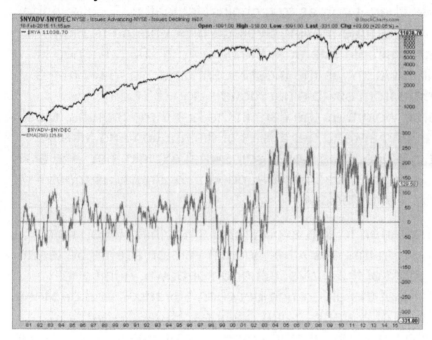

Chart 4-17

Formula: Previous Value + (A – D) smoothed by 200 days.

StockCharts.com Symbol: $NYADV-$NYDEC

References:

Weinstein, Stan. <u>Secrets for Profiting</u> <u>in Bull and Bear Markets</u>. Dow Jones-Irwin, Homewood, IL., 1988

Advance Decline Index – Eakle

Author/Creator: Eakle

Data components required: Advances (A), Declines (D).

Description: This is a smoothed rate of change of the Advance Decline Line. It was originally used as a weekly indicator with a smoothing of 35 weeks and then a 2-week rate of change.

Interpretation: Because of the simplicity of this indicator, using the concept on daily data seemed reasonable. Chart 4-18 shows the Eakle advance decline index using a 10 day (2 weeks) rate of change and a 175 day (35 weeks) smoothing.

Chart 4-18

Author Comments: The only source for this was John McGinley's Technical Trends service. Since the daily version in chart 4-18 did not seem to work very well, here, in chart 4-19 is the weekly version as it was originally designed to be used. Market bottoms seem to be well identified by the downward spikes in the indicator and whenever the indicator is above the zero line, the market is generally bullish. However, it does tend to stay bullish too long and does not seem be work well for tops.

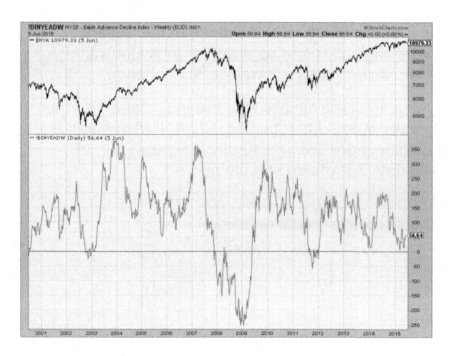

Chart 4-19

Formula: $\sum (A - D)$

StockCharts.com Symbol: !BINYEAD, weekly: !BINYEADW

References:

McGinley, John. <u>Technical Trends</u>. Wilton, CT.

Advance Decline Line - Normalized

Author/Creator: Tushar Chande

Data components required: Advances (A), Declines (D).

Description: This is the adjusted Advance Decline Line normalized with a moving five-day formula similar to that used in George Lane's stochastics. This process shows extremes in the Advance Decline Line. Also like stochastics, the use of 20 for oversold and 80 for overbought works well.

Interpretation: Using a short period such as 5 days makes this more of a trading oscillator. Chande says that oversold values of zero and overbought values of 100 would be good for trading. Chart 4-20 shows the normalized advance decline line for trading as Chande suggests.

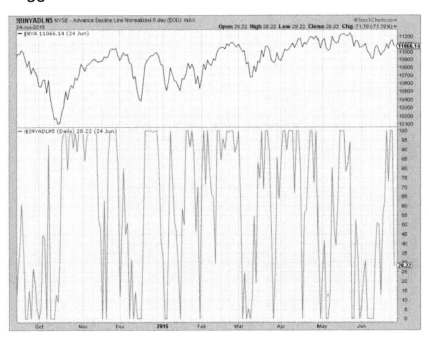

Chart 4-20

Author Comments: Tushar Chande has been a big contributor to the field of technical analysis, so I pay particularly close attention, not only to his work, but try to understand the concept he is revealing. To take this normalizing concept and reduce the signals, I used a 21-day period for the normalization and then smoothed the results with a 7-day exponential average. This makes the indicator slower and better for intermediate analysis. You can see in chart 4-21 that when the indicator is rising and goes above 50, it is the early part of a market rise. After the indicator goes above 80, and then drops back below 80, you can leg out of your long position. Sell all of it when it goes below 50.

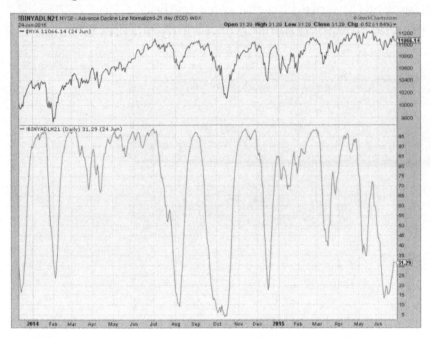

Chart 4-21

Formula: Previous Value + Today's (A – D) = AD, (((AD – lowest value (AD)) / (highest value (AD) – lowest value (A))) * 100

StockCharts.com Symbol: !BINYADLN5 and !BINYADLN21

References:

Chande, Tushar, "Breadth Stix and Other Tricks." <u>Stocks and Commodities</u>, Volume 12, May 1994, pp. 211-214.

Advance Decline Line – Bolton

Also Known As: Bolton Tremblay

Author/Creator: Hamilton Bolton

Data components required: Advances (A), Declines (D), Unchanged (U).

Description: This was an attempt by Bolton to remove downward bias in the Advance Decline Line. It was the square root of the difference of advances and declines, with that difference divided by the unchanged issues. This is an enhanced Advance Decline Line, in that, when the market is strong, it gives a slight push to either the advancing side or the declining side, depending upon which is stronger.

Interpretation: This is yet another version of the Advance Decline Line. Considering its attempt to remove downward bias, this version should definitely be considered. By giving the unchanged issues weight, it can allow for this version to start to slow down its ascent a little sooner than the more traditional version. This follows the logic of the discussion that as a market starts to peak, the number of unchanged issues will expand. Chart 4-22 shows the Bolton version of the Advance Decline Line.

Chart 4-22

Author Comments: Martin Pring uses this version and that is good enough for me. Pring says that Bolton developed this because it was better at reflecting the unweighted indices such as the Value Line composite. Since the Value Line data was not available prior to the 1960s, this gave him a way to evaluate unweighted data for many years prior to that.

There isn't much written about his; I remember it from the old CompuTrac days and found references to it in Pring's and Colby's books, however no charts. I believe the square root of a negative number is the reason you do not find this in charting software or, in fact, charts of it anywhere. I made a few assumptions to overcome it, and believe have displayed it correctly in the chart 4-22. Also, I found the 21-day smoothed version of the ratio to be interesting as shown in chart 4-23.

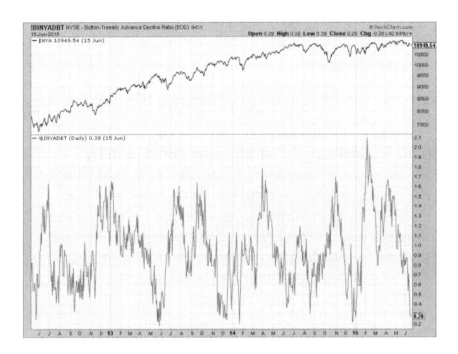

Chart 4-23

Formula: Previous Value + Square Root of ((A – D) / U)

StockCharts.com Symbol: !BINYBADL and !BINYADBT

References:

Dworkin, Fay, "Defining Advance / Decline Indicators." <u>Stocks and Commodities</u>, Volume 8, July 1990, pp. 274-278.

Pring, Martin, "Internal Market Momentum." <u>Stocks and Commodities</u>, Volume 11, July 1993, pp. 298-305.

Pring, Martin J. <u>Technical Analysis Explained</u>. McGraw-Hill, 1985.

Colby, Robert W. <u>The Encyclopedia of Technical Market Indicators</u>. New York: McGraw-Hill, 2003.

Advance Decline Line – Adjusted Total Issues

Also Known As: The Advance Decline Ratio

Author/Creator: Richard Russell

Data components required: Advances (A), Declines (D), Total Issues (TI)

Description: Richard Russell says that this was conceived by Colonel Leonard P. Ayres and James Hughes in 1926, and that it remained relatively obscure until he started his newsletter, Dow Theory Letters, in 1957. This indicator is an attempt to reduce the large increase in issues and normalize the difference between the advances and declines by dividing that difference by the total issues traded. Then is calculated like the Advance Decline Line by adding each successive difference to the previous one.

Interpretation: Looking for divergence with the index is the most common use of the Advance Decline Line, and this version is no different. It is a normal tendency, during bull moves, for there to be more advancing days than declining days, and in down markets, the reverse is true. Chart 4-24 shows the Advance Decline Line adjusted for the total number of issues.

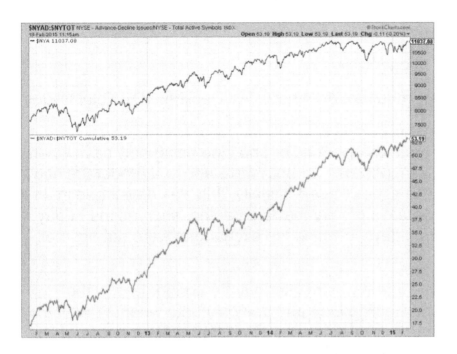

Chart 4-24

Author Comments: Richard Russell was probably one of the first to use the difference between the advances and declines divided by the total issues in his "A-D Ratio" published as a book of charts in 1962. This seems to enhance the more popular Advance Decline Line and offers very good long term divergence patterns. You can see in the above chart that when the market is in a good uptrend, this indicator trends right along with it. However, the first sign of weakness in the price action is readily evident in the adjusted Advance Decline Line.

Formula: $\sum ((A - D) / TI)$

StockCharts.com Symbol: $NYAD:$NYTOT

References:

Russell, Richard, 1975, <u>Dow Theory Letters</u>, San Diego, CA.

Big Movers Only

Author/Creator: Greg Morris

Data components required: Advances (A), Declines (D), Total Issues (TI)

Description: This is the Advance Decline Line using only days when either the advances, declines, or both were above a predetermined percentage of total issues traded. Initially, this was developed in an attempt to remove days of very inactive trading, such as the Friday after Thanksgiving, days in which the exchanges were not open all day, etc.

Interpretation: The intent was to filter out the boring days in the standard Advance Decline Line and use only data when either the number of advances or declines are significant. Long periods of inactivity in the market can still have a bias either upward or downward. It was felt that those trading days did not adequately reflect the underlying trends of the market. By removing a certain percentage of inactive days, this modification to the advance decline line reflects only the more powerful moves in the market. Chart 4-25 shows the Advance Decline Line where days with less than 35% of total issues (either advances or declines) removed. It seems to reflect the market quite well.

Chart 4-25

Author Comments: When I first developed this back in the 1980s, I used a fixed number of 1200 for the limit on whether the advances or declines for that day would be part of this indicator. Like most breadth indicators, adjusting for the big increase in issues traded was necessary. If you look at a long term chart of this indicator, you will see that it will better reveal longer term trends than most Advance Decline Line indicators used in the standard or more generally accepted manner. This is good for keeping the "big picture" in mind during your analysis. Chart 4-26 removes all advance decline data less than 50% of total issues. It is interesting how, during one of the big bull markets in history, from 1988 to 2000, this went down. What does that mean? Somewhere between 35 % and 50% of the large breadth moves of the market were not present in those years. This is also proven true by looking at Zweig's Breadth Thrust (chapter 5) where, beginning in 1984, there were no breadth thrust signals until 2004. This Big Movers line limited to the top 50% breadth days also reflects that.

Chart 4-26

Formula: $\sum (A>\%TI - D>\%TI)$.

StockCharts.com Symbol: !BINYBMO35 and !BINYBMO50

References:

Morris, Greg, 1995, "Indicators and Trading Systems Software," G. Morris Corporation, Dallas, TX.

Advance Decline Line Oscillator

Data components required: Advances (A), Declines (D)

Description: This is a 21-day rate of change of the advance decline line. Rate of change is where you take today's indicator value and subtract the value from 21 days ago.

Interpretation: Like most oscillators this is good for identifying overbought and oversold areas. Putting levels on this indicator, like most oscillators, requires a visual technique because most advance decline line numbers are meaningless by themselves. It all depends on where you start the calculation that determines the numbers (values) that make up the advance decline line. Chart 4-27 below uses zones at +1000 and -1000 and they seem to work very well.

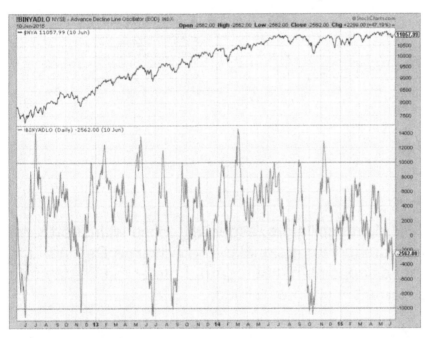

Chart 4-27

Gerald Appel likes to use a 10-day rate of change of the advance decline line and +3000 and -3000 as the zones. He states that if it gets to +5000 or +6000 it is good indicator or market strength. Chart 4-28 shows the Appel version with lines at -3000, 0, +3000, and +6000. Appel also likes to use a 21-day oscillator, which is described at the beginning of this section. He mentions that he also uses this as a divergence indicator with the market.

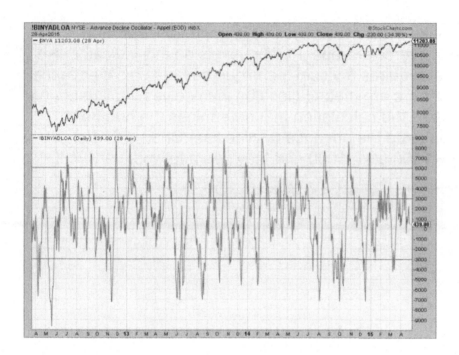

Chart 4-28

Author Comments: Most oscillators, especially those with short term parameters will yield short term signals. The Advance Decline Line Oscillator does not disappoint in that regard. I prefer the 21-day rate of change as the signals are more defined.

Formula: {Cumulated (A-D) - (A-D) input periods ago (ROC)}

StockCharts.com Symbol: !BINYADLO and !BINYADLOA

References:

Appel, Gerald, "Gerald Appel, with Systems and Forecasts." <u>Stocks and Commodities</u>, Volume 12, March 1994, pp. 98-105.

Absolute Breadth Index

Author/Creator: Norman G. Fosback

Data components required: Advances (A), Declines (D)

Description: This indicator was termed by Norman Fosback as a "going nowhere" indicator because you take the absolute value of the difference between advancing issues and declining issues. It does not matter whether there are more or less advances or declines, it is the absolute difference between them that the Absolute Breadth Index measures. It totally disregards market direction. It shows market activity or lack thereof.

Interpretation: The thinking behind the creation of the Absolute Breadth Index is that when the difference between the advances and declines is high, the price changes are also big, which, in turn, can mean the market is more prone to being at a bottom than at a top. This is an indication of good market activity. Similarly, if the difference between the advances and declines is small (low Absolute Breadth Index values), the market is not going anywhere and probably more near a top. This indicates a lack of activity in the market. In chart 4-29 you can easily see that when the Absolute Breadth Index is smoothed by 50 days, it clearly is pointing out market bottoms and tops.

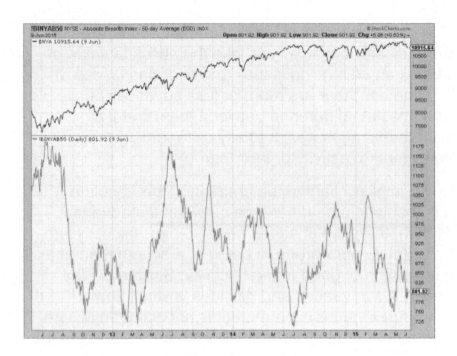

Chart 4-29

Author Comments: This indicator was one of the early ones, as is most of Fosback's work. It is also one of the good ones and because it seems so simplistic, many times I forget to look at it. I prefer to smooth it with 21 days and watch it as it goes over 1100 for bottoms and below 300 for market tops. These are the current settings. Because the number of issues has increased so much in recent years these levels needed to be spread further apart. You can see this in chart 4-30.

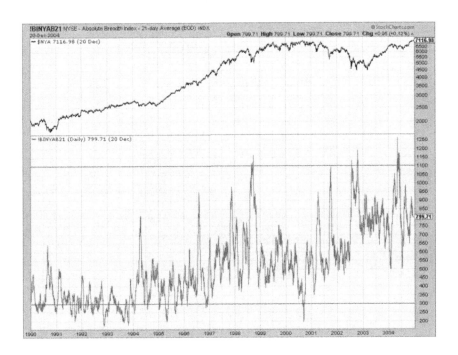

Chart 4-30

During the 1970s and 1980s, the levels that seemed to work best were 250 and 600. This is merely because of less issues being traded. See chart 4-31 below. A more current method of using the Absolute Breadth Index would be the Absolute Breadth Index adjusted for the total issues the way so many indicators from the past can and should be used this way. See Absolute Breadth Index Adjusted in this chapter.

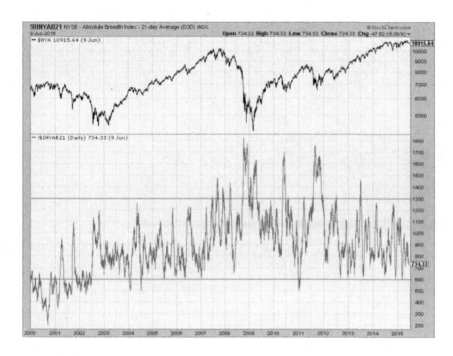

Chart 4-31

Formula: | A – D |

StockCharts.com Symbol: !BINYAB50 and !BINYAB21

References:

Fosback, Norman G. Stock Market Logic, Fort Lauderdale, FL: The Institute for Economic Research, Inc., 1976.

Absolute Breadth Index - Adjusted

Author/Creator: Norman G. Fosback was the creator of the original ABI.

Data components required: Advances (A), Declines (D), Total Issues (TI)

Description: The original version of this indicator was termed by Fosback as a "going nowhere" indicator because you take the absolute value of the difference between advancing issues and declining issues. It does not matter whether there are more advances or declines, it is the absolute difference between them that this indicator measures.

Interpretation: The thinking behind the creation of the Adjusted Absolute Breadth Index is that when the difference between the advances and declines is high, the price changes are also big, which, in turn, can mean the market is more prone to being at a bottom than at a top. Similarly, if the difference between the advances and declines is small (low Absolute Breadth Index values), the market is not going anywhere and probably more near a top.

Author Comments: This is one of those indicators that needed to be adjusted because of the large increase in the number of issued being traded. As with most adjusted indicators, all you need to do is create a ratio. In this case, just divide by the total issues traded. Just like the Absolute Breadth Index, I prefer to smooth it with 21 days and watch it as it goes over 30 for bottoms and below 10 for market tops. Robert Colby, in his book "The Encyclopedia of Technical Market Indicators" further adjusted the formula to multiply by 100 to remove the decimal values of the adjusted absolute breadth index. Chart 4-32 shows the Adjusted Absolute Breadth Index.

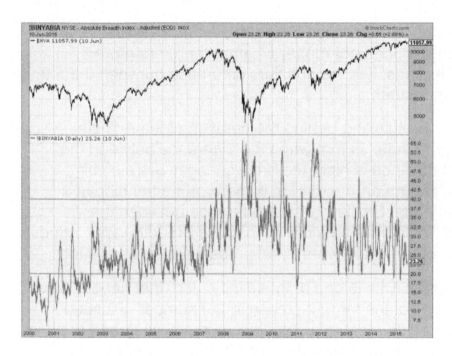

Chart 4-32

Formula: | A – D | / TI * 100

StockCharts.com Symbol: !BINYABIA

References:

Fosback, Norman G. Stock Market Logic, Fort Lauderdale, FL: The Institute for Economic Research, Inc., 1976.

Colby, Robert W. The Encyclopedia of Technical Market Indicators. New York : McGraw-Hill, 2003.

Advance Decline Power

Also Known As: AD Power

Author/Creator: John McGinley / Joe Granville

Data components required: Advances (A), Declines (D), Market Index (MKT).

Description: Originally based upon weekly data, this is the difference between advances and declines divided by the absolute change in the Dow Jones Industrial average.

Interpretation: Originally, the concept was to identify relative strength between the broad market (advances and declines) and the Dow Industrial average (the market). Chart 4-33 is the daily AD Power with a 21-day smoothing.

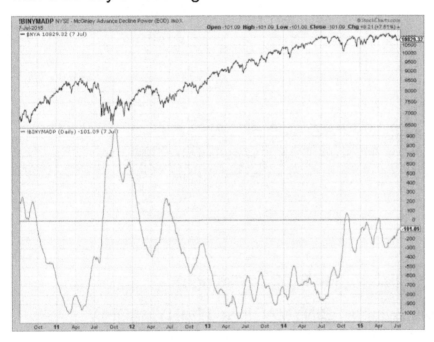

Chart 4-33

Author Comments: By taking a ratio of the advance decline difference and the absolute change in the Dow Industrials, this indicator is relating to momentum or acceleration values. It certainly appears that this indicator is good for identifying significant market bottoms. While it seems to reflect many market tops by its downward spikes, it is somewhat many of the economic indicators that are in use today where they identify twelve of the last eight recessions. In keeping with the original formula, chart 4-33b shows the AD Power index using weekly data. You can see that there isn't that much difference with the daily version.

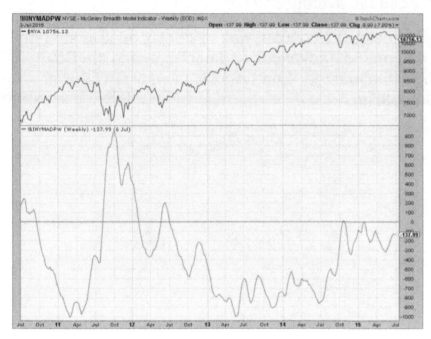

Chart 4-33b

Formula: (A – D) / |MKT – MKT (52 weeks ago)|

StockCharts.com Symbol: !BINYMADP and !BINYMADPW

References:

McGinley, John, Technical Trends, Wilton, Ct.

Coppock Breadth Indicator

Author/Creator: Edwin Sedgwick Chittenden Coppock

Data components required: Advances (A), Declines (D), Total Issues (TI).

Description: This indicator, created in the early 1960s, uses an adjusted advance decline line as its basis. Subtract the declines from the advances and divide that difference by the total issues traded. Then calculate a cumulative total as you would with the advance decline line. A second line is calculated as a weighted moving average of the raw cumulated line. Originally developed as a weekly indicator, the Coppock Breadth Indicator can also be adapted to daily breadth data.

Interpretation: Coppock's interpretation was simple; when the cumulative line crossed its own 15 week weighted moving average a signal was generated. Most times, it is the simple concepts that seem to work the best. Chart 4-34 uses daily data adjusted to a 75 day weighted smooth instead of the 15-week version. When the middle plot is equal to 10, the advance decline line is above its weighted moving average.   When it is at -10, it is below the average.

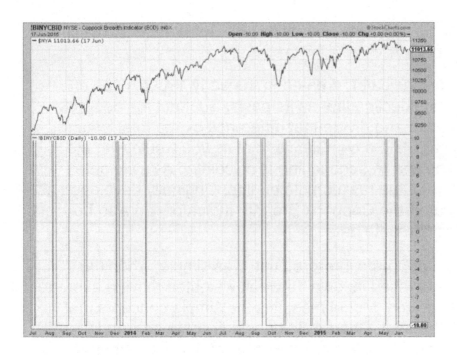

Chart 4-34

Author Comments: Sedge Coppock was as interesting in person as were his early stock market innovations. Most are familiar with his Coppock Curve, not the name he gave it, but one that is generally accepted in the trade. He called it the Trendex Very Long Term Risk Index for Listed Stocks. It was an 11 and 14-month percentage change of the Dow Jones Industrial Average added together and then a 10 month weighted moving average of that. He was once asked why he picked 11 and 14 months for this indicator. He said an undertaker friend told him that the period of time for a grieving family after the death of a close family member was usually between 11 and 14 months.

I had the pleasure of meeting Sedge Coppock in 1988 at the Market Technician's Association (MTA) conference where he was awarded the MTA's annual award for contribution to the field of technical analysis. Prior to that, I had a few communications with him in regard to a local group of analysts in Dallas, Texas, that I was working with. He sent us a tape about his beliefs and observations of almost 40 + years in the stock market. He did not hold back any punches in regard to uninformed investors, those who are always looking for the quick way to profits, and how most will not do the work required to make it in the markets. That tape, and three monographs that he wrote are some of the best investment advice one could ever get.

Formula: Previous Value + (A – D) / TI

StockCharts.com Symbol: !BINYCBID

References:

Coppock, E. S. C., 1977, "Low-Risk Investing," Trendex Research Corp, San Antonio.

Coppock, E. S. C., "Emotions Make Prices," Trendex Research Corp, San Antonio.

Coppock, E. S. C., "Realistic Stock Market Speculation," Trendex Research Corp, San Antonio.

Haurlan Index

Author/Creator: P.N. (Pete) Haurlan and David Holt

Data components required: Advances (A), Declines (D).

Description: The Haurlan Index is an exponential moving average of the advances minus the declines. There are three variations for short, intermediate, and long term analysis.

Interpretation: All three versions give buy signals as it crosses from below the zero line to above it. Sell signals are when it goes from above to below the zero line. Paul Carroll assigned the following buy and sell zones which seem to work well:

Short Term Haurlan Index (3 day smooth):   -550 for buy and +550 for sell.

Intermediate Term Haurlan Index (20 day smooth):   -200 for buy and +200 for sell.

Long Term Haurlan Index (200 day smooth):   he suggests using trendlines.

Gerald Appel also claims that these are ideal for trendline analysis, particularly with the short and intermediate versions. Appel also agrees with Carroll that -550 and +550 for the short version indicate the immediacy of a short term market reversal or consolidation. Chart 4-35 shows the short term version of the Haurlan Index with the thresholds used by Carroll and Appel.

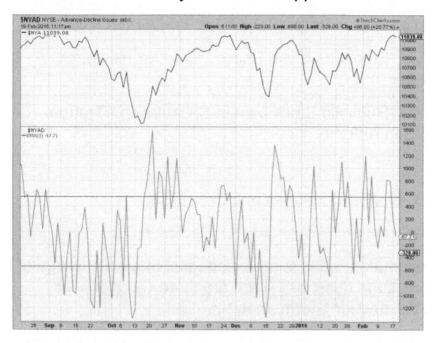

Chart 4-35

Chart 4-36 is the intermediate term Haurlan Index showing the +200 and -200 thresholds.

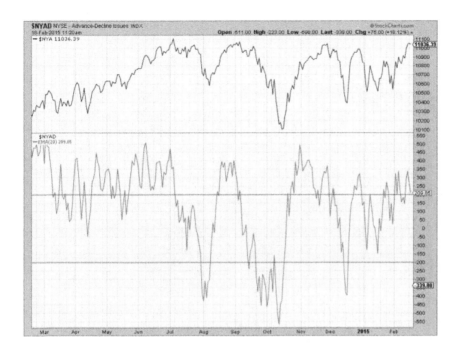

Chart 4-36

Chart 4-37 is the long term Haurlan Index with a couple of trendline breaks identifying market turns.

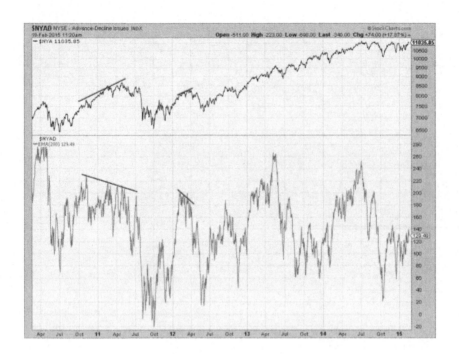

Chart 4-37

Author Comments: This is another twist on the advance decline difference. Some of the best indicators are also the simplest ones. Pete Haurlan was a true rocket scientist who worked for the Jet Propulsion Laboratory. His market interest and contributions to the field were under his advisory firm, Trade Levels.

Formula: Previous Value + (A – D)

StockCharts.com Symbol: $NYAD

References:

Haurlan, P.J., Trade Levels, Inc. Pasadena, CA.

Carroll, Paul E., "The Haurlan Index." Stocks & Commodities, Volume 12, January, 1994, pp. 23-25.

Appel, Gerald. Winning Market Systems. Greenville: Traders Press, 1973.

McClellan Oscillator

Author/Creator: Sherman and Marian McClellan

Data components required: Advances (A), Declines (D).

Description: The McClellan Oscillator is the difference between the 19-day (10% trend) and the 39-day (5% trend) exponential moving averages of the daily net advances minus declines figure. These two smoothing values were used because they reflect the two most dominant short to intermediate cycles in the market. These two exponential averages also were chosen in order to optimize speed in generating a directional signal, while minimizing whipsaws. The oscillator tends to lead the market because it will indicate overbought and oversold situations prior to the market. It will pass through zero at or very soon after an important market turning point.

Interpretation: The McClellan Oscillator is an intermediate term indicator, but it can be used for shorter term timing when it bottoms in oversold areas such as -100 and below. Usually, McClellan Oscillator crossings above the zero line are positive/bullish and below the zero line are negative/bearish. Readings above +100 are overbought readings, while below −100 are oversold. The +130 and -130 levels are also important. When the oscillator drops to -130 and then rallies, quite often the rally will fail and give a good sell signal. The opposite occurs when the oscillator rises to +130. Very negative readings in the -150 area are considered as selling climax levels. Another component of the McClellan Oscillator is divergent pattern formations compared to the market, in particular, a triple top formation of the oscillator. In "Patterns for Profit," there is also mention of using standard trendline analysis with the oscillator. That book further mentions a strong 22-24 week cycle appears in the oscillator, and that was true at the time the book was written. This cycle no longer appears in the patterns of the Oscillator, and it likely disappeared due to changes in U.S. tax laws related to holding periods for determination of capital gains taxes. Chart 4-38 shows the McClellan Oscillator and the +150 and -150 thresholds mentioned above.

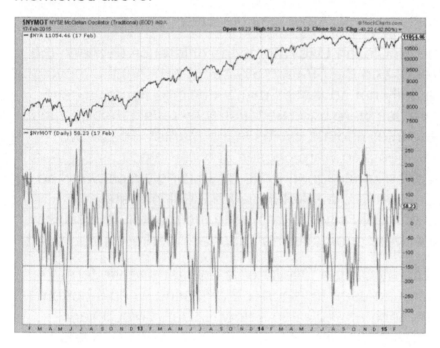

Chart 4-38

Author Comments: Exponential moving averages and percentage of trend smoothing are confusing to most. They really are equal other than small rounding differences. A 19 period exponential average is the same as a 10% trend smoothing. One needs to be cautious to avoid relying on data and results at the beginning of the data file in order to let the indicators adjust to reflect recent data value. See the additional information in chapter 10 (The McClellan Indicators) for the mathematical details.

The McClellan indicators utilize the advance decline line concept. A point often not understood about the advance decline line is that its numerical value has no meaning, since different start points in the A-D data will result in different numerical values for the sum of all previous A-D readings. The A-D Line's relative position to past structures can have importance, such as making a higher high or a divergence relative to prices. Of even greater importance is the A-D Line's acceleration, both up and down. This is why the McClellan indicators are such a significant contribution to breadth analysis.

Sherman McClellan, in an interview in Stocks & Commodities magazine, in 1994, said that McClellan Oscillator readings in the neighborhood of -125 to -130 represented a bearish indication. A reading that low or lower that arises after a prolonged period without deeply negative readings means the market is becoming illiquid. In effect, it can be a warning shot of larger problems to come. A subsequent deeply negative reading does not have the same "warning shot" implications; it is instead the fulfillment of what the warning shot was predicting.

We make mention here of numerical values for the Oscillator, but readers are urged not to focus so closely on the number. Varying amounts of market volatility can affect amplitudes, and so analysis is better done by examining a chart of the Oscillator's path rather than by looking at a single numerical value and drawing conclusions from that. A chart will reveal what levels have marked recent extremes, and will also allow the analyst to spot Oscillator structures which have interpretive significance, such as complex or simple structures and divergences relative to price action.

When the Oscillator crosses through the zero line in one direction, and then makes a direct turn around to head back across zero in the other direction, that is a sign of weakness for that side of the zero line. If, however, the Oscillator builds a "complex" structure on one side of the zero line, doing a lot of chopping up and down without crossing zero, then that implies strength for that side. A complex structure above zero implies that the bulls have control, and although the bears might summon enough energy for a momentary downward correction, further gains should be expected.

Occasionally periods will occur in which neither side of zero will see a complex structure; the Oscillator may just go from a simple structure above zero to a simple structure below zero and back again, meaning that neither side has willingness or ability to take control of the market.

The history of how Sherman and Marian McClellan developed the Oscillator and Summation Index is rich in technical analysis history and development. It begins with contact from Gene Morgan, who hosted "Charting the Market" on KWHY television in the 1960s and who gave the indicators their names. Kennedy Gammage comes into the picture, as does Pete Haurlan. The single best accounting on this was done by Sherman McClellan at the Market Technician's Association meeting on May 14, 2004, when he was awarded the Lifetime Achievement Award. His son, Tom provides this presentation and Sherman's acceptance speech on their site. Go to: http://www.mcoscillator.com/user/MTAspeech.pdf. Tom also was kind enough to add comments on this section and the section on the McClellan Summation Index.

My good friend Tom McClellan has offered the below piece for inclusion in the book.

We have learned a lot about the behavior of the McClellan A-D Oscillator since my parents, Sherman and Marian McClellan, brought it to the public back in 1969. One of the points that we have learned is that the proper way to interpret it depends on the market environment you are in at any given moment.

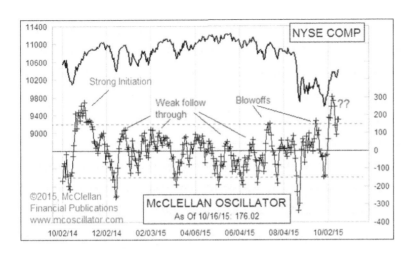

If I were to distill all of the collected wisdom about the McClellan Oscillator into simple sound bites, I would have to break it down according to levels of understanding of the complex messages it can convey. So here, in degrees of increasing sophistication, are the important points:

McClellan Oscillator 101 – Positive is good, negative is bad.

McClellan Oscillator 201 – Overbought and oversold readings are important, as are divergences, although they can sometimes be misleading.

McClellan Oscillator 301 – Complex structures above or below zero convey an important message about which side, bulls or bears, is in control. Conversely, simple across-and-back structures imply a lack of control.

Graduate Level – How one should interpret the McClellan Oscillator is dependent on whether the stock market is in an uptrend or a downtrend.

Now some explanation, as I try to bring you all up to the graduate level in one fell swoop. When the stock market is in an uptrend, if you see the McClellan A-D Oscillator rise up to a level above +150, and the higher the better, it is a sign of strong upward initiation and a promise of even higher highs to follow. Yes, it is an overbought condition, but an overbought reading in an uptrend is not a terminal event as one is in a downtrend.

We saw an example of that back in October 2014, at the left end of the chart above, when the Oscillator climbed up to a high of +271, and stayed at a high level for a long time. It was a message that the worries over the Ebola Panic were done, and that there was still plenty of liquidity available to help lift the overall stock market.

Subsequent rallies were not quite as strong, and we did not see any subsequent instances of strongly positive Oscillator readings. The final price high in May 2015 came with the McClellan A-D Oscillator at a peak reading of only +51, showing the tepid strength in the liquidity stream.

Now we are in a downtrend, and the countertrend rallies have been able to take the Oscillator up to a level which would otherwise be an indication of strong new upward initiation. But the lack of follow through reveals those high readings to be markers of blowoff tops instead of strong new initiation. The latest Oscillator peak rose all the way up to +303, and we thus far are not seeing follow-through.

If the Oscillator continues falling and goes back down through the zero line without building any complexity up above zero, then that will be a "tell" that the recent bounce has been just a countertrend rally, and is not the start of a new uptrend. That is the outcome which I expect to see, and so the Oscillator serves as a great tool for confirmation of expectations.

As an historical example of this principle, this next chart looks back at the period from 2008 to 2009.

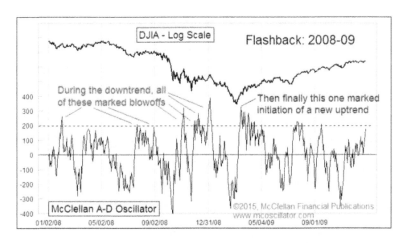

During the whole of the bear market in 2008, we saw several instances of the McClellan A-D Oscillator rising up to very high levels, not just above +150 but up well above +200. And in each case, it marked the end of a countertrend rally rather than the initiation of a new uptrend. It was not until we got past the final bottom in March 2009 that the meaning of the very high Oscillator readings started to change. Each subsequent instance of a very high Oscillator reading marked another bullish wave of upward initiation.

If one had been looking at these readings in real time, it might have been hard to know that the really high readings in late March 2009 were somehow different than the ones all during 2008. So if one had only the McClellan Oscillator as a tool, then it would have been possible to make an initial misinterpretation of the surge higher in March 2009, thinking that it was just another countertrend rally. But the tell in that case was that the Oscillator remained at a high level longer than in all of the countertrend rallies of 2008, and the market refused to stop going up. At some point an honest analyst would have to change his view and accept that there had been a sea-change.

That's easy for me to say now, and it would have been hard to do in real time as it was happening back then, I know. But this serves as a good lesson for us all to remember as we seek to properly interpret what we see in the Oscillator and in the market going forward from here.

By that, I mean that if the +303 McClellan Oscillator reading on Oct. 8 is followed by a prompt downturn and no further upward movement, it will be a tell that we have just seen yet another countertrend rally within what is supposed to be a downtrend lasting until at least April 2016. But if, instead, the Oscillator stays above zero long enough to push the Ratio Adjusted Summation Index above +500, then that will be an entirely different message.

If you want to learn more about the McClellan Oscillator and how to interpret it, start with our Learning Center articles which are free for everyone. Then consider ordering our Advanced Topics Seminar video, which features lessons on how to interpret the McClellan Oscillator plus a whole lot more. And if you would like to order a new eBook-format copy of Sherman and Marian McClellan's original 1970 book, Patterns For Profit, visit our Books and DVDs page.

Many thanks Tom.

More details on the McClellan Indicators can be found in Chapter 10.

Formula: (Today's 19 exp. average of (A – D) – (Today's 39 exp. average of (A – D)

StockCharts.com Symbol: $NYMOT

References:

McClellan, Sherman and Marian. <u>Patterns for Profit</u>. Lakewood, WA: McClellan Financial Publications, Inc., 1976. This book was originally published by Trade Levels in 1970.

McClellan Family Interview, "It's All In the Family: Sherman, Marian, and Tom McClellan." <u>Stocks and Commodities</u>, Volume 12, June 1994, pp. 264-273.

McClellan Summation Index

Author/Creator: Sherman and Marian McClellan

Data components required: Advances (A), Declines (D).

Description: The McClellan Summation Index is the cumulative sum of all daily McClellan Oscillator readings, and provides a long-range view of market breadth. The Summation Index therefore changes each day by the value of the Oscillator, rising when the Oscillator is positive and declining when the Oscillator is negative. The Summation Index has developed a life of its own as time has added additional information to its interpretation. Originally (in the 1960-70s) the summation index moved in the range of +1000 and -1500. Since the Oscillator and Summation Index debuted before the days when computers or even hand-held calculators were available, all calculations were done manually. So that folks would not have to work with negative numbers except under very unusual (and important) circumstances, the McClellans arbitrarily set a neutral level at +1000. This was done by adding 1000 to the calculation. Since the advent of personal computers this is no longer necessary, but is also not easily changed since so much is written about it and so many folks follow it. Tom McClellan (Sherman and Marian's son) told me it was not worth the possible confusion to change it.

Interpretation: A basic mathematical fact is that when the McClellan Oscillator is positive (above the zero line), the McClellan Summation Index will be rising. The levels of the Summation index are as important as the direction. Chart 4-39 shows the McClellan Summation Index back to 1997.

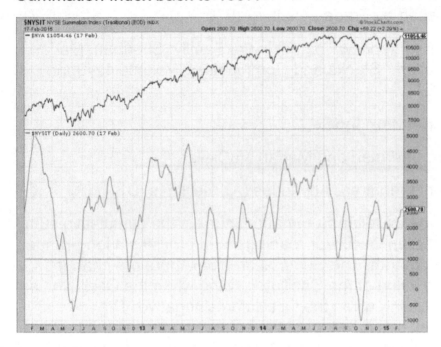

Chart 4-39

Author Comments: This is probably one of the best breadth indicators available. It has a multitude of uses. Not only its direction, but the level it is at is important. It is discussed here in keeping with the conventions used in this book and is further elaborated on in Chapter 10.

The McClellan Summation Index has a number of different calculations. The one that is used by the most analysts, is probably also the one that is not as good as at least one of the others. The use of exponential moving averages (percent of trend) for calculating the summation index is common and actually how the McClellans originally did it. However, in the early 1990s, a bright mathematician named James R. Miekka came up with a modification to the McClellan formula that is today used by the

McClellans, Carl Swenlin, and most of the other purists in the field. While this modification does not affect the oscillator, it does have a significant effect on the summation index which is derived from the oscillator.

One of the problems with the original formula was that as the summation index levels were found to also be important, it was difficult for two different analysts to have exactly the same values. If breadth values from different sources were used, if math errors were present, or if any day's data were missing anywhere in the calculation, then those differences would accumulate and remain in the Summation Index values forever.

Miekka found that the Summation Index could be calculated for any day in history, simply by knowing that day's values for the 10% trend and 5% trend. He created a calibration formula so that the levels will remain the same no matter when you begin the calculation, and any data or calculation errors would eventually be factored out of the Summation Index value just as they are factored out of the 10% trend and 5% trend. The mathematics of Miekka's calculation formula can be found in Chapter 10. In addition, Jim Miekka has offered a McClellan Summation Buy Signal report, also found in Chapter 10.

In their vast research on their indicators, the McClellans found that when the Summation Index went above +3000, it was time to pay attention. The first observation was that whenever that happened, a strong bull market was nearby. From the early 1970s until 1994 (time of their interview), there were seven instances of the summation index breaching +3000. From the chart below, you can see these seven plus the ones in more recent history. The rise to +6000 in April, 2003 was also telling. Looking at the same chart, it is also apparent that when the McClellan Summation Index reaches a deeply negative value on the downside, an important bottom is close at hand. Chart 4-40 shows the McClellan Summation Index using the Miekka formula adjustment (see chapter 10 for more details) with the +3000 and -1200 thresholds.

StockCharts.com Symbol: !BINYMSIM

Chart 4-40

Carl Swenlin and the McClellans also use an adjusted advance decline formula in association with the Miekka modification. This is an attempt to somewhat neutralize the growing effect of the advance decline information on the New York exchange. The ratio used is (A – D) / (A + D). Often a factor of 1000 is used to move the numbers from out of the realm of fractions and into the more normal type numbers. Chart 4-41 shows the McClellan Summation Index using the ratio and the Miekka formula adjustment and is the version used by Carl Swenlin the McClellans today.

StockCharts.com Symbol: !BINYMSIS

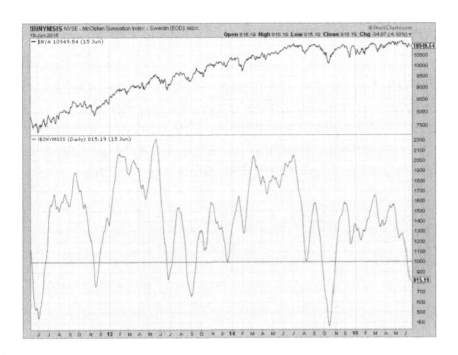

Chart 4-41

Tom McClellan says that when the McClellan Summation Index drops below the zero line, it is a precursor for a bear market. At much deeper levels, the Summation Index can reveal when enough of a decline has taken place, and when traders should begin to look for a strong up move out of that deep bottom. As the market moves up out of a deeply oversold bottom, the Summation Index comes into play again when it either confirms or refutes the strength of the new up move. A move from a deeply oversold level to a very high level within a 5-month period can confirm that a new bull market has been established. Failure to achieve a high enough Summation Index reading after a bear market decline can reveal that the bears are still in control, and the price low needs to be retested or exceeded to the downside.

Another analysis method the McClellans used was to overlay past summation index charts based upon significant market bottoms or low summation readings. This technique helps to anticipate market movements.

Martin Pring claims that using the Summation Index with a 35-day simple moving average crossover offers good results. He also states that using normal trendline analysis on the summation index can lead to changes in market direction. Chart 4-42 shows Pring's use of the McClellan Summation Index with a 35 day moving average.

Chart 4-42

Formula: This is the accumulation of the McClellan Oscillator. SI today = SI yesterday + McO today

StockCharts.com Symbol: $NYSIT

References:

McClellan, Sherman and Marian. <u>Patterns for Profit</u>. Lakewood, WA : McClellan Financial Publications, Inc., 1976. This book was originally published by Trade Levels in 1970.

McClellan Family Interview, "It's All In the Family: Sherman, Marian, and Tom McClellan." <u>Stocks and Commodities</u>, Volume 12, June 1994, pp. 264-273.

Pring, Martin, "Internal Market Momentum." <u>Stocks and Commodities</u>, Volume 11, July 1993, pp. 298-305.

Miekka, James, <u>The Sudbury Bull and Bear Report</u>, St. Petersburg, FL.

Merriman Breadth Model

Author/Creator: Paul Merriman

Data components required: Advances (A), Declines (D), Market Index (MKT)

Description: This indicator uses the advance decline line and the New York Composite Index. It utilizes a relationship between the two in a manner not as complex as the advance decline divergence oscillator, one that is effective.

Interpretation: A buy signal is given when the advance decline line is 2% or more above is 150 day moving average and when the index is 2% or more above its 150 day moving average. A sell signal is given when the advance decline line is 2% or more below its 150 day moving average or the index is 2% or more below its 150 day moving average. In chart 4-43 a buy signal is when the indicator is at +1 and a sell signal is when it is at -1. Multiple signals should be ignored.

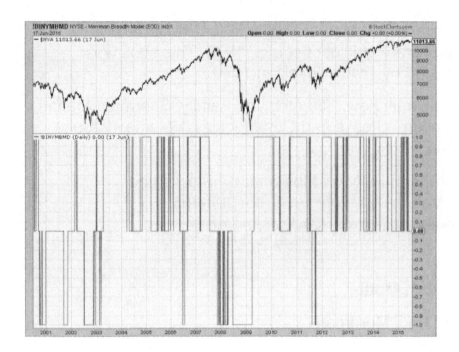

Chart 4-43

Author Comments: This is a simple but quite good concept. It offers double confirmation in order to get into the market where only one of the two components can get you out. I'm not sure how he measures the percentages because the numerical values of the advance decline line can get quite large depending upon where the calculation was started. However, if he is looking at the percentage relative to a moving average of the same values, so this would self-adjust over time.

StockCharts.com Symbol: !BINYMBMD

References:

Merriman, Paul, www.fundadvice.com/modelsexplained.html.

Swenlin IT Breadth Momentum Oscillator

Also known as: ITBM

Author/Creator: Carl Swenlin

Data components required: Advances (A), Declines (D).

Description: The Intermediate Term Breadth Momentum Oscillator is a barometer of breadth. To calculate the ITBM, add the daily McClellan Oscillator (ratio adjusted) to the daily 39-day exponential average, then calculate a 20-day exponential average of the result.

Interpretation: Carl offers this short bit of advice on his indicator: It is better if this indicator is above the zero line and rising. Below the zero line and falling is the worst scenario. Rising is better than falling, even if below the zero line. Above the zero line and rising is best. The absolute value indicates how overbought/oversold the market is. Direction is most important because it indicates whether the market is getting stronger (rising) or weaker (falling). The best condition is for the ITBM to be rising above its 10-EMA (exponential moving average), and the worst is falling below its 10-EMA. It is extremely negative if the ITBM tops below its 10-EMA and below the zero line. Chart 4-44 shows the Swenlin IT Breadth Momentum Oscillator.

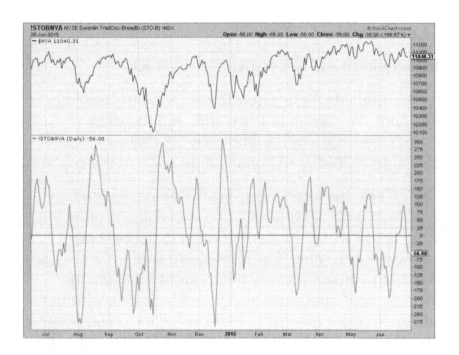

Chart 4-44

Author Comments: Carl Swenlin's website at www.decisionpoint.com is something technical analysts should not miss. Carl has created a number of breadth-based indicators over the years. Carl uses the difference of advances and declines divided by the sum of them for his ratio adjusted version of the McClellan formula. With this indicator, he wanted to develop it so that it would incorporate both the McClellan Oscillator and its components. Carl's version certainly lets you know when to take negative readings seriously.

2015 Update: Decision Point has been completely incorporated into StockCharts.com.

Formula: To calculate the ITBM add the daily McClellan Oscillator (Ratio-Adjusted) to the daily 10% exponential average (Ratio-Adjusted), then calculate a 20-day exponential average (0.10 exponent) of the result.

StockCharts.com Symbol: !STOBNYA

References:

Swenlin, Carl, www.decisionpoint.com, now www.stockcharts.com

McClellan, Sherman and Marian. Patterns for Profit. Lakewood, WA: McClellan Financial Publications, Inc., 1976

Swenlin Trading Oscillator – Breadth

Also known as: STO-B

Author/Creator: Carl Swenlin

Data components required: Advances (A), Declines (D)

Description: The Swenlin Trading Oscillator – Breadth was designed for short-term trading. It is a 5-day simple moving average of a 4-day exponential average of the daily advances minus declines divided by the total daily advances and declines times 1000. This is the ratio that is common in Swenlin's work.

Interpretation: The double smoothing of the short-term data results in a reliable oscillator that persists in one direction, usually tops near short-term market tops, and bottoms near short-term market bottoms. As with most indicators, the primary trend of the market will determine how you will use the indicator. In a bull market, the tops will not be very reliable. In a bear market, the bottoms will not be very reliable. The indicator is shown in chart 4-45.

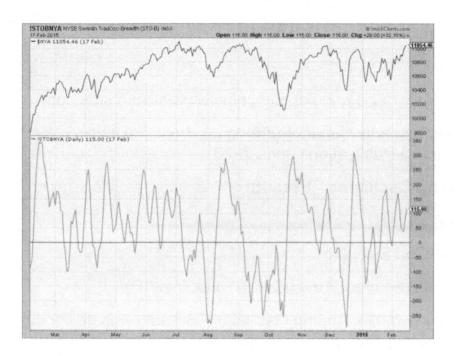

Chart 4-45

Author Comments: Carl Swenlin has created a good trading vehicle with his Swenlin Trading Oscillator.

Formula: The STO is a 5-day simple moving average of a 4-day exponential moving average of the daily advances minus declines divided by the total daily advances and declines times 1000. (A-D)/(A+D)*1000. First you must calculate the average value of (A-D)/(A+D)*1000 for the last four days before you can begin the exponential weighting. Next you can begin calculating the exponential average. The following is a key for the symbols in the formula. pdEMA = Prior Day's Average (Begin with simple MA, thereafter pdEMA is an exponential average.) (A-D)/(A+D)*1000 = Current day's advances minus declines divided by the total advances and declines times 1000. The formula for the EMA is: ((A-D)/(A+D)*1000)*0.5)+pdEMA All that remains is to calculate a 5-day simple moving average of the EMA.

StockCharts.com Symbol: !STOBNYA

References:

Swenlin, Carl, www.decisionpoint.com, now www.stockcharts.com

Zahorchak Method

Author/Creator: Michael G. Zahorchak

Data components required: Advances (A), Declines (D), Market Index (MKT).

Description: In his 1977 book, The Art of Low Risk Investing, Michael Zahorchak lays out a complete investing and analysis plan using moving averages on the New York Composite Index and the advance decline line. Zahorchak, who was assistant vice-president of the American Stock Exchange, developed this methodology using only weekly data. Basically you must maintain a 5, 15, and 40 week moving average on the advance decline line, the New York composite index (Zahorchak used the Dow Industrial Average), and any stocks that you wish to analyze and invest in.

Interpretation: Zahorchak defines how to move from a down trend to an up-trend and also talks about periods of indecision. Basically, when the advance decline line and the market average are both above their 40 week (200 day) moving averages, the market is in an up-trend. Identification of a market top is when a combination of the 5 and 15 period averages begin to break down. Similarly, a bottom occurs when they start to rise. The chart below was developed using daily data, substituting the appropriate number of days for the weeks used by Zahorchak (15 weeks = 75 days). Daily data has more oscillations, but the method works just the same.

The indicator in chart 4-46 is scaled from -15 to +15. As various components of this method take affect the indicator rises or falls based upon the sum of all of its components. The most bullish is

+15 and the most bearish is -15. Using the zero-line crossing for signals seems to work well. One could also develop more extravagant signals using various levels to enhance the timing. Always keep in mind that this was a long term approach to identifying trends and is not for trading.

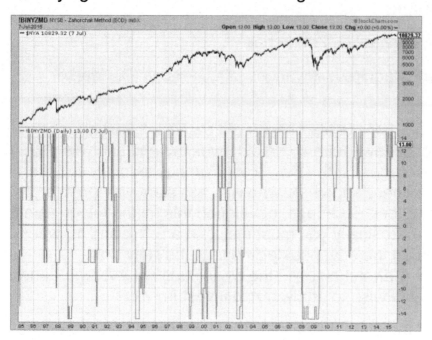

Chart 4-46

Author Comments: This was one of the first books that cemented my thinking into taking a technical approach to investing and market analysis. It is a shame the book is out of print, because Zahorchak covers all the basics from emotions, to Wall Street myths, to how to control all the outside influences that can cause you to make bad decisions in the market. I would do this method injustice if I did not include the signals using weekly data. On the weekly chart (chart 4-47) one can see that whenever the indicator is above +8, the market is rising and when below -8 it is not. Noteworthy, is the fact that the indicator dropped to +4 the first week in October, 1987. This is a good methodology for keeping yourself on the right side of the market. It is not for trading.

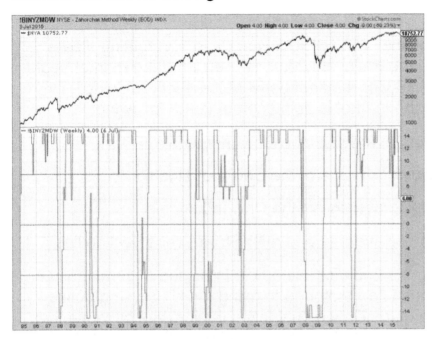

Chart 4-47

Details on the Zahorchak Measure

Let's start off with a review of the Zahorchak Measure in considerable detail. Zahorchak states that there is often no correlation between the price of a stock and its fundamentals. He further states that fundamentals will tell you whether or not investors will be attracted to a stock. Zahorchak clearly believes that the markets move regularly from bull market periods to bear market periods. These switches from bear to bull and back again are not due to economic conditions but a switch in investor psychology from optimism to pessimism. He also believes that stocks move in herds and have a tendency to go up and down together in these bull and bear markets, with just enough exceptions to prove the rule. He was really big on spending lots of time on selecting a shopping list of

137

stocks as potential purchases; no less than 25 and no more than 100. He preferred cyclical stocks that moved well with bull and bear periods.

"Only the market itself can tell you what to do. Everything else is irrelevant. While the irrelevant items tell you what the market ought to be doing, this may or may not be what it actually is doing." To determine what the market is doing compute the following:

1 - 5 week moving average of the Dow Industrials

2 – 15 week moving average of the Dow Industrials

3 – 40 week moving average of the Dow Industrials

4 – 15 week moving average of the NYSE advance decline line.

Note: Rereading the book for this article I realized at some point in the last 4 decades I had switched to using the NYSE Composite average instead of the Dow Industrials. I think it was because the advance decline line uses the NYSE stocks, so figured using the index of those stocks made more sense. I seriously doubt it makes a difference.

Zahorchak then discusses the timing of the market because the primary trend tells you when to buy stocks and when to avoid them, however, it does not tell you when to sell them. Once stocks have been bought, their trend action tells you when to sell. Note: Keyword here is 'their.' He then goes into the four basic market conditions.

1 – Bull market.

2 – Sideways periods in a bull market. He goes into considerable discussion on why investors make terrible decision during these types of markets.

3 – Bear market.

4 – Again, an uncertain period within a bear market. Again, much discussion about all the mistakes investors make during this period.

In the table 4-1 below, +40 or –40 mean that the price is above (+) or below (-) the 40-week average. Up means the moving average is moving higher each week. Down means the moving average is moving lower.

| General Market | | | AD Line | Investment Posture |
| NYSE Composite Average | | | | |
5 week	15 week	40 week	15 week	
-40	-40	Down	Down	Bear market - avoid new purchaese
-40	-40	Up	Down	Bear market - avoid new purchaese
Up/-40	-40	Down	Down	Uncertain (probably bear rally)
40	-40	Down	Down	Uncertain (Possibly first sign of bull - BUY)
-40	-40	Down	Up	Uncertain (Possibly first sign of bull - BUY)
40	-40	Down	Up	Second sign of bull - BUY
40	40	Down	Up	Buy aggressively or stay invested
40	40	Up	Up	Bull market - stay invested
-40	40	Up	Up	Uncertain (stay invested - no buying)
40	40	Up	Down	Uncertain (stay invested - no buying)
+/-40	-40	Up	Up	Bear market
+/-40	-40	Up	Down	Bear market

Table 4-1

The timing of the purchase and sale of individual stocks is provided in Table 4-2. The AD Line is not used here since there is no advance decline information on an individual stock.

| Individual Stocks | | | Investment Posture |
| NYSE Composite Average | | | |
5 week	15 week	40 week	
40	40	Up	Hold, regardless of general market
40	40	Down	Hold, regardless of general market
-15	40	Up	Hold if Bull - Sell if Bear
-15	40	Down	Hold if Bull - Sell if Bear
-40	40	Up	Hold if Bull - Sell if Bear
-40	40	Down	Hold if Bull - Sell if Bear
40	-40	Up	Buy in early Bull - Avoid in Bear
40	-40	Down	Buy in early Bull - Avoid in Bear
-40	-40	Up/Down	Avoid, regardless of general market

Table 4-2

2015 Update. When we were converting the Zahorchak Measure into StockCharts.com's symbol catalog, we had a difficult time because I had tinkered with the original formula trying to improve it. I finally got the correct formula taken care of but want to add the ZM2 version for both the weekly and daily Zahorchak Measure. When Bill Shelby and I started to program the Zahorchak Measure into StockCharts.com's format so it would be included in the symbol catalog, we had trouble getting started. The reason was actually my fading memory as I had tinkered with the Zahorchak Measure over the decades and in the process thought I had made a few changes and improved it somewhat. Once I realized I was giving Bill the code to the "tinkered" version and sent him the correct code we were off and running. After reviewing both sets of code I decided to also include my alternate version.

I had noticed that during market bottoms and especially tops there was a lot of noise in the measure; while it still yielding reasonable signals. This generally happens when a short term average is dancing with a long term average, which in this case is the 5 week versus the 40 week. So I simply removed the buy and sell requirements for those two relationships and it removed much of the noise without affecting the timeliness. Chart 4-48 below shows the weekly modified ZM for the past 35 years. You might notice that with the 5/40 relationship removed the ZM now only moves from +10 to -10. Chart 4-49 shows the weekly modified ZM for last 10 years.

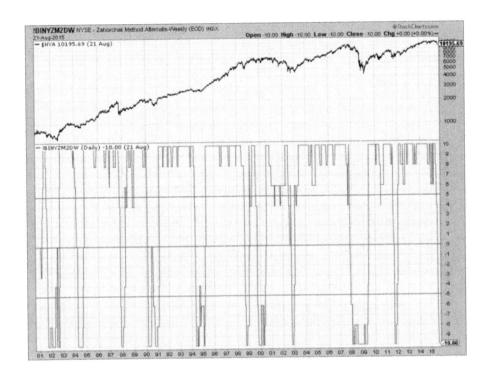

Chart 4-48

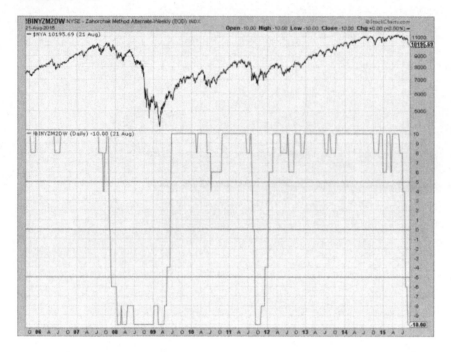

Chart 4-49

Since I modified the weekly we went ahead and did the same thing for the daily version. Chart 4-50 shows the daily alternate ZM for the past 10 years.

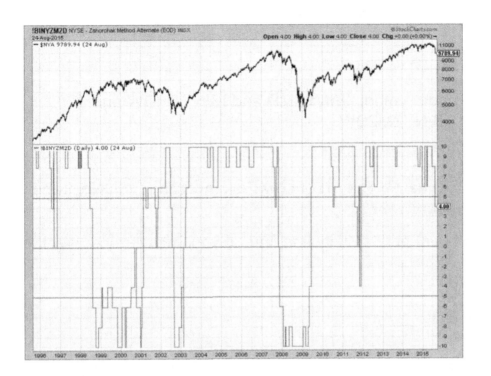

143

Chart 4-50

Formula: $\sum (A - D)$ weekly

StockCharts.com Symbol: !BINYZMD and !BINYZMDW and !BIZM2D and !BINYZM2DW

References:

Zahorchak, Michael G. The Art of Low Risk Investing. Van Nostrand Reinhold Company, 1977.

This book is out of print a difficult to find. If you uncover one, buy it.

CH 5 - Advance Decline Ratio Indicators

Advances / Declines

The breadth indicators in this section utilize the ratio of the advancing issues and the declining issues as their primary relationship.

Advance Decline Ratio Indicators

Advance / Decline Ratio

Breadth Thrust

Breadth Thrust Continuation

Duarte Market Thrust Indicator

Eliades Sign of the Bear

Hughes Breadth Momentum Oscillator

Panic Thrust

STIX – Short Term Trading Index

Advance / Decline Ratio

Data components required: Advances (A), Declines (D)

Description: This is the ratio of advancing issues and declining issues (Advances divided by Declines).

Interpretation: Martin Zweig liked to watch this ratio over a 10-day period. He said it was very rare for the 10-day ratio to reach 2-to-1 (2.0) or more. It seems that the level of 1.8 is better with more recent data. Both levels are shown on chart 5-1.

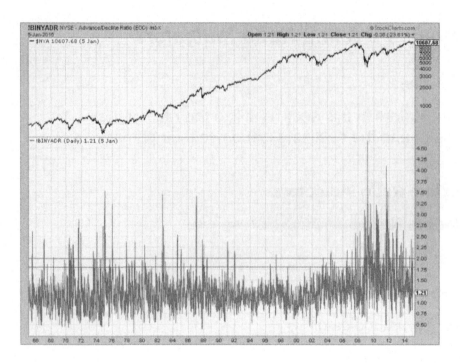

Chart 5-1

Author Comments: Ratios and differences account for many different variations of technical indicators. If you take the 10-day difference of price and plot it next to the 10-day ratio of price, you will get a similarly shaped line, only the values are different. Another interesting discovery was that the ratio of advances and declines was called the overbought oversold index by Norman Fosback (Steve Achelis used the difference of advances and declines for the overbought oversold index). Fosback says that the ten-day average of the ratio is good for determining overbought and oversold areas in the market. He says that the market is oversold when the advances are at least 25% fewer than the declines (0.75 on chart 5-2). The market is overbought when the ratio shows that the number of advances is at least 25% more than the declines (1.25 on chart 5-2). Fosback states that this indicator has not tested well and is probably overrated. I added a line at 1.70, which means advances outnumber declines by about 58%. It is clear that since the low in

146

2009, the overbought area has increased significantly. Chart 5-2 shows that the Advance Decline Ratio seems to better reflect overbought with today's breadth numbers. This is one of the issues I have with any overbought oversold indicator, the levels change over time, so it makes it unreliable if used in an isolated condition.

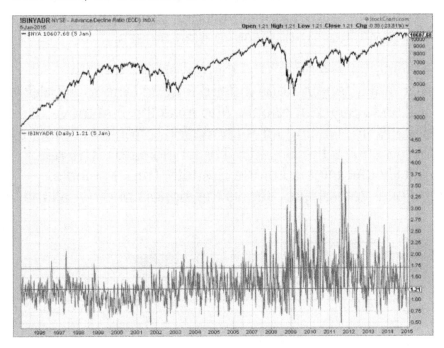

Chart 5-2

Formula: (A / D)

StockCharts.com Symbol: !BINYADR (please note, this is the 10-day arithmetic average of A/D; if you want the raw ratio you can use: $NYADV:$NYDEC).

References:

Fosback, Norman G. <u>Stock Market Logic</u>, Fort Lauderdale, FL: The Institute for Economic Research, Inc., 1976.

Breadth Thrust

Author/Creator: Martin Zweig

Data components required: Advances (A), Declines (D)

Description: Breadth Thrust is a 10-day exponential average of the advances divided by the sum of the advances plus the declines. A Breadth Thrust signal occurs when this indicator goes from under 0.40 to above 0.615 within a 10-day time period or less.

Interpretation: Between 1944 and 2014 there were 13 thrusts. Martin Zweig says that strength does indeed tend to lead to greater strength. He goes on to say that people who miss the first move of an explosive rally and are waiting for a correction, often miss most of the action. Chart 5-3 shows the Breadth Thrust indicator. The red digital version quickly identifies all of the Breadth Thrust signals. Remember, the digital version just shows the signals and not all the analog noise.

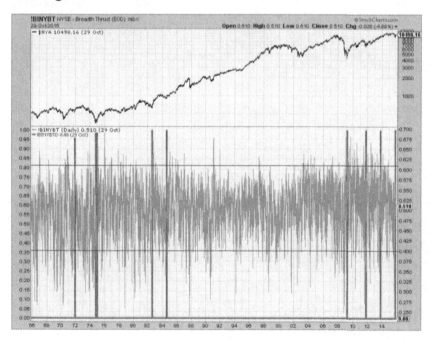

Chart 5-3

Author Comments: I wish I had a dime for every time I have seen this indicator misquoted or used incorrectly. The component that is usually overlooked is that it must go from oversold to overbought within 10 days.   Since 1965 there have been only 9 Breadth Thrust signals as shown in charts 5-3. Here are the dates:

December 3, 1971	March 18, 2009
October 10, 1974	October 14, 2011
January 3, 1975	October 18, 2013
August 20, 1982	October 7, 2015
August 3, 1984	

Those intimately familiar with the market over the last 40+ years will recognize the second and third dates as the first bottom of the giant 1973-74 bear market, the 1982 date as within a week of the beginning of the biggest bull market in history, and the 1984 date as one that coincides with a good market bottom. The March 18, 2009 was about a week after a huge bull market.

Robert Colby tested this indicator over 62 years of data and found that by using 0.659 for a buy signal and dropping below 0.366 for a sell signal worked well. However, he used a simple moving average instead of an exponential one, and it appears he did not use the 10 periods for the signal to occur. However, that does not detract from the importance of his results and further offers another use of the breadth thrust concept.

As I always do, I ask what I can do to this indicator to improve it. I can increase the days to give a signal, say to 15 days. This would give the indicator more time to reach its goal of going above .615. I can change the smoothing from 10 to 8 (to make it faster), and even change the type of smoothing from exponential to arithmetic (to make it slower). All of these may or may not yield better results. The problem here is that one is deviating from the initial concept and trying to build a better mousetrap. Martin Zweig's concept was that the market sometimes launches like a rocket and he was attempted to define that with his Breadth Thrust. The first thing I tried was to change from using an exponential average to using a simple moving average. It didn't provide any improvement. I think tried a shorter period for the exponential average (8 periods) and it gave many more signals because it was able to travel from .4 to .615 quicker, however, it didn't appear to drastically improve the original work.

Formula: (A / A + D)

StockCharts.com Formula: !BNYBT and !BINYBTD

References:

Achelis, Steven B. <u>Technical Analysis from A to Z.</u> New York: McGraw-Hill, 1995.

Colby, Robert W. <u>The Encyclopedia of Technical Market Indicators</u>. New York: McGraw-Hill, 2003.

Breadth Thrust Continuation

Author/Creator: Gerald Appel

Data components required: Advances (A), Declines (D)

Description: Breadth Thrust is a 10-day exponential average of the advances divided by the sum of the advances plus the declines. A Breadth Thrust occurs when this indicator goes from under 0.40 to above 0.615 in a 10-day time period or less. A Breadth Thrust Continuation is when it goes above 0.615. This means the likelihood of the market continuing its upward move is great.

Interpretation: A Breadth Thrust Continuation signal is given whenever it goes above 0.615 without the requirement for it to come from below 0.40 in ten days. That continuation signal is good until it then drops below 0.50. On chart 5-4, the upward spikes denote the Breadth Thrust Continuation signals with the sell signals being the downward spikes. Subsequent sell spikes should be ignored. They only come into play after an upward buy spike.

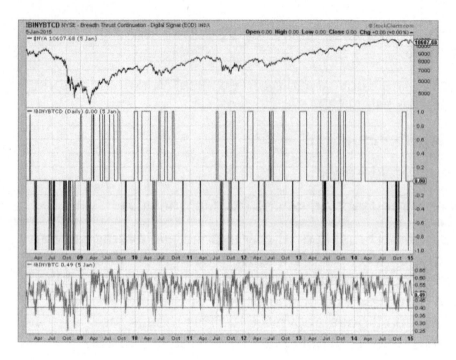

Chart 5-4

Author Comments: Tom McClellan added an additional rule stating that the continuation signal expires after 50 days, but can restart that timing (50 days) with any subsequent move above 0.615. Since 1965 there have been 31 Breadth Thrust Continuation signals.

Formula: (A / A + D)

StockCharts.com Formula: !BINYBTC and !BINYBTCD

References:

McClellan, Tom, "The McClellan Market Report," November 19, 2004.

Achelis, Steven B. Technical Analysis from A to Z. New York: McGraw-Hill, 1995.

Colby, Robert W. The Encyclopedia of Technical Market Indicators. New York: McGraw-Hill, 2003.

Duarte Market Thrust Indicator

Also Known As: Bi-weekly Market Thrust Indicator (BMTI)

Author/Creator: Dr. Joe Duarte

Data components required: Weekly Data, Advances (A), Declines (D).

Description: The Bi-weekly Market Thrust Indicator (BMTI) is a measure of market momentum, and is based on the often-overlooked weekly variation of the advance decline line. It is a predictor of stock prices over the six months after a signal occurs. Based on Martin Zweig's Ten Day Advance Decline Ratio, BMTI uses weekly data, as opposed to Zweig's daily data. The difference is that Zweig captured the market's advance decline ratio for ten straight days, looking for a two to one ratio of advancing over declining stocks on a rolling basis, while BMTI focuses on weekly data. To calculate BMTI take the weekly advance-decline data and add the advances and the declines for two weeks.

Interpretation: Using this weekly indicator, signals are generated for buying only whenever the ratio is equal to two or greater. If you bought a market average on one of these signals and held for at least six months, your return would be good. Chart 5-5 shows the Duarte Market Thrust Indicator.

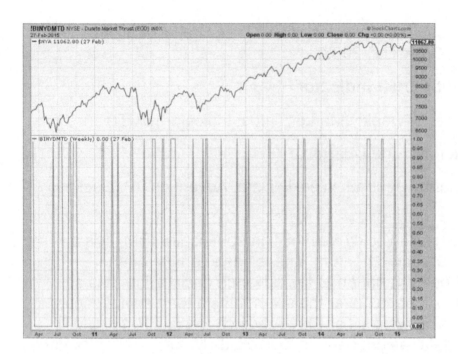

Chart 5-5

Author Comments: One of the important concepts that Dr. Duarte identified with this indicator is what he calls a super cluster. This is when the BMTI gives several consecutive signals. It means that upside momentum is huge and the market can stay bullish for up to a year. The super clusters in charts 5-7 are denoted by the wider spikes. The wider the spike on the chart, means more consecutive signals, and the better the indication.

Formula: (A / D) (weekly values)

References:

Duarte, Joe, www.joe-duarte.com.

Zweig, Martin E. Winning on Wall Street. New York: Warner Books, 1986.

Eliades Sign of the Bear

Author/Creator: Peter Eliades

Data components required: Advances (A), Declines (D).

Description: Peter Eliades first wrote about his in 1992 after noting a lack of volatility in the advance decline numbers. After apparently much research, back to 1940, he came up with three rules required to identify the "sign of the bear."

A. There must be a streak of 21-27 consecutive days (trading) where the daily advance/decline ratio remains above 0.65 and below 1.95.

B. That steak mentioned above must end with a downside break which means the advance/decline ratio is less than 0.65.

C. The downside break must be confirmed by either a two-day average advance/decline ratio or a three-day average advance/decline ratio following the end of the streak being below 0.75.

Interpretation: This is not an indicator that gives many signals. In the paper that Eliades has on his website, www.stockmarketcycles.com, there have only been 7 "sign of the bear" signals since the late 1920s. Yes, that is right, over the last 90+ years. April, 1998 and September, 2000 were the last two signals. In chart 5-6, the third parameter is shown in the middle of the chart and can be used for verification. When you consider that parameter, the early signals in the 1990s will go away, leaving only the 1998 and 2000 signals. Personally, an indicator that only gives 7 signals in 90 years is not of much value. However, these things can teach you about market action and help you create others.

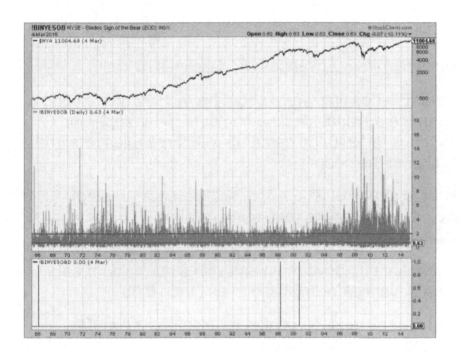

Chart 5-6

Author Comments: The first rule (A) addresses the lack of volatility that he first noticed when deriving this indicator. Originally it was just 21 days. The second rule (B) requires for a day to have at least 1.5 times more declines than advances. The third rule (C) is a way to give the breakout some time for confirmation. This is an indicator that one needs to be aware of. You should visit his website and read the paper he wrote on "the sign of the bear."

StockCharts.com symbol: !BINYESOB and !BNYESOBD

References:

Eliades, Peter, www.StockMarketCycles.com,

Hughes Breadth Momentum Oscillator

Author/Creator: James F. Hughes

Data components required: Advances (A), Declines (D), Unchanged (U).

Description: This ratio indicator uses all the breadth movement (advances, declines, unchanged) issues in its formula. It is the difference of advances and declines as the numerator and the sum of the advances, declines, and unchanged as the denominator. This sum is also the total issues. Hughes defined selling climaxes as when the declines were over 70% of total issues while advances were less than 15% of total issues.

Interpretation: This is an oscillator that utilizes all components of issue-oriented breadth. Putting overbought and oversold zone will make this a good short term oscillator. The shorter the term that you want to work with, the shorter the smoothing you should use. Chart 5-7 uses 21 days and would be good for intermediate term analysis.

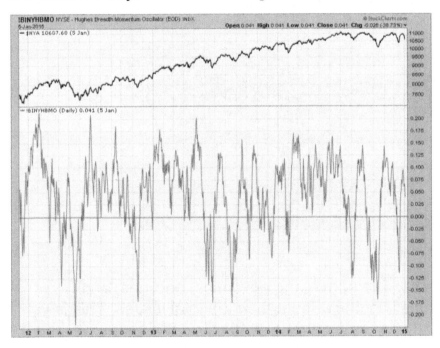

Chart 5-7

Hughes Breadth Momentum % Oscillator was a creation of Robert Colby as an attempt to avoid using negative numbers and fractions and have it oscillate around 100. Overbought and oversold zones at 87 and 110 seem to work well. Colby's modification, while not changing the concept of the indicator is a good improvement. Chart 5-8 is that modification further smoothed by 21 days (red line). The red line is the indicator you should use. It was decided to use the raw version of this indicator and show the smoothing as an overlay. This way you can see how you can change the smoothing to your desired value.

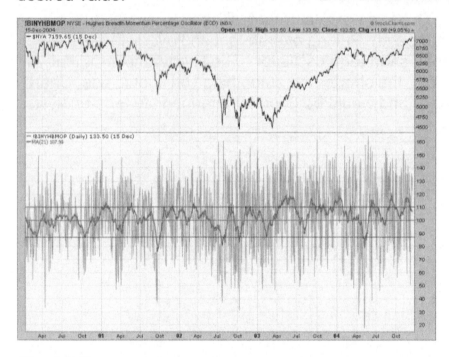

Chart 5-8

Author Comments: The sum of the advances, declines, and unchanged issues is nothing more than the total issues. This is yet another way to derive a ratio that should utilize the same overbought and oversold zones over time. If Total Issues traded is available, and one is entering this data manually, one could use that as the denominator instead.

Formula: (A − D) / (A + D + U) or (A − D) / TI

StockCharts.com Formula: !BINYHBMO and !BINYHBMOD

References:

Colby, Robert W. The Encyclopedia of Technical Market Indicators. New York: McGraw-Hill, 2003.

Dworkin, Fay H., "Defining Advance/Decline Issues," Stocks & Commodities, Volume 8, July 1990, pp. 274-278.

Panic Thrust

Data components required: Advances (A), Declines (D).

Description: This indicator is a method to determine overreaction to market extremes. Simple to calculate and, while not always accurate, will certainly alert you to those extremes.

Interpretation: Whenever the ratio of advances to declines is greater than 4, a buy signal is given. This means that there were more than 4 times as many advancing issues as there were declining issues. Chart 5-9 shows all instances where the advances outnumbered the declines by four to one.

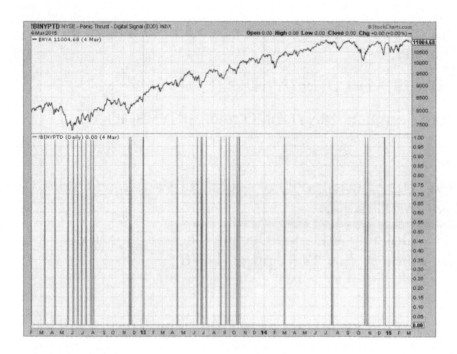

Chart 5-9

Author Comments: There is no doubt that when markets go to extremes, people react differently. In this case, the attempt to pick a bottom based on an extremely oversold condition is identified. This indicator was created after experimenting with a number of different ratios and found that four to one was reliable.

Formula: (A / D) > 4

StockCharts.com symbol: !BINYPTD

STIX

Author/Creator: The Polymetric Report

Data components required: Advances (A), Declines (D).

Description: STIX is an acronym for Short Term Trading Index. It is the advances divided by the sum of the advances and declines.

Then you exponentially smooth it with a 21 day moving average to get STIX.

Interpretation: Low STIX readings are bearish and high readings are bullish. STIX has a normal range in the 42% and 58% range. Somewhat overbought is in the range of 56% to 58% and oversold in the range of 42% and 44%. Chart 5-10 shows STIX with the above mentioned thresholds.

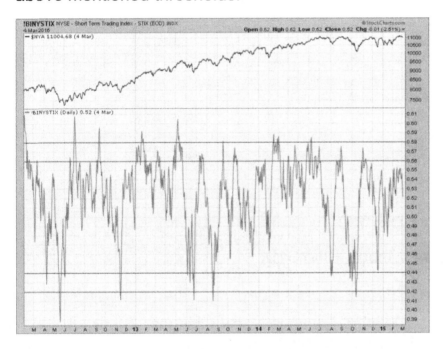

Chart 5-10

Author Comments: Because this is a ratio of advances to the sum of advances plus declines, the overbought and oversold zones mentioned by Fay Dworkin in his 1990 article still appear to be good ones. A slight further enhancement might be to additionally smooth STIX with a simple 10-day average. Chart 5-11 shows the 10-day simple average (red line) of STIX. One can see that the additional smoothing removed many of the signals and keep the really good ones.

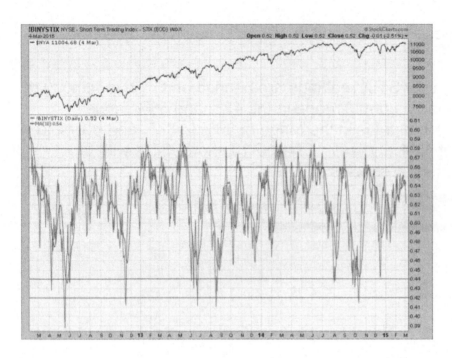

Chart 5-11

Formula: (A / (A + D)) *100

StockCharts.com symbol: !BINYSTIX

References:

Dworkin, Fay H., "Defining Advance/Decline Issues," <u>Stocks & Commodities</u>, Volume 8, July 1990, pp. 274-278.

Chande, Tushar, "Breadth Stix and Other Tricks," <u>Stocks & Commodities</u>, Volume 12, May 1994, pp. 211-214.

CH 6 - Advance Decline Miscellaneous

The breadth indicators in the section could not be categorized as using the difference or the ratio of the advances and declines, so they are in the miscellaneous section.

Advance Decline Miscellaneous Indicators

Advances / Issues Traded

Advance Decline Divergence Oscillator

Advance Decline Diffusion Index

Breadth Climax

Declining Issues TRIX

Disparity Index

Dynamic Synthesis

Unchanged Issues

Velocity Index

Advances / Issues Traded

Also known as: Schultz AT

Author/Creator: Schultz

Data components required: Advances (A), Total Issues (TI)

Description: This indicator looks at only the advancing issues relative to the total issues, calculated as a ratio.

Interpretation: Schultz did not use total issues, but summed the advances, declines, and unchanged issues which would yield the same result. Chart 6-1 shows that in its raw from (unsmoothed), this would be a difficult indicator to use. However, if you put threshold values on the oscillator, you can see it helps identify the spikes relative to market action.

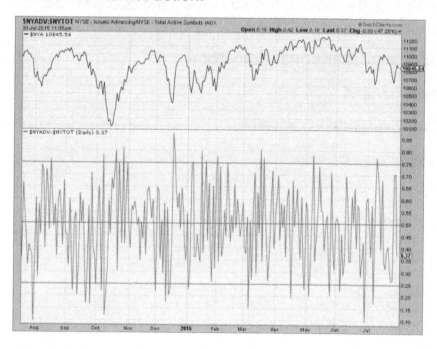

Chart 6-1

Author Comments: Other than a brief reference in a very old CompuTrac software manual, I have not been able to find out any more about this indicator or about Mr./Mrs. Schultz. I spoke with Tim Slater, the founder of CompuTrac and he was gracious enough to look through his old files to see if he could find any reference. Tim called me back a few weeks later and was of the belief that the indicator was obtained from Dunn and Hargitt, however he could not uncover any further information.

2015 Update: We now know all about the Schultz AT – see the article below by George Schade.

Like many indicators, smoothing this one will greatly enhance its usefulness. It is apparent from chart 6-2 that the advancing issues will lead almost all market up moves.

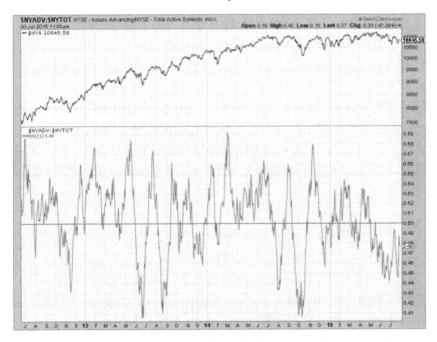

Chart 6-2

My good friend George Schade, the lawyer, the excellent technical analyst, the market historian, the superb researcher, and the one who has dampened a few of my brusque writings into less offensive prose has given me permission to reproduce an article he wrote in 2011 about the origins of the now misnamed indicator Schultz AT. It is presented below with some minor editing on my part to reduce the number of paragraphs and removal of the Endnotes. I also enlarged the chart significantly. I have inserted a few notes which begin with: **Note**. Any errors perceived or real are my fault.

___

SCHULTZ AT - THE MISNAMED INDICATOR

BY GEORGE SCHADE JR., CMT

Tracing an indicator's origin is an exciting hunt. Gregory Morris and Robert Colby have written about the "Schultz AT" measure of market breadth. Morris asked who Schultz was but did not get a complete answer, while Colby suggested that AT had been named after John W. Schulz (no "t" in the surname). AT's formula is simple, namely, the total number of advancing issues is divided by the number of total issues traded. The non-accumulated ratios are charted daily or smoothed preferably with a short term moving average. Neither Harry D. Schultz nor John W. Schulz originated the AT indicator, but both popularized it. Harold M. Gartley created AT and wrote about it in 1935.

I.   John W. Schulz

John W. Schulz was an early member of the Market Technicians Association ("MTA"). In 1979, he received the MTA Annual Award. According to Ralph Acampora, Schulz was a primary drafter of the charter MTA Constitution. In 1972, Schulz wrote the MTA's Principles and Policies document associated with the constitution. The Market Technician Association Journal (now the Journal of Technical Analysis) reprinted an article in 1979 written by Schulz concerning the Kondratieff Wave.

Between 1959 and 1976, Schulz worked for at least three Wall Street firms. At the last firm, as Managing Director of Brean Murray, Foster Securities, Inc., he wrote a market letter entitled The Technical Review. From October 1, 1959, to March 15, 1976, he wrote a column for Forbes magazine. The column was initially entitled Technical Perspective and later Technician's Perspective. Schulz was part of the highly regarded group of writers at Forbes that included Heinz H. Biel, Lucien O. Hooper, and Sidney B. Lurie.

In 1962, Schulz wrote The Intelligent Chartist which is available in the MTA Library. **Note**: I just checked and Amazon has it for $499;

my copy is not for sale. In the book's last section, Schulz described the data he analyzed to measure market movements. He considered the number of daily advances, declines, and unchanged - the issues traded - to be "perhaps the most enlightening of the" daily market numbers."

He wrote: *"In my opinion, the daily number of issues advancing is more useful by far. This part of the market is shown … as a percentage of all issues traded for the day. I make no further adjustment to this (or any other) figure [such as moving averages]; but the raw data seem preferable to me; despite the wide variations over brief periods, the trend of the variations themselves becomes quite clearly apparent. A similar line could be plotted for the percentage of issues declining. But this, too, would add to the clutter; and anyway, the issues-down factor is more or less implicit in its opposite, - the issues-up line."*

Schulz called the percentage of daily advances to issues traded the "issues- up line." Because the "issues-up line alone can serve as an early indicator of changes in trend direction," he compared it to the Dow Jones Industrial Average to detect divergences.vi For this purposes, he advised using the issues-up line together with volume and the cumulative advance-decline line. Schulz used AT, but he was not its originator. He conceded that "there is nothing especially original about my approach to this material; and the data themselves have long been recognized as useful and significant and are in the toolkit of most careful technicians."

II.   Harry D. Schultz

For over 45 years, Harry D. Schultz produced the "International Harry Schultz Letter." Reportedly, he published the last issue in December 2010. He frequently wrote on financial panics and crashes. An interview held on July 11, 2010, is enlightening. In 1962, Schultz wrote Bear Market Investing Strategies in which he described the "percent of advances index" indicator as follows (the 17th indicator on his list of 18): "*Percent of advances index. Divide the daily advances by the issues traded. This is another way of approaching the overbought–oversold problem. A 10-day moving average is probably best. In charting it, you'll discover how to interpret it, for the extremes become obvious cues. When it falls below 40%, it's a signal of weakness ahead.*"

The "percent of advances index" is the same as the "Schultz AT" indicator. Most likely this description is the basis for naming the indicator after Harry D. Schultz. Interestingly, John Schulz and Harry Schultz published about AT the same year - 1962. Unlike Schulz, Schultz smoothed AT with a 10-day moving average. In Bear Market Investing Strategies, Schultz wrote about the stock market volume work of Harold M. Gartley, "a great technician in the 1930s." Gartley closes this wonderful story because he originated AT.

III.   Harold M. Gartley (1899-1972)

In 1966, Schultz edited what has become a primary source for historical research, namely, A Treasury of Wall Street Wisdom. The book contains the chapter on volume found in Gartley's classic book Profits in the Stock Market. Schultz's knowledge of Gartley's work is significant because Gartley created a market breadth indicator that was the ratio of daily advances divided by the number of total issues traded, the same indicator that John Schulz and Harry Schultz described almost 30 years later. Gartley received a degree in Commercial Science and a Master's Degree in Business Administration from New York University. Beginning in 1912, he worked in Wall Street as a stockbroker, adviser, analyst, instructor, and financial public relations counsel. By 1932, he was an adjunct lecturer at the Columbia Business School when Benjamin Graham taught there.

Gartley began studying breadth of the market in 1931. A year later, in a Barron's article, Gartley included a chart that showed daily advances and declines. The article did not describe or show the ratio of advances and total issues traded. AT appeared in chapter 15 of Gartley's Profits in the Stock Market published in 1935. Chapter 15, entitled "Breadth-of-the-Market," headlined: *"Although this subject has been studied by many market students, with the exception of the author's work, we know of no published material."* It is possible that the market breadth work of Leonard P. Ayres and James F. Hughes was either not fully known to Gartley or as comprehensive as he may have desired.

Gartley wrote that the "reason we study the general statistics of the market is to obtain what the old time trader called 'a better feel of the market'." He believed in analyzing breadth of the market numbers because:" the value of this type of study cannot be overemphasized as a timing device providing considerable aid to the technical student. It is believed that no single branch of stock market trend research will yield greater results. This contention is based on the belief that the growth and deterioration of bullish and bearish market sentiment is clearly reflected in the general market statistics, providing that adequate analysis is made."

The market-derived statistics are the same used today, namely:

1.   Number of issues traded

2.   Number of advances

3.   Number of declines

4.   Number of prices unchanged

5.   Number of new highs

6.   Number of new lows

7.   Total volume

8.   Ratio of trading in the 15 most active stocks to total volume

Gartley's market letter as well as other financial publications provided the data. The Wall Street Journal was reporting New York Stock Exchange advances, declines, and unchanged by February 19, 1932, and so was Barron's by May 1, 1933. Gartley emphasized that "these statistics must be considerably refined, in order to be of any practical value." Even "after a year or two, it was found that considerable refinement was necessary, and even after several years of experience no arrangement of the data has been found which reliably reflects each successive intermediate turning point."

Refinement led to AT. According to Gartley: "*Experience with the raw data … soon showed that it had to be somewhat refined if it was to be useful. So the idea was conceived to reduce all the data to some uniform basis, and, instead of using just the number of advances and declines, a ratio was prepared wherein the percentage of the advances and the declines, as compared to the total issues traded each day, was computed.*"

In chapter 15 of Profits in the Stock Market, Gartley showed the results of using a 7-day moving average of the ratios of daily advances and declines compared to the number of total issues traded. He found that when the 7- day moving average of the ratio of advances to total issues traded exceeds 60%, it is time to consider selling stocks, and when the 7-day moving average of the ratio of declines to total issues traded rises above 60%, it is time to buy stocks especially if a decline has been in progress for some time. Gartley found these indicators useful to determine intermediate trend reversals, but they also developed some rather consistent minor trend signals. A nominal distinction is that Gartley used a 7-

day moving average while Harry Schultz suggested a 10-day moving average.

In 1981, the Market Technicians Association Journal reprinted an article that Gartley wrote in August 1937, which essentially was chapter 15 of Profits in the Stock Market. The article is entitled Breadth of the Market Trends. Gartley's AT is shown in Chart 1 below as it appeared in the Journal's article. Line 1 shows the number of unchanged in June and July, 1932. Line 1A shows the ratio of unchanged divided by total issues traded in August through November, 1932. Line 2 shows the number of advances in June and July, 1932. Line 2A shows the ratio of advances divided by total issues traded in August through November, 1932. Lines 3 and 3A show the Standard Statistics Daily 90-Stock Index for comparison purposes. Lines 4 and 4A show the same for daily declines in the same time periods.

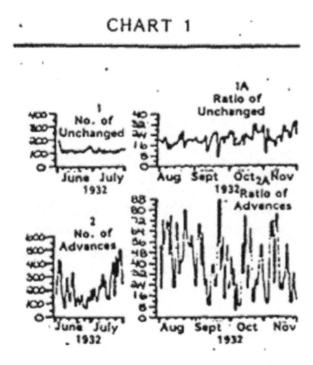

CHART 1

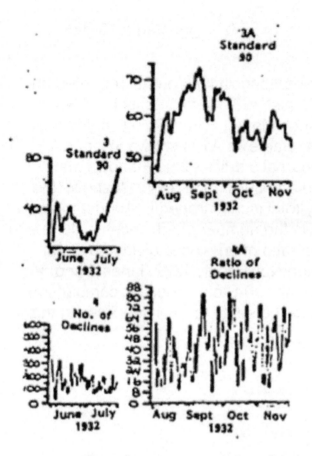

Chart 1. The First Showing of Advances/Total Issues Traded.

Note: I (Greg) broke the original graphic into a top section and bottom section so I could enlarge them.

Chart 2 in Gartley's article shows the 7-day moving average of both advances and declines compared to total issues traded between June, 1932, and April 1937. Chart 2 is not shown here because its reproduction is not as clear as that of Chart 1.

IV.   Conclusion

Harold M. Gartley originated the Advances/Total Issues Traded as well as the Declines/Total Issues Traded indicators. John Schulz and

Harry Shultz popularized AT but cannot be credited with its invention. Morris' inquiry is answered. Harold M. Gartley originated Advances/Total Issues Traded as Harry Shultz and John Schulz used it fifty years ago. And finally, to borrow liberally from Shakespeare's Romeo and Juliet:

> *"What's in a name? That which is called Schultz AT*
>
> *By its proper name Gartley AT would be as true."*

Thanks George.

Back with Greg - In the early 1990s, Norm North and I had created a simple Point and Figure charting software that downloaded daily data from Warner Computer. I sent a number of copies out to my short list of folks I knew used Point and Figure, one was John W. Schulz; the same John Schulz mentioned by George and also a founding member of the MTA (Market Technicians Association. John Schulz called me one day to thank me and asked if I would help him get the software going as he claimed he was completely not at home with a computer. Over the next few months we spoke a couple of times a week, usually in the evening and eventually I had him set up to download data every evening, chart it with the box size and reversal period he wanted, and then print it. He was a gentleman 100% of the time. We talked about the markets often – he had a fascinating understanding of the markets. One day I received a large package and in it was his book, "The Intelligent Chartist," along with many hand-drawn point and figure charts. He asked me if I would like to be on his fax list. I said yes and for a couple of years until he died I received hundreds of hand-drawn charts. Not once did I ask him why he did not use my software.

Formula: (A / TI)

References:

1984 CompuTrac software manual.

Advance Decline Divergence Oscillator

Author/Creator: Arthur Merrill

Data components required: Advances (A), Declines (D), Unchanged (U) Market Index (MKT).

Description: This was Arthur Merrill's Disparity Index; an attempt to see how a breadth indicator performed relative to a market index. He stated that he did not like the subjectivity of visually looking at a chart of each one. Here is what he said: "The comparison isn't easy, since the market average is in dollars, and the advance decline line is an accumulation which could start anywhere." He made the comparison into an oscillator. Rather than subtracting one index from the other, he calculated a simple least squares regression line. The calculation is the same as a least squares trend, except the ordinal statistics are the Dow Jones Industrial Average, and the abscissa statistics are the advance decline accumulation (advance decline line). To make the oscillator, he compares the Dow with the least squares line, and then calculated the percentage that the Dow was above or below the line. I used the NYSE Composite in these examples.

Interpretation: If the Advance Decline Divergence Oscillator is positive, the NYSE Composite is pulling ahead of the Advance decline Line. Assuming a better breadth indicator over prices, a positive value is bearish and a negative value is bullish. Art Merrill also used signals based upon 2/3 of a standard deviation. It was bullish when it was below -0.7 and bearish was when it was above +5.4. Chart 6-3 is a modified version of Art Merrill's Advance Decline Divergence Oscillator. It normalizes the market price data and also the advance decline data, then looks at the difference between the two. A period for normalization of one year (252 days) was used. While considerably different than Merrill's work, the concept is identical. Chart 6-3 clearly shows the concept that Art Merrill was talking about. The top plot is the NYSE Composite Index and the bottom plot is the AD Divergence Oscillator.

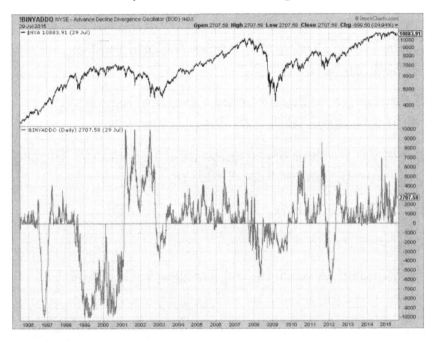

Chart 6-3

Author Comments: You can see from chart 6-3 that whenever the advance decline line is stronger relative to the NYSE Composite, the oscillator is above the zero line. It is apparent from this indicator that the advance decline line is a very early warning indicator of future market direction, especially at market tops. And this is good because most indicators are better at identifying market bottoms.

Arthur Merrill also included in the advance decline calculation Edmund Tabell's adjusted AD value by dividing the difference between advances and declines by the unchanged issues. Edmund Tabell figured that if the unchanged issues were low, then there was a great deal of conviction in the market.

175

Formula: $\sum ((A - D) / U) / MKT$

StockCharts.com Symbol: !BINYADDO

References:

Merrill, Arthur, "More Trend Direction." <u>Stocks & Commodities</u>, Volume 6, June, 1988, pp. 218.

Merrill, Arthur, "Fitting a Trendline by Least Squares." <u>Stocks & Commodities</u>, Volume 6, July, 1988, pp. 254.

Merrill, Arthur, "Advance Decline divergence as an oscillator." <u>Stocks & Commodities</u>, Volume 6, September, 1988, pp. 354.

Advance Decline Diffusion Index

Author/Creator: Richard Carlin

Data components required: Advances (A), Declines (D), Total Issues.

Description: This is a 10 day moving average of the percentage of advancing issues over total issues.

Interpretation: According to Carlin, simply watch for change in direction ahead of the appropriate market. This is not unlike the advance decline line interpretation, but much shorter term in nature. Carlin also says that when it descends from a high level while the market continues to rise, a sell signal is at hand. Complementarily, when it rises ahead of the market a buy signal is given. He also suggests using it with weekly data. Chart 6-4 shows the AD Diffusion Index.

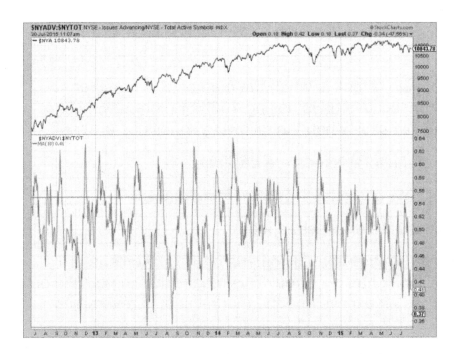

Chart 6-4

Author Comments: I'm confused at the name for his relatively simple indicator. Where do the declines come into play and what does it diffuse? There was only a single source of information on this indicator that I could find. Because a good bull market will have ever expanding advancing issues, this could offer a divergent indicator for long up moves.

Formula: (A / TI) * 100 for 10 days.

References:

Carlin, Richard K., PhD, "Technical analysis of industry groups." Stocks & Commodities. Volume 6, November, 1988, pp. 408-410.

Breadth Climax

Author/Creator: Gerald Appel

Data components required: Advances (A), Declines (D), Unchanged (U).

Description: A buying climax is when the market puts together no more than two consecutive days having 1000 or more advancing issues. A selling climax is when the following conditions are met:

1. At least 70% of the total issues are declines.

2. No more than 15% of the total issues are advances.

3. Less than 150 issues are unchanged.

Interpretation: When either the buy criteria or the sell criteria are met, a Breadth Climax has occurred. This means that the buying or selling has reached an excess and the market should reverse its previous trend.

Author Comments: Gerald Appel developed this system over 30 years ago. The breadth numbers have changed dramatically since then. I took the basic concept he was using and found a better set of parameters. A buying climax occurs when there are two consecutive days where the advances are greater than 65% of the total issues. A selling climax is when the following conditions are met (only slightly different that Appel's):

1. At least 75% of the total issues are declines.

2. No more than 15% of the issues are advances.

3. There are less than 150 issues unchanged.

Chart 6-5 shows the buying climaxes as upward spikes and the selling climaxes as downward spikes.

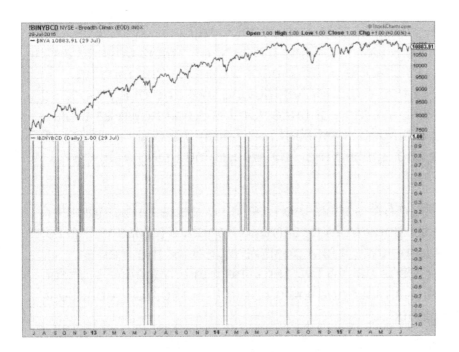

Chart 6-5

Chart 6-5 fairly well identifies periods in the market when sharp declines or advances have occurred. The long period between 1988 and 2001, without any buying climaxes falls in line with a number of other indicators similar to this one, such as Martin Zweig's Breadth Thrust. In a bull market, after it gets underway, there are few, if any, buying climaxes.

StockCharts.com Symbol: !BINYBCD

References:

Appel, Gerald. <u>Winning</u> <u>Market Systems.</u> Greenville, SC: Traders Press, 1973.

Declining Issues Trix

Author/Creator: Gilbert Raff

Data components required: Declines (D).

Description: The Trix indicator was developed by Jack Hutson, publisher of Stocks & Commodities magazine. Trix is defined as the one period percent change of an x-period exponential moving average of an x-period exponential moving average of an x-period exponential moving average of price. Or it is also known as triple exponential smoothing. Gilbert Raff has taken the daily number of declining issues and applied the Trix smoothing using a 35-day period.

Interpretation: Chart 6-6 shows the Declining Issues Trix indicator. When the indicator goes from positive to negative (crosses the zero line from above to below), it is a positive signal for the market. Similarly, when it rises above the zero line it is a negative sign for the market. This is an inverted indicator in that regard, because it uses declining issues.

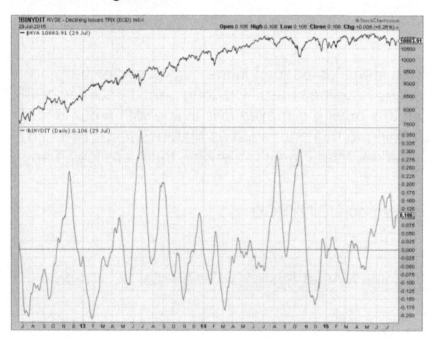

Chart 6-6

Author Comments: This seems to work fairly well when the market is trending well. However, it has many whipsaws during sideways market action. The extremes in this indicator seem to identify market tops and bottoms. Using this with a short term simple moving average might generate some good signals. You know I have to do this, chart 6-7 is the Advances TRIX. At first glance it appears to just be the complement of the declining issues Trix, but closer examination will reveal that it is not. Using the Advancing Issues Trix with a 10-day smoothing (dotted line) seems to give a good way to use this. When the indicator is above the zero line and it drops below its 10 day average a sell signal is generated. When the indicator is below the zero line and it rises above its 10 day average a buy signal occurs.

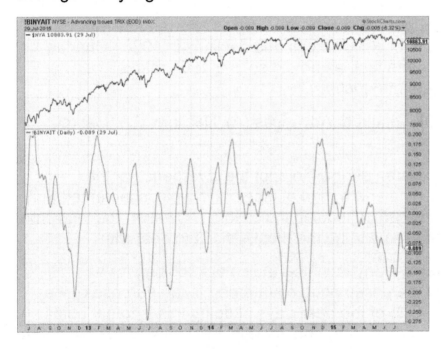

Chart 6-7

Formula: Exponentially smooth the declines 3 times and then take a one-day rate of change.

StockCharts.com Symbol: !BINYAIT and !BINYDIT

References:

Raff, Gilbert, "Exponentially Smoothing the Daily Number of Declines." Stocks & Commodities, January 1992, pp. 15-18.

MetaStock Professional, Equis International, Salt Lake City, UT.

Disparity Index

Also known as: Advance Decline Divergence Oscillator

Author/Creator: James Alphier, in an October, 1988 article said that James Hughes had written on the subject of the divergence between the advance decline line and the market indices. Hughes was the first person to whom Col. Leonard P. Ayres showed this new idea of counting the number of advances and declines in 1926. Charles Dow may have been first, as he did so in a 1901 market commentary (see Introduction).

Data components required: Advances (A), Declines (D), Market Index (MKT).

Description: This is an attempt to spot the divergence of the advance decline line and a market index. It is well documented that such divergences can be leading indications, however, the lead time is the issue that seems to be the most difficult to deal with.

Interpretation: Like many technical indicators, looking for a divergence with the price based counterpart is the purpose of the Disparity Index. One of the best ways of doing this is to put both indicators on the same chart and visually determine when they were diverging. In fact, this is how it is done most of the time because of the visual capabilities. Chart 6-8 shows the New York Composite index on the top plot and the Advance Decline Line on the bottom plot.

Chart 6-8

Author Comments: I have attempted to create an indicator that shows the divergence between the advance decline line and the market index. The concept was to first normalize the components over the long term. This would give them equal weighting in the overall calculation. Secondly, I then smoothed, exponentially, the difference over a 10-day period. I worked with a number of different smoothing values, but the 10-day period was long enough to give the divergence I wanted to see, and short enough to be timely. The longer the valued used the better the divergence showed up, but was almost too late to be beneficial. Very similar to the divergence indicator Art Merrill created, chart 6-9 shows positive whenever the breadth (Advance Decline Line) is outperforming the price (market index). The top plot is both the New York Composite Index (solid line) and the Advance Decline Line (dotted line).

183

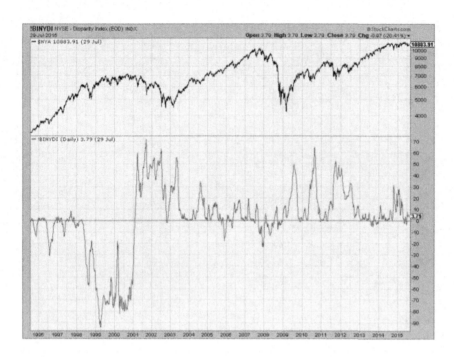

Chart 6-9

Formula: (Previous Value + (A – D)) / MKT

StockCharts.com Symbol: !BINYDI

References:

Alphier, James, "The Tragic Neglect of the Old Masters." <u>Stocks & Commodities</u>, Volume 6, October, 1988, pp. 395-396.

Dynamic Synthesis

Author/Creator: Walter A. Heiby

Data components required: Advances (A), Declines (D), Unchanged Issues (U), Market Index (MKT).

Description: In 1965, Walter Heiby wrote about a method to help determine market tops and bottoms. To use his technique one has to take the 10-day average of advancing issues, the 10-day average of declining issues, and the 10 average of unchanged issues, each plotted separately. The plots need to further divide the plots into quarters, starting over every 50 days. Said a different way, we are looking for new 10 day highs or lows in the advances, declines, and unchanged. The new highs or lows are based upon the last 50 days.

Interpretation: Heiby states that the unchanged issues normally move in the same manner as the advancing issues and opposite that of the declining issues. There is a strong tendency on the part of the unchanged issues to be low at good buying opportunities and to be high near rally tops. Chart 6-10 shows the New York Index and the components of Heiby's Dynamic Synthesis. You can see that September, 2001 gave a good buying opportunity based upon Heiby's analysis. Similarly, October, 2002 did also. Remember the issues plot must be in the top or bottom quartile in order for the signal to be generated. These plots did not adhere to Heiby's desire to look at new highs and lows only over the last 50 days, as there did not seem to by many signals.

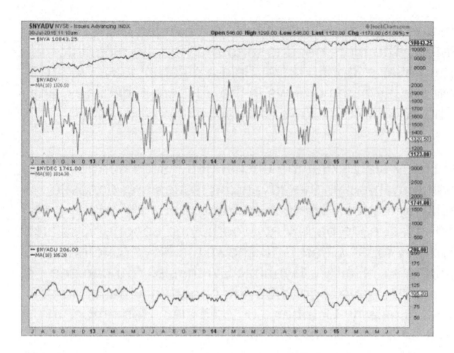

Chart 6-10

Buy Signal Criteria:

1. The market index must be in the bottom quartile.

2. The advances index must be in the top quartile.

3. The advances index must be greater than the declines index.

4. The unchanged issues must be in the top quartile.

Sell Signal Criteria:

1. The market index must be in the top quartile.

2. The advances index must be in the bottom quartile.

3. The decline index must be in the top quartile.

4. The advances index must be less than the declines index.

186

5. The unchanged index must not be in the lowest quartile.

Author Comments: With the big changes in pricing on the New York Stock Exchange in 1997 (pricing went to sixteenths from eighths) and early, 2001 (went to decimal pricing - cents), the unchanged issues are distorted so one has to ensure you are viewing like data, even when adjusting the individual issues on a percentage of total issues. This is especially true with the unchanged issues since they were the most affected by the pricing changes. Chart 6-11 shows the three components adjusted for total issues during a 6-year period of exceptional market volatility. One can spot numerous occurrences of Heiby's theory.

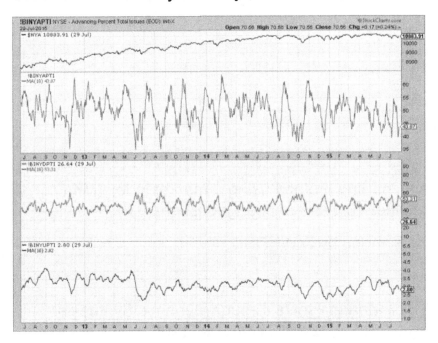

Chart 6-11

Normalizing the various components of the Heiby dynamic synthesis over a fifty-day period and creating buy and sell signals based upon the parameters above, takes out the visual chart subjectivity. Chart 6-12 shows Heiby's signals with the up spikes being buy signals and the down spikes being sell signals. There are entirely too many sell signals, but I decided not to try to fix it.

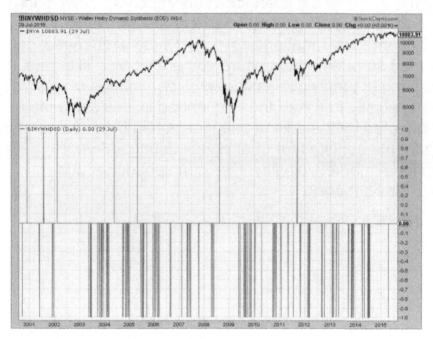

Chart 6-12

Formula: This is a charting method using a market index (MKT), advances (A), declines (D), and unchanged issues (U).

StockCharts.com Symbol: !BNYWHDSD

References:

Heiby, Walter. <u>Stock Market Profits through Dynamic Synthesis</u>. Chicago: The Institute of Dynamic Synthesis, 1965.

Unchanged Issues

Data components required: Unchanged (U).

Description: Looking at the unchanged issues that traded is a new twist and researched by Anthony Tabell.   Earlier writings were by

Walter Heiby in 1965.

Interpretation: On days with a high number of unchanged issues, and the market was up based upon breadth, there had to be fewer advances, and even fewer declines than normal. This could mean that a market top is being put into place as issues refuse to advance further. In fact, it is normal for the number of unchanged issues to increase as the market peaks. During a market decline, a low number of unchanged issues usually indicate the decline will continue. Because of the usual quick and sharp patterns generated at market bottoms, the unchanged issues will tend to be low, initially, as the decrease in the number of declines is overtaken by the rapid rise in advancing issues. Tabell says that the low number of unchanged issues is generally bullish over a one-year period. Chart 6-13 shows the raw unchanged data.

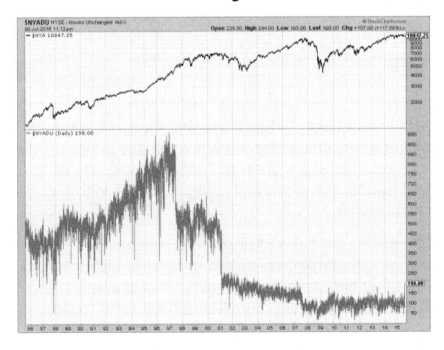

Chart 6-13

Smoothing the raw unchanged issues by 21 days presents a similar shaped chart (chart 6-14) but somewhat easier to read and use.

Chart 6-14

Author Comments: Theoretically, when there are a large number of issues not advancing or declining, the market is usually in the process of topping. Looking at the chart of unchanged issues as a percentage of total issues, a low reading is more bullish, with the high readings being bearish.

There are three things on the chart of unchanged issues that bothered me. One was the large increase in unchanged issues from 1991 to 1997. The other two were the significant drops in mid-1997 and January, 2002. The large drop in unchanged issues in June, 1997 was the beginning step to decimalization by moving to the use sixteenths (1/16) or about 6.25 cents in pricing. Previously, the smallest price move was in eighths (1/8) or 12.5 cents. The large drop in January, 2002 was when the New York Exchange changed from using fractions to using decimals. A stock can now be an advancing or a declining issue with only a one cent move.

If you look at the chart of unchanged issues above, you will quickly notice that the unchanged issues continue to climb as the market rallied during the period from 1991 to 1997. Why is this? It is because of the large growth in overall issues on the New York Stock Exchange during that time period. This is why many single breadth components must be used as a ratio. I divided the unchanged issues by the total issues and then smoothed it by 21 days. Notice in chart 6-15 that the increase in the period from 1991 to 1997 went away. Yes, there was growth in the number of issues, but not in just the unchanged issues.

Chart 6-15

Because of the two steps in the middle of 1997 and early 2001 to get to the decimalization of minimum price changes in trading, using the unchanged issues by themselves should be done in steps to eliminate the two significant drops in unchanged issues. Chart 6-15b shows the unchanged issues as a percentage of total issues over a two-year period starting in early-1987. You can see that as the market rallied off of the low set in October, 1987, the unchanged issues continued to climb. This seems to follow the logic of the unchanged issues talked about earlier in this section.

Chart 6-15b

Formula: (U).

StockCharts.com Symbol: !BINYUPTI

References:

Jaffe, Charles A., "Unchanged Stocks." <u>Stocks & Commodities</u>, Volume 8, January 1990, pp. 44.

Velocity Index

Data components required: Advances (A), Declines (D), Unchanged (U).

Description: This indicator measures the unchanged issues and advancing issues relative to total issues. It takes one half of the unchanged issues and the advancing issues and then divides that sum by the total issues.

Interpretation: Moves in the Velocity Index greater than +10 and -12 normally indicate continued movement in that direction. Keep in mind that this is not much different than the advances as a percent of total issues. The addition of using one half of the unchanged issues would imply that this indicator would be coincident at market tops as the advancing issues dry up. Chart 6-16 shows the Velocity Index.

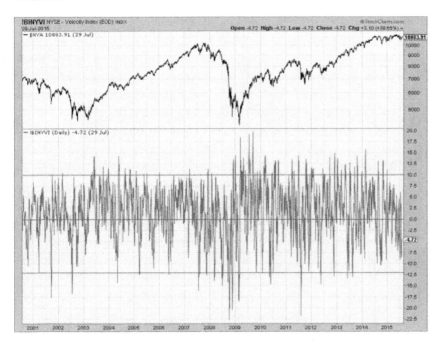

Chart 6-16

Author Comments: I put his indicator into a breadth formula package I created over 25 years ago. I cannot find any additional information on it or who created it. It wasn't me.

Formula: (U/2 + A) / (A + D + U)

StockCharts.com Symbol: !BINYVI

References:

Morris, Greg, "Indicators and Trading Systems Software," G. Morris Corporation, Dallas, TX.

CH 7 - New High New Low Indicators

This Chapter contains all the indicators that are dedicated to using New Highs and/or New Lows.

New High New Low Indicators

High Low Difference

New Highs – New Lows

New High New Low Line

New Highs & New Lows Oscillator

New Highs & New Lows Derivations

High Low Ratio

New Highs / New Lows Ratio

High Low Miscellaneous

New Highs & New Lows

New Highs % Total Issues

New Lows % Total Issues

High Low Logic Index

High Low Validation

High Low Difference

New Highs – New Lows

Data components required: New Highs (H), New Lows (L).

Description: This is the difference between the daily new highs and new lows. If the new highs outnumber the new lows, the indicator will be above the zero line. If the new lows outnumber the new highs, it will be below the zero line. Without some sort of smoothing or rate of change it is a very noisy oscillator.

Interpretation: Basically it can be used as an overbought oversold oscillator, similar to the advance decline overbought oversold indicator. Chart 7-1 shows that by smoothing it by 21 days takes out much of the noise and then can be used for bullish and bearish signals as it crosses the zero line.

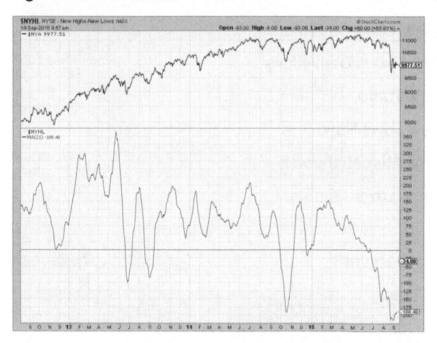

Chart 7-1

Author Comments: In its raw form this is not useable other than to get a feel for the number of new highs relative to the number of new lows. A better derivation for this would be to look at the difference as a percentage of total issues. Tim Hayes of Ned Davis Research gives the following information using weekly data. When this weekly indicator is above 8.8% it is bullish and when it is below -3.6% it is bearish.   Chart 7-2 shows Hayes' thresholds along with an overlay for identifying buy and sell signals. Whenever the difference is above the upper (8.8%) threshold the value is +30 and when below the lower (-3.6%) threshold it is -30.

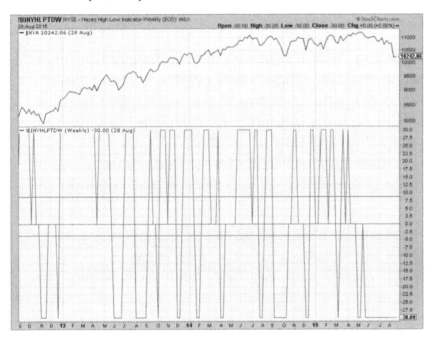

Chart7-2

Formula: (H – L)

StockCharts.com Symbol: !BINYHLPTDW

References:

Hayes, Timothy. The Research Driven Investor. McGraw-Hill, 2001.

Author Note: This is a great book, but unfortunately it is out of print. I strongly recommend it if you can find a copy.

New High New Low Line

Data components required: New Highs (H), New Lows (L).

Description: The New High New Low Line plots the difference between the number of stocks hitting new 52-week highs and those hitting 52-week lows and then adds that difference to the value from the previous day. It is constructed like the advance-decline line and can be interpreted in a similar way.

Interpretation: When the spread between the number of new highs and lows is widening, the New High New Low line is rising, which is positive. Any serious divergence between the NH-NL line and the stock average can be an early warning of a possible trend change. Whenever this cumulative line (shown in chart 7-3) changes direction it is an important move in the market that cannot be ignored. Divergence of this indicator with price is also a good technique.

Chart 7-3

Author Comments: If this indicator changes direction, it is important. To remove some small whipsaws, one can smooth it with a 21-day arithmetic average.   Again, when this indicator changes direction you should pay attention, because the market is also changing direction, as shown in chart 7-4.

Chart 7-4

Formula: $\sum (H - L)$.

New Highs & New Lows Oscillator

Data components required: New Highs (H), New Lows (L).

Description: This is the difference between the new highs and new lows, then put into a relationship like the advances and declines are with the McClellan Oscillator.

Interpretation: Chart 7-5 shows that the crossing of the zero line seems to be very effective. However, it does produce too many whipsaws to be used for anything other than short term trading.

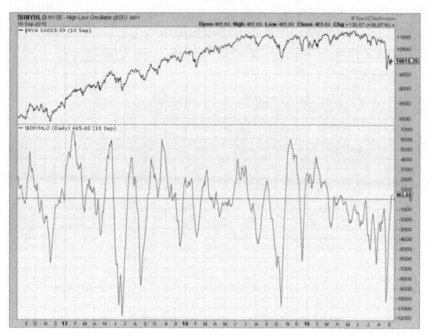

Chart 7-5

Author Comments: I like the McClellan concept of looking at the difference between two different smoothings and tend to like highs and lows a little better than advances and declines. Keep in mind that the new highs and new lows have a much different relationship with each other than the advances and declines do. This is because of the fact that a new high or new low is based upon data over the last year, and advance or decline is based on yesterday's data. This is a good indicator. Gerald Appel likes to smooth it by 10 days. Smoothing it by 15 days makes it work very well, as shown in chart 7-6.

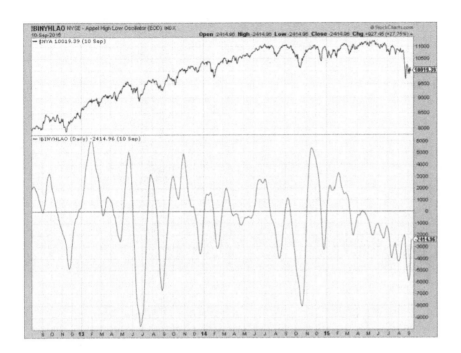

Chart 7-6

While creating the above chart, I accidentally put the wrong formula
in the indicator builder and created a chart of the 19-day exponential
average of new highs minus the 39-day exponential average of new
lows. There seems to be some merit in this; observe in chart 7-7
how it works as it crosses the zero line.

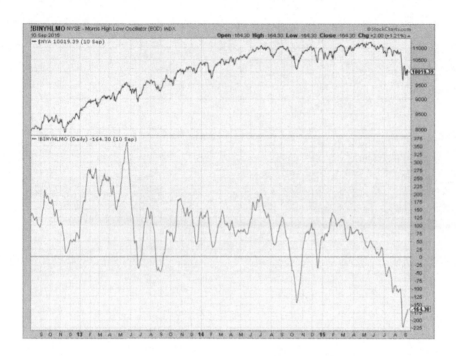

Chart 7-7

Formula: 19-day exp. average (H – L) - 39 day exp average (H – L).

StockCharts.com Symbol: !BINYHLO, !BINYHLAO, !BINYHLMO

References:

Appel, Gerald, "Gerald Appel, with Systems and Forecasts." Stocks & Commodities, Volume 12, March 1994, pp. 98-105.

New Highs - New Lows Derivations

Data components required: New Highs (H), New Lows (L).

Description: These are two indicators based upon two popular price-based technical indicators, Welles Wilder's relative strength index (RSI), and Stochastics (%K). While those indicators used price, these derivations use the difference between the new highs and new lows.

Interpretation: The RSI version uses the difference between the RSI of new highs and the RSI of new lows. Like the price-based RSI, in trending markets, this indicator is not telling us much. From chart 7-8 we can see that crossing the zero line seems to work best. There is a zero line here since this is the difference between two RSI calculations. The more common price-based RSI oscillated between zero and 100.

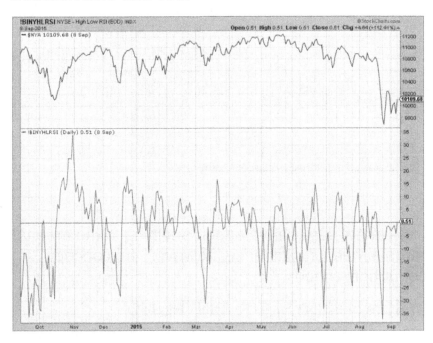

Chart 7-8

The Stochastic version of the high low difference was created the same way as the RSI version. Basically a difference between the stochastic of the new highs minus the stochastic of the new lows. Chart 7-9 is using a 65-day period for the stochastics.

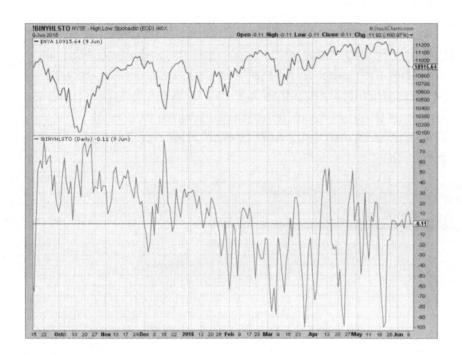

Chart 7-9

Author Comments: I'm not sure I have added anything to the arsenal of breadth indicators already in existence, however, the concept could certainly be further refined.

StockCharts.com Symbol: !BINYHLRSI, !BINYHLSTO

High Low Ratio

New Highs / New Lows Ratio

Data components required: New Highs (H), New Lows (L).

Description: This is the new highs divided by the new lows. Since the possibility of there being a day with zero new lows (you cannot divide by zero – it is undefined), this indicator must be smoothed, by smoothing the individual components before doing the division.

Interpretation: Chart 7-10 shows this ratio smoothed with a 21-day simple average. Most of the down spikes are just after market lows.

When the market is declining there are not many new highs being made, but once it starts to rally, new highs come quickly. Watching the upward moves for a reversal can assist in identifying tops. Also, chart 7-10 uses semi-logarithmic scaling for the indicator to better reflect the changes over such a long time period.

Chart 7-10

Gerald Appel uses a 10 day smoothing as shown in chart 7-11. He states that when this indicator falls to 30 and turns up it is a buy signal. When it gets above 90, the market is strong and will continue for some time. He says anytime the indicator stays over 70, you can stay in the market.

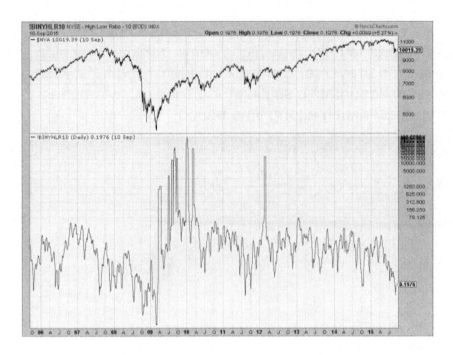

Chart 7-11

Author Comments: Notice the period on chart 7-11, near the 1987 crash and how this indicator did not register much movement. Why? The crash in October was sharp and quick, and recovered quickly. New highs and new lows data covers the preceding year. There was a strong market up move from 1984 until the crash preventing any new highs to occur off of the 1987 crash bottom. Said a little differently to ensure you understand it, as the market rallied off of that October bottom, the action did not produce new highs because the drop was so sharp and quick.

Abraham Cohen from Investor's Intelligence, used a 10-day average of new highs divided by the sum of new highs and new lows. This was also a stable part of Art Merrill's and John McGinley's Technical Trends service. Chart 7-12 shows Cohen's version.

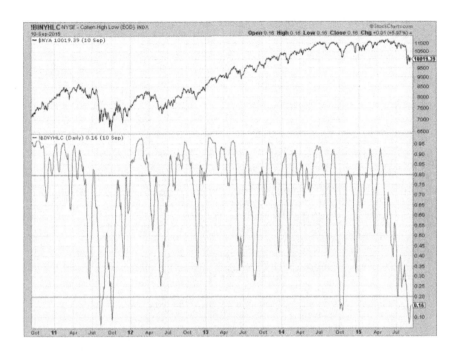

Chart 7-12

Arthur Merrill tested an indicator that used new highs divided by the sum of new highs and new lows using a percentage over a ten-day period. With the usual Arthur Merrill thoroughness, testing was done over a ten-year period using this indicator and the Dow Industrial Average. It turned out that the indicator worked well as an overbought and oversold indication showing an excess of new highs is bearish and an excess of new lows is bullish. Chart 7-13 shows this, but also shows that long periods of extended moves will keep the indicator in an overbought or oversold area. This is to be expected since up moves that are longer than 52 weeks will continue to generate new highs with each up day, and similarly for down moves and new lows. I have attempted to identify the validity of this thinking with the High Low Validation Index later in this section.

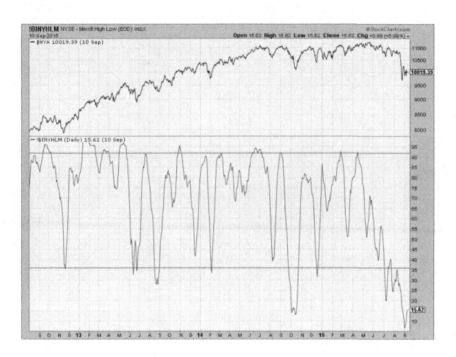

Chart 7-13

In 1993, Tim Hayes, of Ned Davis Research said that using weekly new highs is a very good leading indicator for a market top. As of late 1993, out of 14 indicators this was the second best in his testing. He states that the weekly new highs indicator was 100% successful in leading nine bull markets, doing so by a median of 34 weeks and with a range of 71 weeks. It appears that this simple indicator continues to do well. Chart 7-14 shows this. This is not an indicator using the ratio, but just the weekly new highs.

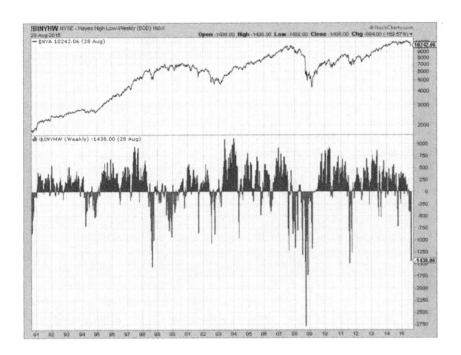

Chart 7-14

The third best indicator out of the Tim Hayes' study mentioned above was a daily ratio of new highs to the sum of new highs and new lows, smoothed by 55 days. Hayes claims it has a better record than the advance decline indicators. Determination of it signaling a market top is done by a divergence in the indicator. All divergences have been identified in chart 7-15. Also, Hayes says that when it is below .21, the market is oversold, again, as shown by the line in chart 7-15.

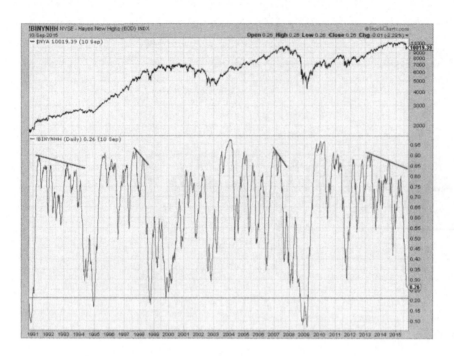

Chart 7-15

Formula: (H / L), (H / (H + L))

StockCharts.com Symbol: !BINYHLR21, !BINYHLR10, !BINYHLC, !BINYHLM, !BINYHW, !BINYNHH

References:

Appel, Gerald, "Gerald Appel, with Systems and Forecasts." Stocks & Commodities, Volume 12, March 1994, pp. 98-105.

Merrill, Arthur, 1985, Technical Trends, Merrill Analysis.

Merrill, Arthur, "New Highs / New Lows." Stocks & Commodities, Volume 8, June 1990, pp. 228-229.

Hayes, Tim, "Leading Indices at Bull Market Peaks." Stocks & Commodities, Volume 11, December 1993, 483-488.

High Low Miscellaneous

New Highs & New Lows

Data components required: New Highs (H), New Lows (L).

Description: This is merely the act of displaying both the new highs and new lows as separate lines, each arithmetically smoothed by 10 days. This makes it somewhat subjective and not good for detailed analysis, but good for a general picture of the breadth of the market in accordance with new highs and new lows.

Interpretation: From chart 7-16 you can see that in normal times, the new highs are above the new lows during market rises and below the new lows during market declines. This is as one would expect, so looking for the early reversal of this would possibly lead to turns in the market. The two plots in the middle show this; the new lows being the dotted line and the new highs being the solid line. In the bottom plot, when the line is above zero, it shows a value of +1, and means the new highs are greater than the new lows. If below the zero line at -1, the new lows are above the new highs.

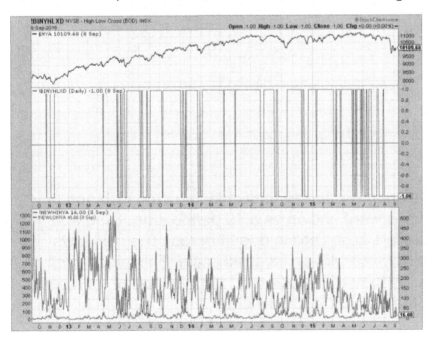

Chart 7-16

Author Comments: An awareness of the number of stocks making new highs and new lows is an important part of breadth analysis. I prefer to remove as much subjectivity from the analysis as possible. Chart 7-17 is a chart showing the new highs and new lows each smoothed by a 10 period average, then showing it as +1 when the new high average is above the new low average, and -1 when the new high average is below the new low average.

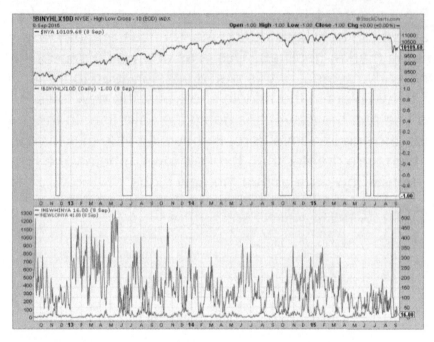

Chart 7-17

Mike Burk shows an unusual way to display the new high and new low data. New highs were shown as a 19 period smoothing and normalized on a scale from zero to one hundred. The new lows were shown similarly but with an inverted scale. This meant that as new lows increased they would descend from the top of the chart. They share a common high value, whether it is new highs or new lows. Also, the normalizations are for periods of about one hundred trading days.

Chart 7-18 shows Burk's charting convention. The number of new lows (dotted line) relative to the range of new lows over the last 100 days helps identify market bottoms with fairly good accuracy. The number of hew highs, again relative the range of new highs over the last 100 days shows market tops but only after the number of new highs starts to drop.

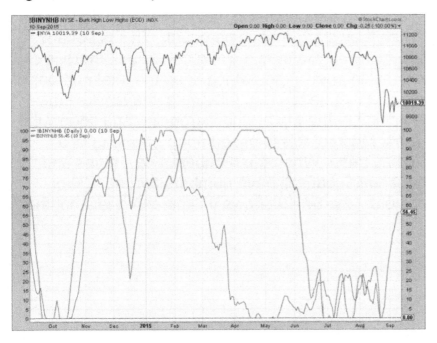

Chart 7-18

Formula: (H + L)

StockCharts.com Symbol: !BINYHLXD, !BINYHLX10D, !BINYNHB

References:

Burk, Mike, "New High and New Low Indicators." <u>Stocks & Commodities</u>, Volume 8, May 1990, pp. 197-198.

New Highs % Total Issues

Data components required: New Highs (NH), Total Issues (TI).

Description: Probably the best way to look at a single data component is to put it into perspective with a related, but more global, breadth component. Here we take the new highs as a percentage of total issues.

Interpretation: Leading up to a market top, the number of new highs is considerably more than the number of new lows. The first warning sign is when they start to become equal. This is because as a top is formed, many stocks stop making new highs, there is a churning of issues making new highs which keep the total number of them from declining. Once the top is in full swing, the stocks that peaked at the beginning of the top are now dropping and soon will be making new lows. Much of this is based upon how long of a topping process it has been. When the number of new highs and new lows are about equal, but still have numbers around 100 or more of each, look out. Chart 7-19 shows this percentage smoothed by 21 days.

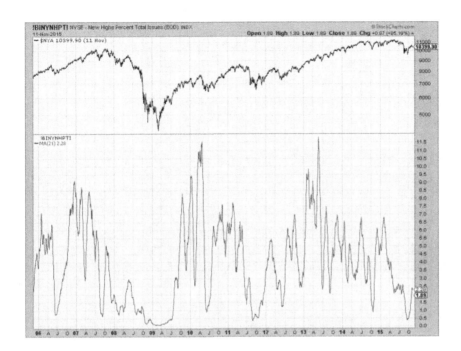

Chart 7-19

Author Comments: At times I believe that new high and new low data is better than the advance decline data for identifying market trends and turning points. Hew highs, like advances, will drive the market higher. Chart 7-20 shows the percentage of new highs viewed as a rate of change, and again, smoothed by 21 days.

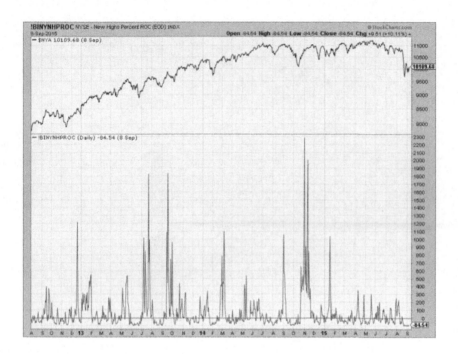

Chart 7-20

Tim Hayes, of Ned Davis Research, looks at this indicator and claims that when the weekly new highs as a percentage of total issues exceed 30% for the first time in a new year, it is bullish. Similarly, when the weekly new lows as a percentage of total issues, is below 1.95%, it is bullish and when above 7.2% it is bearish. Chart 7-21 shows the new highs in the middle plot and the new lows in the bottom plot with the Hayes thresholds shown.

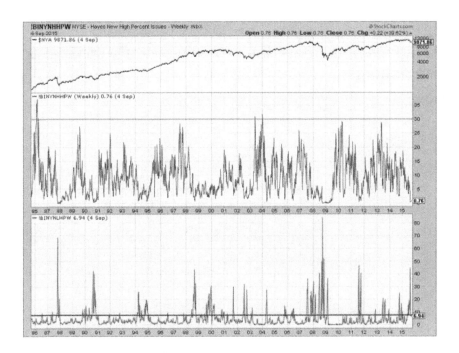

Chart 7-21

Formula: (H / TI) *100

StockCharts.com Symbol: !BINYNHPTI, !BINYNHPROC, !BINYNHHPW

References:

Davis, Ned. Being Right or Making Money. Ned Davis Research, 1991.

New Lows % Total Issues

Data components required: New Lows (NL), Total Issues (TI).

Description: This is the number of stocks hitting a new low for the first time in the last 52 weeks relative to the total issues traded.

Interpretation: New lows will show you additional information about the health of the market. Chart 7-22 shows this with the percentage smoothed over 21 days. As expected because of the sharp tendency of the markets at bottoms, the new lows usually spike at or very near to those bottoms.

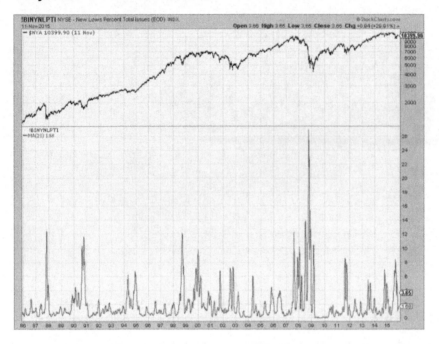

Chart 7-22

Author Comments: Mike Burk claims that the new lows are best at defining cycles in the market, and not particularly useful for day to day trading. Chart 7-23 is the rate of change chart similar to that used in the new high percentage section.

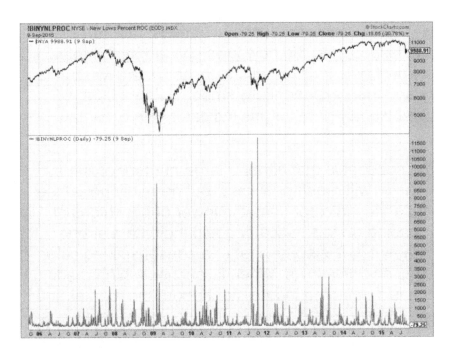

Chart 7-23

Tim Hayes of Ned Davis Research offers buy and sell information on the weekly new lows as a percentage of total issues – look under New Highs % Total Issues earlier in this section.

Formula: (L / TI) * 100

StockCharts.com Symbol: !BINYNLPTI, !BINYNLPROC

References:

Burk, Mike, "New High and New Low Indicators." <u>Stocks & Commodities</u>, Volume 8, May 1990, pp. 197-198.

High Low Logic Index

Author/Creator: Norman Fosback

Data components required: New Highs (H), New Lows (L).

Description: This is an indicator that uses two ratios: the new highs divided by the total issues, and the new lows divided by the total issues. The High Low Logic Index uses the lesser of the two ratios on any given day and then exponentially smooths it by 50 days. Note: Fosback used weekly data for this indicator with a 10-day smoothing.

Interpretation: The concept is that either a large number of issues will reach new highs or will reach new lows, but normally not at the same time. Because the indicator uses the lower of new highs or new lows, a low reading on this indicator could indicate a strong trend. If you think about it, it is somewhat of a consensus indicator based on new highs and new lows. When it reaches a high reading, it means that there is something inconsistent about the market and it is not a good sign. Chart 7-24 also shows the individual new highs and new lows (dotted line) in the middle and the high low logic index on the bottom. This chart uses daily data adjusted for Fosback's parameters. You can see in chart 7-24 that when the market is trending, the indicator is at its low points.

Chart 7-24

Chart 7-25 uses weekly data as preferred by Norman Fosback.
Close examination of the daily and weekly versions does not yield
much difference. This is because new high and new low data is
based upon a much larger time frame.

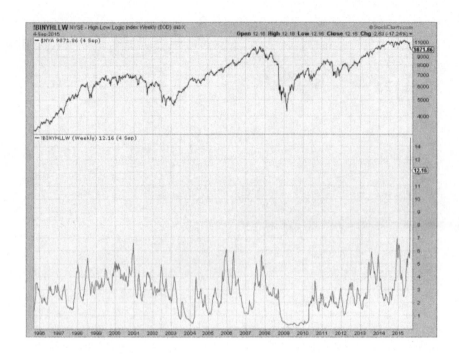

Chart 7-25

Gerald Appel uses a slight modification to this indicator. He uses the lesser of the two ratios of new highs to total issues and new lows to total issues. Because he also used weekly data for the new highs and new lows, I adjusted his sell parameter to 2.4 as shown in chart 7-26. This version seems to identify tops when it rises above 2.4.

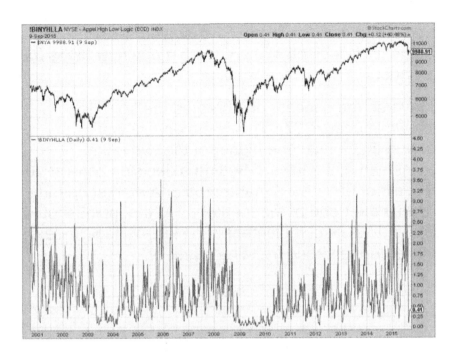

Chart 7-26

Author Comments: I think that the weekly data was easier to work with when there were no personal computers and that accounts for its use in some of this older indicators. I also believe there isn't much difference in using weekly data versus daily data in regard to new highs and new lows since they are based on prices 52 weeks (252 days) ago. If an issue reaches a new high on Monday, it means it is the highest high value for that issue in a year. If the weekly new highs (Friday close) also reflect that, it is within less than 2% of representing the time of the new high. And that is the worst case scenario. The other days of the week are even closer, with Friday being the same as the weekly.

This unique concept is somewhat similar in concept to Wilder's Directional Movement. The steady moves of the indicator either up or down can represent good trending markets. Look at the period between 1992 and 1997 (chart 7-25), a time of continuous market

223

upwards movement. The high low logic index stayed at low readings much of the time, indicating there were many new highs (or new lows) being made.

I figured I would reverse the concept and created the Low High Logic Index as shown in chart 7-27. This is the opposite of Fosback's indicator in that it uses the higher of the two ratios mentioned above instead of the lower. Setting a decision zone at 10 tells us that we are either at a new a market top or a market bottom. The good news is that the trend of the market up to that point should tell us which it will be. Like its complement, the high low logic index, it stays at low values during strong trending markets.

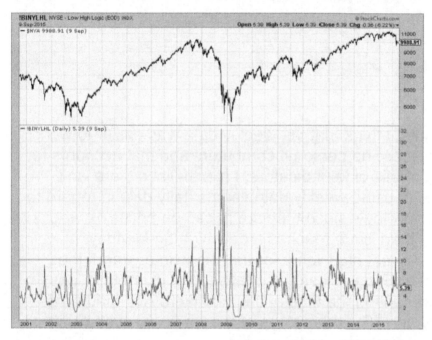

Chart 7-27

Formula: Previous Value + ((H / TI) or (L / TI) (exponentially smoothed by 50 days).

StockCharts.com Symbol: !BINYHLL, !BINYHLLW, !BINYHLLA, !BINYLHL

References:

Fosback, Norman G. Stock Market Logic, Fort Lauderdale, FL: The Institute for Economic Research, Inc., 1976.

Appel, Gerald, "Gerald Appel with Systems and Forecasts." Stocks and Commodities, Volume 12, March 1994, pp. 98-105.

High Low Validation

Author/Creator: Greg Morris

Data components required: New Highs (H), New Lows (L), Market Index (MKT).

Description: This is an attempt to help validate new high and new low data and, to be honest, is still a "work in progress." If you consider the facts relating to new highs and new lows, you will see the necessity for this. A new high means that the closing price reached a high that it had not seen in the last year (52 weeks). Similarly, a new low is at a low not seen for at least a year. This indicator tries to identify when the new high or new low is determined to be good or bad using the following line of thinking.

Consider that prices have been in a narrow range for over a year. Something then triggers an event that causes the market to move out of that trading range to the upside. This will immediately cause almost every stock that moves with the market to also become a new high. New highs are generally the force that keeps good up moves going. The new lows in this scenario will dry up, as expected. Now consider that the market has had a steady advance for quite some time. The number of new highs will generally continue to remain high as most stocks will rise with the market. Of course there will be drops as the market makes it corrections on its path to higher prices. When the number of new highs starts to dry up, you will probably notice that the number of unchanged issues starts to increase slightly because a lot of stocks will just cease to participate in the continuing rise. New lows will not happen for some time because the market is just starting to form a top. The number of new lows will increase as the market forms its broad top, while the number of new highs gets smaller and smaller. It will be the time frame of this topping action that determines when the new lows will start to kick in. Remember, you cannot have a new low until an issue is at a new low price over the last year.

When the market declines and you start to see fewer new lows, it means the market is losing its downside momentum. Why is this so? It is because some issues have already bottomed and are not continuing to make new lows. This is tied to the rotational effect, sometimes caused by various market sectors hitting bottoms at different times.

Interpretation: Chart 7-28 is an attempt to show this visually. Up spikes (solid green line) equal to +2 represent good new highs. Up spikes (shorter green line) equal to +1 represent bad new highs. Similarly, down spikes (solid red line) at -2 equates to good new lows and -1 (shorter red line) equates to bad new lows. You might read that again since it is not obvious. I wanted to keep the new highs as the up spikes and the new lows as the down spikes. Short up spikes are bad new highs and short down spikes are bad new lows. Bad, in this case means they did not conform to the theory talked about above.

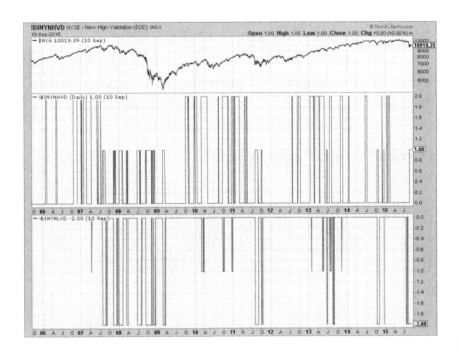

Chart 7-28

Author Comments: This method of trying to determine when the new highs and new lows are truly good ones, involves the rate of change of the market, a smoothed value of each component relative to the total issues traded, and their relationship with each other. For example, if the market is in a rally (rate of change high) and the new highs are increasing, any new lows that appear are not good ones.

StockCharts.com Symbol: !BINYNHVD, !BINYNLVD

CH 8 - Up Volume Down Volume Indicators

The breadth indicators in this section utilize either up volume, down volume, or both in their calculation. Please do not confuse this with the plethora of technical indicators that use total volume.

Up Volume and Down Volume Indicators

Up Volume

Down Volume

Changed Volume

Up & Down Volume

McClellan Oscillator – Volume

McClellan Summation Index – Volume

Merriman Volume Model

Swenlin IT Volume Momentum Oscillator

Swenlin Trading Oscillator – Volume

Up Volume Down Volume Line

Cumulative Volume Ratio

Up Down On Balance Volume (OBV)

Volume Percentage Ratio

Upside – Downside Volume

Upside / Downside Volume Ratio

Zweig Up Volume Indicator

Up Volume

Data components required: Up Volume (UV)

Description: This is the total amount of volume that is in the advancing issues on a daily basis.

Interpretation: By itself, it is a noisy number and almost unusable, however, smoothing it by 21 days gives some interesting information about the market. Volume generally precedes market highs. Many say that the up volume fuels the market's rise. If this smoothed indicator is not making new highs with the market, be on the alert. Chart 8-1 is the 21-day smooth of the up volume.

Chart 8-1

Gerald Appel likes to look at up volume smoothed over 10 days. He says that if the market makes a new high and the up volume (10-day average) does not also make a new high within about six weeks, be alert for a market top. Leigh Stevens says that up volume is a true test of buying interest. He also uses a 10-day average of up volume for his analysis. He watches a baseline in up volume which is at 525 – 550 million shares. The mid-point of his range (537 million) is shown on chart 8-2. Clearly when that was written, the volume has increased dramatically and is no longer valid.

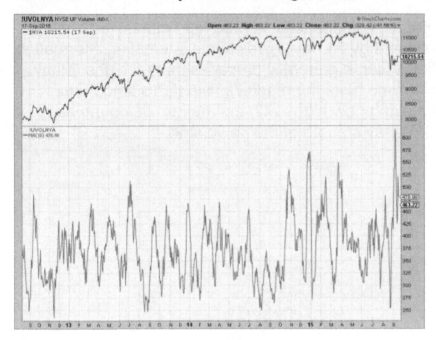

Chart 8-2

Author Comments: John McGinley liked to use up volume as a percentage of total volume with a three-week average. His reason was that up volume was the motor of the market; without it the market will drop. In order for the market to just remain even, it must have up volume.

I think detrending a data set such as this is better than looking at the raw data, even if it is smoothed as in the example prior to this. Chart 8-3 shows the up volume relative to its 21-day average, with the results further smoothed by 10 days. You can spot periods of strong up volume associated with good up market moves. However, once the market starts to weaken, this indicator turns around quickly. It does not mean the up move is over, but the good strong up volume associated with its initial launch is no longer present. Keep in mind that as long as this indicator is above the zero line the up volume is still above is moving average. A longer term moving average would avoid many of the whipsaws but would reduce the timing.

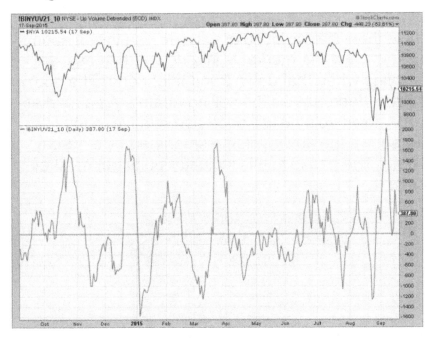

Chart 8-3

Formula: UV

StockCharts.com Symbol: !BINYUV21_10

References:

Appel, Gerald, "Gerald Appel, with Systems and Forecasts." Stocks and Commodities, Volume 12, March 1994, 98-105.

Stevens, Leigh, "Spotting Index Tops and Bottoms." <u>Stocks and Commodities</u>, August 2004, pp 23-26.

Down Volume

Data components required: Down Volume (DV).

Description: This is the total volume of all issues that declined in price for the day.

Interpretation: While there are no popular ways to use this, it seems that it should be used when the market is in a down trend as it will assist you in identifying when that down trend might end. The down volume should start to decrease as the selling abates. As a market starts to bottom, the down volume will decrease relative to total volume. Chart 8-4 shows the down volume smoothed by a 10-day average (dotted line). The peaks in this indicator point out most of the market bottoms.

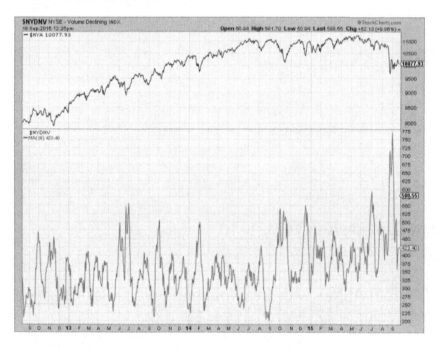

Chart 8-4

Author Comments: Using raw data, even though it is smoothed is not as good as using the raw data relative to a smoothed value of it. This is called detrending. Chart 8-5 is showing the down volume relative to its 21-day average, with the result further smoothed by 10 days (the same thing that was done with the up volume in the previous section).

Chart 8-5

Formula: (DV)

StockCharts.com Symbol: !BINYDV21_10

Changed Volume

Data components required: Up Volume (UV), Down Volume (DV).

Description: This represents all the shares on a particular exchange that changed in price for the day. It includes the up volume and the down volume. Total volume is different, in that it includes the

233

unchanged issues volume. You could also subtract the unchanged volume from the total volume to arrive at the same value.

Interpretation: The volume used here is the active volume for the day. Because of decimalization, this indicator needs to be looked at in stages, similar to the unchanged issues. Decimalization caused a giant decrease in unchanged issues, so this would cause a giant increase in the changed or active issues. Chart 8-6 shows this indicator since 1996 to show the decimalization that occurred in January, 2001.

Chart 8-6

Author Comments: One might be able to tie this to the fact that as markets start their topping process, the number of unchanged issues should start to increase. If the unchanged volume increases this would assist and also help to confirm it. Therefore, if the changed volume were to decrease this might offer the same interpretation. This could be construed to be more important than total volume by some.

Formula: (UV + DV).

StockCharts.com Symbol: !BINYCV21

Up & Down Volume

Data components required: Up Volume (UV), Down Volume (DV).

Description: A chart showing the up volume and down volume on the same plot will tell a lot about where volume is flowing. Smoothing each of them will make it much easier to use and interpret.

Interpretation: In chart 8-7, the up volume is the solid line and the down volume is the dotted line. You can see how the up volume generally increases during up moves and the down volume increases during down moves. This is normal market action and is to be expected. It is the deviation from this that you need to watch for.

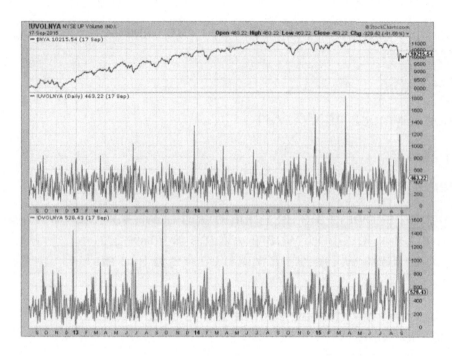

Chart 8-7

Author Comments: You can see that as a market drops in price, the down volume steadily increases and peaks right at the market bottom. Just after the market bottom, up volume rises quickly and continues to dominate throughout the upward move. You can also see that even small corrections in the market will cause the up and down volume to react significantly. Trends in the market are shown when one of the lines remains above or below the other for extended periods of time.

Formula: (UV), (DV)

McClellan Oscillator – Volume

Author/Creator: Sherman and Marian McClellan

Data components required: Up Volume (UV), Down Volume (DV).

Description: This is the McClellan Oscillator but instead of using advances and declines data, up volume and down volume data are used. The calculation is exactly the same, only the data components are changed.

Interpretation: Using the analogy that volume precedes price, the McClellan Oscillator using up and down volume should be used in the same manner as the advance decline based McClellan oscillator. Look for extreme readings to warn against market turning points. Keep this in mind: the market cannot go up in a healthy way without good accompanying up volume. It can certainly fall much easier. Trendline analysis of the McClellan Oscillator - Volume is also a good technique when using this indicator. Chart 8-8 shows the McClellan Oscillator - Volume.

Chart 8-8

Author Comments: From chart 8-8, it appears that watching this indicator as it crosses from below to above the zero line will almost nail the market bottoms, including those that are just trading rallies. This is probably because changes in the market are more quickly reflected in the up and down volume.

The McClellan Volume Oscillator also has importance when one compares it to the McClellan Advance Decline Oscillator. When the two disagree, such as if one moves above the zero line while the other does not, it is usually the Volume Oscillator that tells the truer story. Volume is not always the correct one, but that is the tendency and any disagreement is a sign for the analyst to be concerned.

Volume also differs from Advance Decline numbers in that Volume numbers are theoretically limitless, whereas the difference between Advances and Declines can never be greater than the number of issues traded. Big volume trading days can therefore have a bigger impact on volume breadth indicators like the McClellan Volume Oscillator. Conversely, small volume days like the day after Thanksgiving can have only a minimal contribution to changing the volume-based oscillator, while the Advance Decline Oscillator does not know the difference.

My thanks go to Tom McClellan who reviewed this section and the following one on the McClellan Summation Index – Volume.

Formula: (Today's 19 exp. average of (UV – DV) – (Today's 39 exp. average of (UV – DV)

StockCharts.com Symbol: !VMCOSINYA

References:

McClellan, Sherman and Marian. Patterns for Profit. Lakewood, WA: McClellan Financial Publications, Inc., 1976. This book was originally published by Trade Levels in 1970.

McClellan Family Interview, "It's All In the Family: Sherman, Marian, and Tom McClellan." Stocks and Commodities, Volume 12, June

1994, pp. 264-273.

McClellan Summation Index - Volume

Author/Creator: Sherman and Marian McClellan

Data components required: Up Volume (UV), Down Volume (DV).

Description: Like the McClellan Oscillator that uses volume, this is the McClellan Summation Index using up volume and down volume instead of the advances and declines. The calculations are identical, just the breadth components have changed.

Interpretation: As with the McClellan Advance Decline Summation Index, the Volume Summation Index indicates the prevailing trend for the market based its direction of movement. It also makes for a nice intermediate term overbought/oversold indicator when it reaches extreme values. The McClellan Volume Summation Index is shown in chart 8-9.

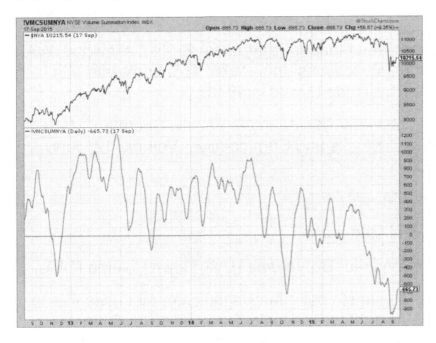

Chart 8-9

Author Comments: Because of the large increases in daily trading volume over the years, making a ratio adjustment of the daily Up and Down Volume figures is even more important than for the A-D numbers when trying to make long-term historical comparisons. The McClellans do this adjustment in the same way for Volume that they do for Advance Decline, by dividing the Up Down Volume difference by the total of Up plus Down Volume. The one drawback is that this equalizes all trading days, so big or small volume days do not have the same impact that they would in the raw calculations.

Formula: This is the accumulation of the volume based McClellan Oscillator.

$$VOLSUM_{TODAY} = VOLSUM_{YESTERDAY} + VOLOSC_{TODAY}$$

StockCharts.com Symbol: !VMCSUMNYA

References:

McClellan, Sherman and Marian. Patterns for Profit. Lakewood, WA: McClellan Financial Publications, Inc., 1976. This book was originally published by Trade Levels in 1970.

McClellan Family Interview, "It's All In the Family: Sherman, Marian, and Tom McClellan." Stocks and Commodities, Volume 12, June 1994, pp. 264-273.

Merriman Volume Model

Author/Creator: Paul Merriman

Data components required: Up Volume (UV), Down Volume (DV).

Description: This is a simple but effective indicator that uses the up and down volume as a ratio. One looks for extreme levels to determine market strength or weakness. Merriman initially created this indicator using the up and down volume from the Nasdaq market.

Interpretation: When the sum of the up volume over the last eight trading days divided by the sum of the down volume over the last eight days is greater than 1.5, a buy signal is generated. A sell signal is when the eight-day ratio of the sums is equal to 0.8. Merriman's logic is simple, in an up market you can expect more up volume and in a down market you can expect more down volume. Chart 8-10 is the indicator using New York breadth data. Ignore repetitive signals in the chart.

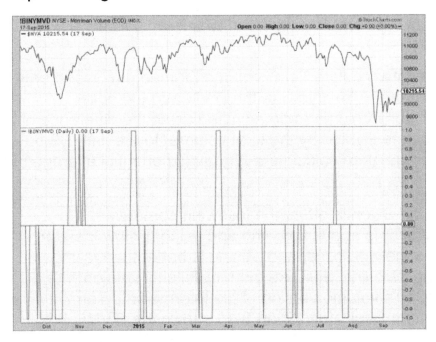

Chart 8-10

Author Comments: Paul Merriman has created a fairly simple but reliable indicator for determining market turns based upon volume. While he originally used Nasdaq data, the use of New York data seems to work just as well.

Formula: 8-day sum of UV / 8 day sum of DV

StockCharts.com Symbol: !BINYMVD

References:

Merriman, Paul, www.fundadvice.com/modelsexplained.html.

Swenlin IT Volume Momentum Oscillator

Also known as: ITVM

Author/Creator: Carl Swenlin

Data components required: Up Volume (UV), Down Volume (DV), Total Volume (V).

Description: The Intermediate Term Volume Momentum Oscillator is a barometer of breadth. To calculate the ITVM add the daily McClellan Oscillator - Volume (ratio adjusted using the difference of up and down volume divided by the total volume) to the daily 39-day exponential average, then calculate a 20-day exponential average of the result.

Interpretation: Carl Swenlin offers the following comments: It is better if this indicator is above zero line and rising. Below the zero line and falling is the worst scenario. Rising is better than falling, even if below the zero line. Just like the McClellan's version with volume, this is Carl's volume version of his Intermediate Term Breadth Momentum Oscillator. Chart 8-11 shows the ITVM.

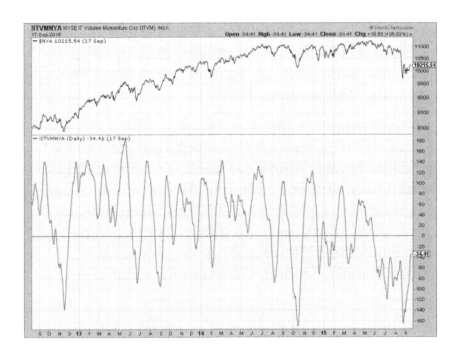

Chart 8-11

Author Comments: The indicator troughs seem to pinpoint market bottoms and the peaks point out the loss of upside momentum.

StockCharts.com Symbol: !ITVMNYA

References:

Swenlin, Carl, www.decisionpoint.com.

Swenlin Trading Oscillator – Volume

Also known as: STO-V

Author/Creator: Carl Swenlin

Data components required: Up Volume (UV), Down Volume (DV), Total Volume (V).

Description: The Swenlin Trading Oscillator – Volume was designed for short-term trading. It is a 5-day simple moving average of a 4-day exponential average of the daily up volume minus down volume divided by the total daily volume times 1000.

Interpretation: Carl Swenlin offers these comments: The double smoothing of the short-term data results in a reliable oscillator that persists in one direction, usually tops near short-term market tops, and bottoms near short-term market bottoms. As with most indicators, the primary trend of the market will determine how you will use the indicator. In a bull market, the tops will not be very reliable. In a bear market, the bottoms will not be very reliable. Chart 8-12 shows the Swenlin Trading Oscillator for Volume.

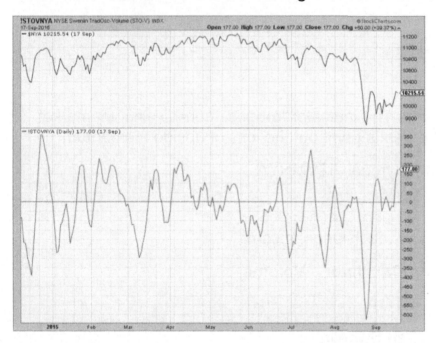

Chart 8-12

Author Comments: You can see that this indicator will generally cross the zero line after a market makes a top or bottom, but will not be far behind it.

StockCharts.com Symbol: !STOVNYA

References:

Swenlin, Carl, www.decisionpoint.com.

Up Volume Down Volume Line

Data components required: Up Volume (UV), Down Volume (DV).

Description: The Up Volume Down Volume Line is a variation of the advance decline line concept, except that it uses up and down volume instead of advances and declines.

Interpretation: This indicator can be used the same way as the advance decline line. Look for divergence patterns with the market. Using trendline analysis will also help you identify market turning points. Chart 8-13 shows the Up Volume Down Volume Line.

Chart 8-13

Author Comments: Dick Arms would tell you that this is a much better advance decline line because it incorporates volume. Volume drives the market and this indicator will certainly hint at when a bullish run is ending.

Formula: $\sum(UV - DV)$.

Cumulative Volume Ratio

Author/Creator: John C. Lawlor

Data components required: Up Volume (UV), Down Volume (DV).

Description: This is an indicator that sums the up volume for the last 50 days and divides it by the sum of the down volume over the last 50 days.

Interpretation: This will indicate the momentum of volume over a predetermined time period. For example, if the number of days used is 50, and the ratio is equal to 4, it means there was an average of 4 times as much up volume as there was down volume over the last 50 days. Likewise, if the value of the ratio (up volume/down volume) over 50 days, is -3, it means that 3 times more down volume than up volume occurred during that time frame. One can also see from chart 8-14 that divergence with price seems to be an early indicator of market direction.

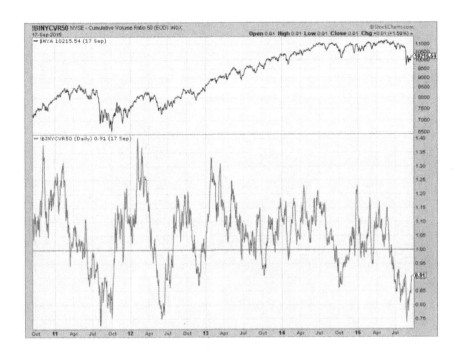

Chart 8-14

Author Comments: Lawlor developed a methodology in which he
identified cyclicality in the Cumulative Volume Ratio. This seemed
to be more prevalent when using the ratio over a 10-day period.
While not precise in identifying significant tops and bottoms, it did
seem to show short term price peaks with some consistency. Chart
8-15 is shown with a 10 period ratio and its 10 period cyclicality
(dotted sine wave).

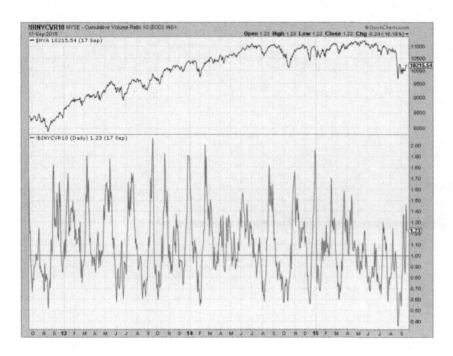

Chart 8-15

Formula: Previous Value + (UV for 50 days / DV for 50 days)

StockCharts.com Symbol: !BINYCVR50, !BINYCVR10

References:

Lawlor, John, "Cumulative Volume and Momentum." <u>Stocks & Commodities</u>, February 1988, pp. 67-69.

Up Down OBV

Author/Creator: Greg Morris

Data components required: Up Volume (UV), Down Volume (DV) Market Index (MKT).

Description: This is a unique take off from Joseph Granville's On Balance Volume (OBV). On Balance Volume added the day's volume when the closing price was higher than the previous day and subtracted the volume for the day when the closing price was lower than that of the previous day. The Up Down OBV uses a similar concept of determining the change in closing prices, but uses Up Volume if the close is higher and Down Volume if the close is lower. The daily values are accumulated similar to the way the advance decline line is calculated.

Interpretation: It would seem that increases in Up Volume associated with the price closing up would cause this indicator to reflect moves in the market in an exaggerated sense, and similarly on down moves. Chart 8-16 shows that it seems to reflect market action much like Granville's OBV.

Chart 8-16

Author Comments: This is a difficult one to interpret and one has to be careful not to read too much into these types of indicators. In chart 8-17 you can see that, similar to Granvilles' OBV, you can spot divergences with price.

Chart 8-17

I think using this as an oscillator would produce better results and offer more interpretive value. Chart 8-18 is the Up Down OBV Oscillator and when referring to the peaks and troughs, it aligns well with the market. This is the Up Down OBV with a 21-day rate of change. Up markets will keep the indicator above the zero line and down markets will keep it below zero.

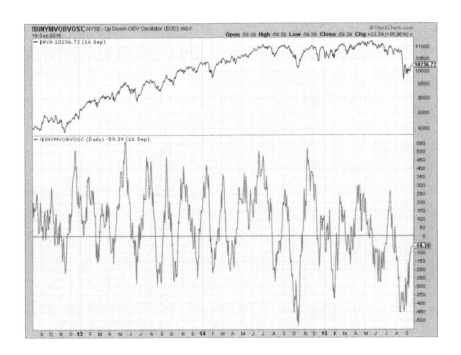

Chart 8-18

StockCharts.com Symbol: !BINYMVOBV and !BINYMVOBVOSC

Volume Percentage Ratio

Author/Creator: Mike Burk

Data components required: Up Volume (UV), Down Volume (DV) Total Volume (V).

Description: The volume percentage ratio is a 19 period exponential average of the down volume as a percentage of the total volume subtracted from a 19 period exponential average of the up volume as a percentage of the total volume.

Interpretation: Burk states that volume is best used as a confirming indication of the market. When viewing a plot of the Volume Percentage Ratio such as in chart 8-19, it is the relative position that

251

is important and not the actual values. Burk also says that it is best used as a short term indicator, usually over periods of 50 to 75 days.

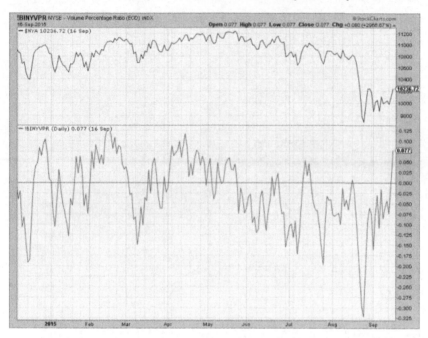

Chart 8-19

Author Comments: It seems that the Volume Percentage Ratio is fairly good a calling market bottoms, but offers little in calling tops. Of course, that falls in line with most short term indicators and is not surprising.

Formula: 19 exp. avg. (UV % TV) – 19 exp. avg. (DV % TV)

StockCharts.com Symbol: !BINYVPR

References:

Burk, Mike, "Volume Percentage Ratio." Stocks & Commodities, Volume 7, December 1989, pp. 453-455.

Upside - Downside Volume

Data components required: Up Volume (UV), Down Volume (DV).

Description: This is calculated the same as the advances minus declines except using up volume and down volume. Also, any variations of those indicators would apply here.

Interpretation: Chart 8-20 shows that it is generally best if smoothed and used as it crosses the zero line. In chart 8-20 the up down volume difference is smoothed by 21 days.

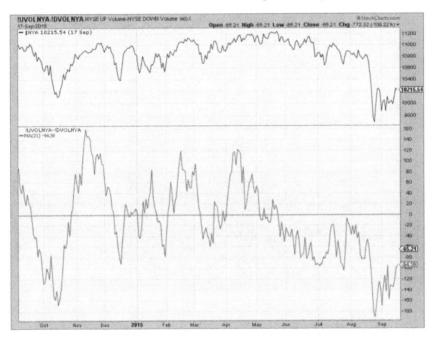

Chart 8-20

Author Comments: To be honest, I do not find much in the way of importance of difference with this one. Since this book is the complete guide, it has to be here.

Formula: (UV – DV)

Upside / Downside Volume Ratio

Data components required: Up Volume (UV), Down Volume (DV).

Description: This is the ratio of up volume to down volume (up volume divided by down volume).

Interpretation: Chart 8-21 shows that spikes to the upside represent up volume that is significantly more than down volume. Remember that a ratio of positive numbers will always yield a positive number.

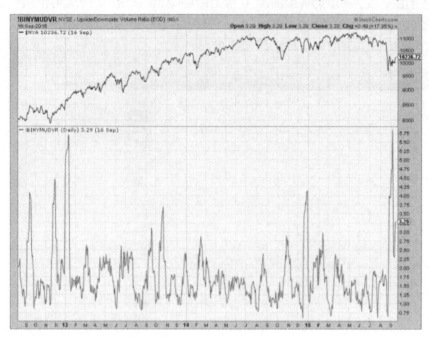

Chart 8-21

Author Comments: William O'Neil, founder and publisher of Investor's Business Daily, mentions the upside/downside volume indicator in his book, "How to Make Money in Stocks." He states that an impending upturn in the market occurs when, after a decline of 10-12%, while the market continues to drop, the upside/downside volume will start to shift.

Larry McMillan, author of numerous books on options, uses a 50-day sum of up volume divided by a 50-day sum of down volume. Larry says that if the ratio is greater than 3.0, it is excellent volume, if greater than 2.0, it is very good volume, 1.0 is neutral, less than 0.8 is poor, and less than 0.5 is terrible. This ratio attempts to measure whether stock traders are participating with good buying volume on days that the market is up. While Larry uses this primarily on individual stocks, chart 8-22 shows the upside downside volume using the data from the New York Stock Exchange.

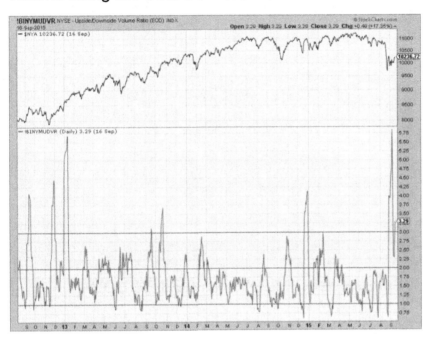

Chart 8-22

Another version of up and down volume was written about by Dennis Peterson, a frequent contributor to Stocks and Commodities magazine. This version uses a three-day sum of the ratio of up volume to changed volume (up volume plus down volume) and then divided by 3. The division serves no real purpose other than to reduce the large scaling numbers. Peterson's version is shown in chart 8-23.

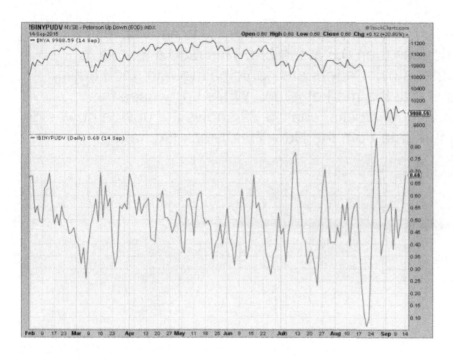

Chart 8-23

Formula: (UV / DV)

StockCharts.com Symbol: !BINYMUDVR and !BINYPUDV

References:

O'Neil, William J., How to Make Money in Stocks. McGraw-Hill, 1988.

McMillan, Larry, www.theoptionstrategist.com.

Peterson, Dennis, "Market Breadth: Volume." Stocks and Commodities, Volume 19, February 2001, pp. 57-60.

Zweig Up Volume Indicator

Show Zweig Double 9 Down Volume Ratio and Zweig Double 9 Up volume ratio.

Author/Creator: Martin Zweig

Data components required: Up Volume (UV), Down Volume (DV).

Description: This is another of Dr. Martin Zweig's momentum indicators. This one uses a ratio of up volume and down volume. This ratio shows the powerful thrust of the market and cannot be ignored.

Interpretation: Whenever the ratio reaches 9 to 1, a good buying opportunity exists. There have been many signals given since 1965. The biggest ratio ever was on August 17, 1982, the beginning of an 18-year bull market. The chart below shows each occurrence of the 9 to 1 up volume ratio since late 2007, identified by the down spikes that go down to -9. You will notice in chart 8-24 that they generally happen near significant, certainly tradable, market bottoms.

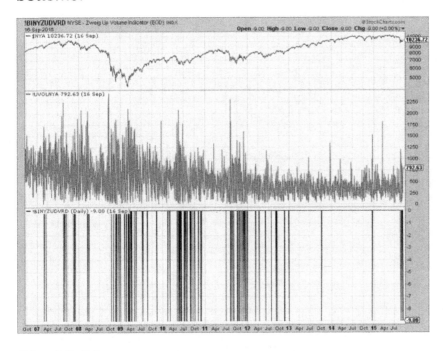

Chart 8-24

A further concept from Dr. Zweig is to expand the 9 to 1 ratio of up volume to down volume to state that anytime there are two signals in any 3-month period, the evidence suggests a strong market to follow. Notice in chart 8-25 that these "double nine" signals are after the market bottoms. They are identified as the longer of the down spikes and go down to -18, whereas the down spikes that go down only to -9 are the regular ones mentioned earlier. The longer down spikes are the second of the 9-to-1 ratios to occur in a 3-month period. They won't be good market bottom signals, but will give you an opportunity to get onboard a strong market. They are almost confirmation that a good upward move is underway and considered as a continuation of the first 9-to1 down spike.

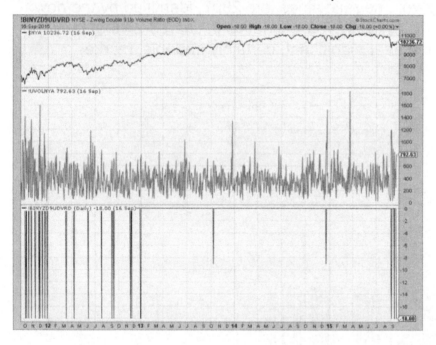

Chart 8-25

Author Comments: I took his concept one step further and identified all the down volume days in which the down volume was 9 times greater than the up volume. There were many more signals for

258

both the regular 9 to 1 ratio and also the "double nine" signals. Chart 8-26 shows the double nine signals as the down spikes that go down to -18 and the regular nine-to-one ratios are the shorter down spikes (dotted lines). The October 19, 1987 "Black Monday" market plunge distorts the chart, because there was over 500 times more down volume that up volume on that day. That is the reason chart 8-26 does not display data back to that date. After studying this data for some time, I think it is best to keep it in the "nice to know" category. I do not see any trading opportunities or investing strategies that can make use of this. When you think about it, down volume in excess is usually from panic situations, many times they are near market bottoms as it is during capitulation, but mostly during only one day panics. The down volume 9-to1 ratios could be the first indication that the ensuing rally might be a good one.

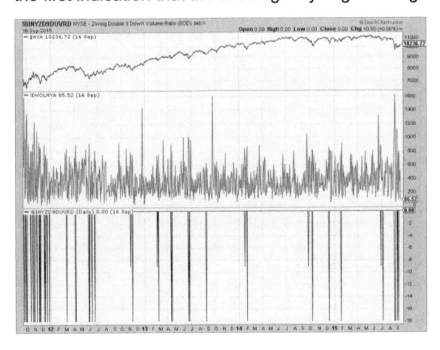

Chart 8-26

StockCharts.com Symbol: !BINYZUDVRD, !BINYZD9UDVRD, !BINYZD9DUVRD

References:

Zweig, Martin E. <u>Winning</u> <u>on Wall Street</u>. New York: Warner Books, 1986.

CH 9 - Composite Indicators

The breadth indicators in this section utilize different categories of breadth components for their calculation. Some use all breadth components, and some use only two or three components.

Composite Indicators

Arms Index

Arms Open Index

Bretz TRIN-5

Cash Flow Index

Composite Tape Index

Dysart Positive Negative Volume

Eliades New TRIN

Haller Theory

Hindenburg Omen

Market Thrust

McClellan Oscillator with Volume

McClellan Summation Index with Volume

Meyers Systems

Moving Balance Indicator

Technical Index

Titanic Syndrome

Trend Exhaustion Index

Arms' Index

Also known as: TRIN and MKDS

Author/Creator: Richard W. Arms

Data components required: Advances (A), Declines (D), Up Volume (UV), Down Volume (DV)

Description: The Arms Index (TRIN) is the ratio between advancing issues and declining issues divided by the ratio between the up volume and the down volume. Said differently, it is the ratio of the volume of declining stocks divided by the volume of advancing stocks. A rising line above 1.0 reflects more volume in declining issues and is negative. A falling line below 1.0 reflects more volume in rising stocks and is positive. The Arms index trends in the opposite direction of the market and is considered an inverse indicator.

Special Treat: I asked my good friend Dick Arms if he would write a short piece for this book about what his thought process was when creating the Arms Index. The next two paragraphs are from the man himself. Thanks Dick.

The Arms Index was my first invention in a long career of developing technical methods over the years and writing about them in my six books on technical analysis. It was way back in 1967, and I was a young retail broker for the now defunct firm of EF Hutton. We had just moved into a new modern office with the latest in quotation equipment. Those machines on every desk allowed one to see, on a tiny screen, the four factors that make up the index: Advances, Declines, Advancing Volume and Declining Volume. It seemed logical to me to combine these in an equation that would answer the question: "Are the advancing stocks getting their fair share of the volume?" I merely wrote them down as they appeared on my screen and made each a fraction. I started by calculating the first ratio, then the second ratio, and then the comparison of the two ratios.

After a few weeks of playing with the results I showed it to a prominent analyst in the New York office, Newton Zinder. He showed it around to others and before long Barron's had me write an article about it. From then on it took on a life of its own, and I went on to develop other things such as Equivolume Charting and now Arms Candlevolume charting. The beauty of the Arms Index is that it is so much based upon the core forces of the market place that no matter how closely followed it self-adjusts and cannot, therefore, self-destruct. It was originally called TRIN because the first users were calling it the Trader's Index. Thanks to the efforts of many other technical analyst supporters it is now generally called the Arms Index.

Thanks Dick

TRIN came from its original name of Short Term TRading INdex. When computers came along and everyone started attaching their names to their creations (appropriately so), it was changed to Arms Index. The first known writing on it appeared in Barrons in 1967.

Interpretation: Newton Zinder, of E. F. Hutton and Co. has identified the bullishness of the Arms Index when two consecutive days had readings of 2.0 or greater. To produce levels like this there must be a large number of declines compared to advances, plus those declines must garner most of the volume for that day. It represents almost a panic type of selling for the day.

Chart 9-1 is the Arms Index in its basic form. A line is drawn at an Arms Index value of 2.0, showing the extreme levels of large volume going into declining stocks. Remember that this is an inverse (upside down) indicator. You can quickly see that it is volatile and difficult to interpret in this basic form. The following different ways to chart and use the Arms Index will add significantly to its merit.

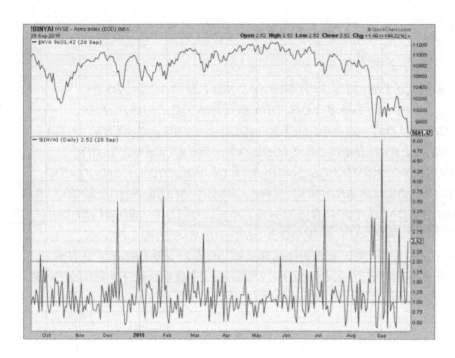

Chart 9-1

Richard Arms has stated that he uses a 21-day smoothing for intermediate forecasts and 55 days for longer term use. In 1991, Richard Arms talked about an oscillator using the 21-day smoothing and the 55-day smoothing of the Arms Index. Whenever the 21-day average dropped below the 55-day average, it was giving a buy signal (remember, this is an inverted indicator), and whenever the 21-day average went above the 55-day average, a sell signal was generated. Richard Arms called this indicator the "Cross Your Arms" indicator. Arms further refined his use of this indicator by suggesting that you use it as an intermediate term market direction indicator, and when it is bullish look for buys only. Likewise, if it is bearish, look only for selling opportunities. A lot like the old saying – don't fight the tape. A little known fact is that Richard Arms preferred exponential smoothing instead of arithmetic. Thomas Aspray wrote about such an oscillator but used a 10-day average and a 30-day average for his indicator. The "cross your arms" indicator is shown in chart 9-2.

Chart 9-2

Another of Arms' uses of his indicator, the Arms Index, is to plot a 4-day average of it and put Bollinger bands around a 13-day simple average. He states that it is very short-term and only used for trading. When it moves outside the bands a signal is given. Again, keep in mind that this is an inverse indicator, so when it breaks out of the top band a buy signal is given and when it breaks out below the bottom band, a sell signal is given. Chart 9-3 shows this method, with the Bollinger bands being the red lines.

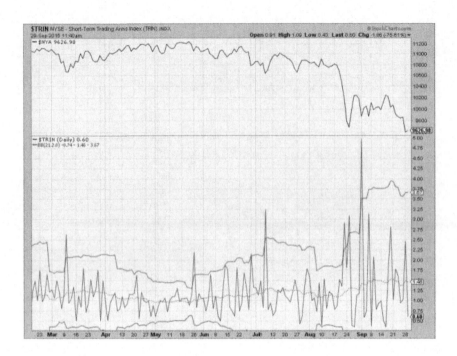

Chart 9-3

Steven Achelis, founder of Equis International, suggests using a 4 day moving average for short term work, a 21 day moving average for intermediate term work, and a 55 day moving average for long term work. These values are in line with Arms' suggestions. You can see a plot of the Arms Index with a 21-day smoothing in chart 9-4. Trendlines are shown pointing out some obvious divergences with the market.

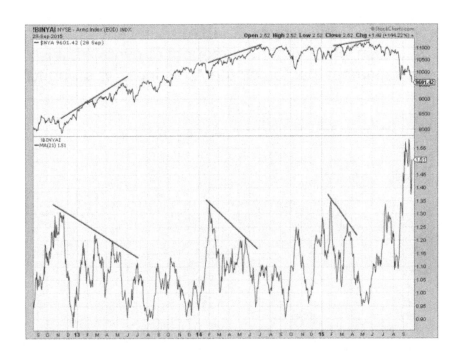

Chart 9-4

Notice in the preceding chart how it builds higher and higher during the topping process of the market. This is because the Arms Index is not a true ratio, in that it theoretically has no limit to the upside, but cannot go below zero on the downside, giving it an upside bias. Smoothing it will not change this bias. Another popular way to interpret this indicator is to construct a 10-day moving average of its daily values. A 10-day Arms Index over 1.20 is oversold; a 10-day Arms index below .80 is overbought, as shown in chart 9-5. A further enhancement, which is strictly visual appeal, is to invert the indicator so that up is bullish and down is bearish, which is more in line with most indicators. This can easily be accomplished by dividing 1 by the indicator. If you do this then the Arms Index over 1.20 is overbought and when below .80, it is oversold. You can quickly see that using this as a trading tool will generate entirely too many false signals. I just prefer to monitor it to keep a mental focus on where the volume is going, into advancing stocks or declining stocks. In general, because of swings in market sentiment, the Arms Index can be bullish when either overbought or oversold. It is the rapid change in sentiment that forces the Arms Index to swing to extremes.

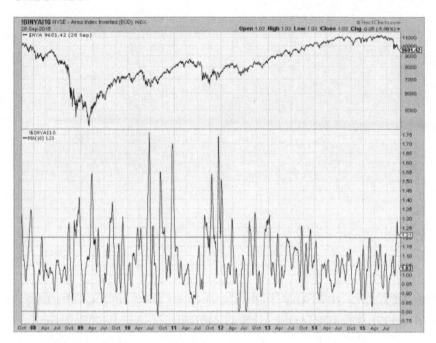

Chart 9-5

In 1987, James Alphier and Bill Kuhn wrote an article in Stocks & Commodities magazine after a comprehensive study of the market using a daily Arms Index reading of 2.65 or greater. They showed the performance of the S&P 500 Index 3, 6, 9, and 12 months after the Arms Index gave a 2.65 reading. A cursory glance at their table revealed that the market was usually higher over different time periods after the big selling day when the Arms Index went above 2.65. The question they wanted to answer was: "Does it pay to go along and panic with the herd?" Their answer: "It does not." Remember, that when the Arms Index is at a high, it means that most of the volume is going into the declining issues. Many times this extreme selling can be a form of panic and a selling climax. Another very interesting note that they made was that after a 2.65 reading, a key trading low came a short time later. The chart below shows the Arms Index when values are greater than 2.65. Each down spike at the bottom of chart 9-6 identifies a day when the Arms Index is greater than 2.65.

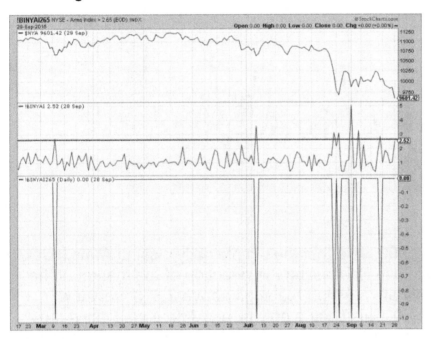

Chart 9-6

Tim Hayes at Ned Davis Research uses a 40-day average of the Arms Index for their intermediate-term work. He says that the Arms Index is a good measure of the quality of volume in the market, more on an intermediate to short term basis. Buy signals occur when the indicator increases to 1.12 or at least to .968 and then reverses. Sell indications are readings below .798 or a decrease to at least .928 and then back above the level. Chart 9-7 is a plot of the 40-day average of the Arms Index (TRIN).

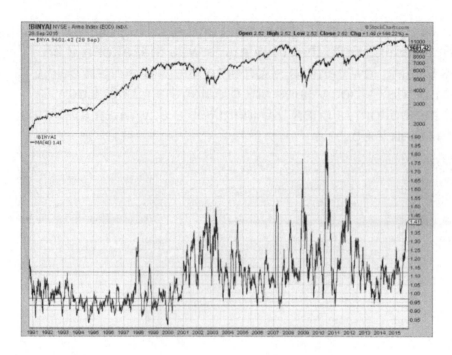

Chart 9-7

Arthur Merrill in 1992, said that the simple daily closing Arms Index seems to be useful in forecasting the direction of the market of the following day only at very high readings above 2.3, or very low readings below 0.4. This occurs only rarely. Arthur was using the prices of the Dow Jones Industrial Average for this analysis and only 435 days (less than 2 years) of market data.

Author Comments: The Arms Index and the Advance Decline Line are the two most over analyzed breadth indicators I know of. That is certainly a measure of their popularity. There are many derivations of the Arms Index, some good, some not so good. This section has presented most of them. One thing that stands out is that the bullishness of the Arms Index is related to the number of declining issues. This is a little hard to grasp until you study the formula.

I have always found the raw Arms Index difficult to use for trading, other than a quick picture of where volume is flowing, either into advancing stocks or declining stocks. I much prefer to invert it, smooth it, and set up zones for bullish and bearish readings. Richard Arms told me at a technical analysis conference in Dallas, Texas, in the early 1990s that he wished he had inverted it in the beginning because of the interpretation problems most folks had with using an inverted indicator. Inverting it does not affect its interpretation in any way, it just uses the more popular "up is bullish and down is bearish" convention. Also, Richard Arms is of the belief that volume is the most important component of the market. To make his point during his presentation, Dick made the comment that when he left his office to go to lunch, he told his secretary that he would be back in about 35 million shares. He also said in a 1991 interview for Stocks & Commodities magazine, that if the market were a wristwatch, it would be divided into shares, not hours.

In reference to Arms 4-day average of the Arms Index and the 15% bands around the 13-day average shown in chart 9-3, it looks to me that the concept is quite good, but even better if you wait until the 4-day smoothed value returns within the bands before generating a signal. In other words, a buy signal is given after the 4-day average goes above the upper band and then drops below it. Likewise, a sell signal is given when it comes from below to above the lower band. This interpretation was done by using a cursor and visually looking at the data from 1965 to early 2005.

Robert Nurock, the chief elf on the Wall Street Week television show, who created the Wall Street Week Index, used the Arms Index as one of that index's components. A bullish signal was given when the 10-day average of the Arms Index was above 1.2 and bearish when below 0.8.

Formula: (A / D) / (UV / DV)

StockCharts.com's Symbols: !BINYAI, !BINYAIO2155, !BINYAI10, !BINYAI265

References:

Arms, Richard W. Jr. <u>The Arms Index</u> <u>(TRIN).</u> Dow Jones-Irwin, 1989.

Arms, Richard W., "Cross Your Arms." <u>Stocks & Commodities</u>, Volume 9, May 1991, pp. 177-179.

Achelis, Steven B. <u>Technical Analysis from A to Z.</u> New York: McGraw-Hill, 1995.

Alphier, James and Kuhn, Bill, "A Helping Hand from the Arms Index." <u>Stocks & Commodities</u>, Volume 5, April 1987, pp. 142-143.

Aspray, Thomas, "NYSE technical indicators: diagnosing market bottoms." <u>Stocks & Commodities</u>, Volume 6, June 1987, pp. 227-231.

Merrill, Arthur, "Volume Indices." <u>Stocks & Commodities</u>, Volume 7, September 1989, pp. 301-303.

Hayes, Tim, "Tim Hayes: Running with the Trend." <u>Stocks & Commodities</u>, Volume 9, August 1991, pp. 310-315.

Davis, Ned. <u>Being</u> <u>Right or Making Money</u>. Ned Davis Research, 1991.

Arms' Open Index

Author/Creator: Suggested by Harvey Wilbur, recommended by John McGinley and Peter Eliades.

Data components required: Advances (A), Declines (D), Up Volume (UV), Down Volume (DV).

Description: This is a smoothed version of Richard Arms' Short Term Trading Index or Arms Index, however, it smooths the individual components prior to doing the multiple divisions. Wilbur used a 10 period moving average for the smoothing each of the components.

Interpretation: Steve Achelis states that readings above .9 are bearish and below .9 are bullish. While it seems to pick tops and bottoms at times, other times seem to not do so, as shown in chart 9-8.

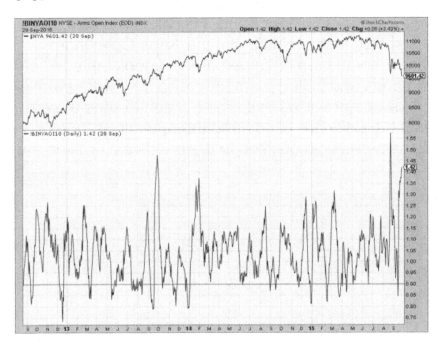

Chart 9-8

Author Comments: Personally, I'll stick with Dick Arms original index, but display it upside down so it is more intuitive for me and then give it a 10-day smoothing. I use the Arms Index for a short term picture of the markets; to assist in determining where the volume is going, either into advances or declines. I can see the merits of the Arms Open (prefer Open Arms – sounds more inviting), but also prefer to just use a smoothed version of TRIN (Arms Index). However, Wilbur wasn't finished with the Arms Index and his modifications to it.

In November, 1992, Harley Wilbur presented, in my opinion, the best modification to the continuously modified Arms Index. He normalized it relative to its own volatility. First of all, he took the Arms Open Index using 10 day averages, took a 10-day average of that, and then normalized it with typical two standard deviation Bollinger bands. This made the indicator oscillate essentially between zero and 100, with zero being the lower Bollinger band and 100 representing the upper Bollinger band. He called this indicator Trin10. Chart 9-9 shows in the middle plot the Arms Open index with Bollinger bands. If you then imagined that you took the ends of the two Bollinger bands and pulled them taught so they were parallel straight lines, the lower plot shows this. The horizontal lines at zero and 100 are in fact the Bollinger bands and the open arms index is displayed with its same relative position to the bands as it was in the middle plot.

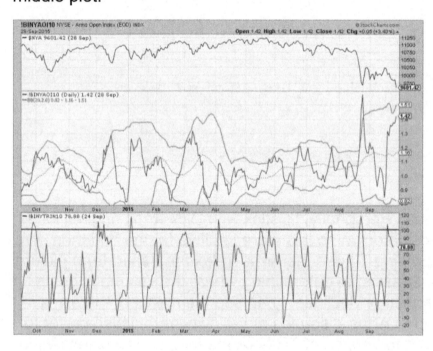

Chart 9-9

Wilbur next weighted the Trin10 with a five period weighted moving average as shown in chart 9-10. A weighted average is one that has a linear weighting with the most recent having the greatest weight and the oldest having the least. Wilbur suggested the trading strategy was to buy on an uptick from below 20 and sell on a downtick from above 80. Wilbur readily admitted that it did not always work, but rated it good enough to keep in the technician's arsenal. I certainly agree.

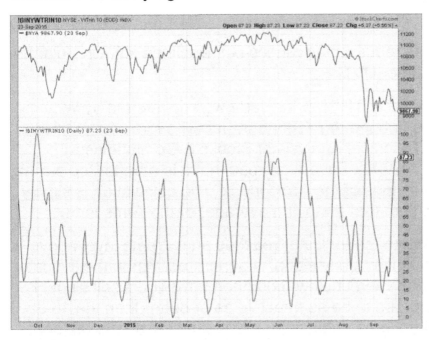

Chart 9-10

Formula: TRIN = (A / D) / (UV / DV), (TRIN – LowerBB) / (UpperBB – LowerBB).

StockCharts.com's Symbols: !BINYAOI10, !BINYTRIN10

References:

Achelis, Steven B. Technical Analysis from A to Z. New York: McGraw-Hill, 1995.

Wilbur, Harley, "A Twist on the Arms Index." Stocks and Commodities, Volume 10, November 1992, pp. 449-453.

Merrill, Arthur, "Closing Arms." Stocks and Commodities, Volume 10, April 1992, pp. 148-150.

Bretz TRIN-5

Show: Bretz TRIN-5 (inverted)

Author/Creator: W. G. Bretz

Data components required: Advances (A), Declines (D), Up Volume (UV), Down Volume (DV).

Description: The Bretz TRIN -5 Indicator was developed by W.G. Bretz, and it was dubbed the TRIN-5 by Jerry Favors who published an article on it (Technical Analysis of Stocks & Commodities Magazine; March 1992). Favors claimed that it is a better top picker than the other versions of the Arms Index. The calculation is simply a 5-day moving sum (not a moving average) of the Arms Index.

Interpretation: When the indicator reaches an extreme level above 6.00, then turns down, a buy signal is generated. When the indicator reaches an extreme level below 4.00, then turns up, a sell signal is generated. It appears to be as effective as or better than the 10 day TRIN at market bottoms and it is far more effective at market tops and is shown in chart 9-11.

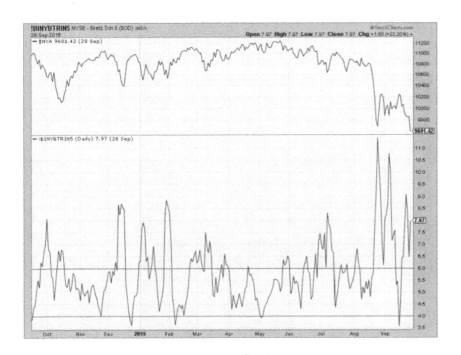

Chart 9-11

Author Comments: Carl Swenlin does what most of us do with Arms Index related indicators and derivations, he inverts it so that the more normal appearance of overbought and oversold are correct and more intuitive. Chart 9-12 shows it as inverted with the calculation so that overbought is up and oversold is down. The interpretation now is that when this indicator rises from below 4 and turns up, a buy signal has been generated. And when it goes from above 6 and turns down a sell signal is generated. Personally I like to see buy signals when it goes from below 4 and then goes above 6 before it generates a buy signal. Likewise, when it drops from above 6 and goes below 4, a sell signal is given.

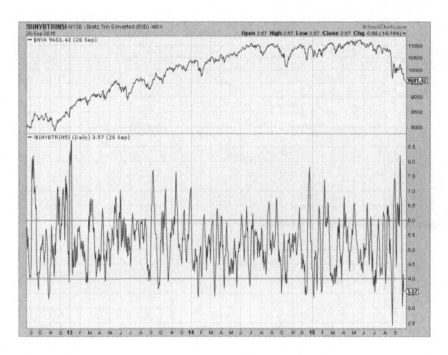

Chart 9-12

Formula: (A / D) / (UV / DV) summed over the last 5 days.

StockCharts.com's Symbols: !BINYBTRIN5, !BINYBTRIN5I

References:

Bretz, W.G. <u>Juncture Recognition in the Stock Market</u>. Vantage Press, 1972.

Favors, Jerry, "The Trin-5." <u>Stocks and Commodities</u>, Volume 10, March 1992, pp. 125-126.

Cash Flow Index

Also known as: see The Technical Index

Author/Creator: William Mason

Data components required: Advances (A), Declines (D), Up Volume (UV), Down Volume (DV), New Highs (H), New Lows (L), Total Issues (TI), Volume (V).

Description: The Cash Flow Index is created by taking the net difference of the advances and declines, up and down volume, and new highs and new lows; expressing them as a percentage of their respective base, combining them to get a new value; and multiplying it by the volume for the day, then accumulating the daily values. Mason said that the reason for using percentages is that no single parameter will dominate.

Interpretation: Most indicators of cash flow are measuring price and volume or two non-neutralizing components of market statistics. Using it to help confirm new highs in the market would be about the only way I can think of that this would be effective. Chart 9-13 is the cash flow index developed by Mason.

Chart 9-13

Author Comments: I have only found a few sentences on this indicator by William Mason. It is a derivation of the Technical Index he developed with a daily total volume component added to it. Since one of the components in the Technical Index is the up volume down volume difference and total volume ratio, adding the total volume as a multiplier seems to dampen, and almost hinder, the usefulness of this indicator. It renders the ratio ineffective, and makes the volume contribution only that of the difference between the up and down volume. One might improve it by detrending it with a moving average of 50 days or so.

Formula: Previous Value + Today's (V * ((A – D) / TI) + ((UV – DV) / V) + ((H – L) / TI))

StockCharts.com's Symbol: !BINYCFI

References:

Mason, William, "Master Oscillator." <u>Stocks and Commodities</u>, Volume 7, April 1989, pp. 109-111.

Composite Tape Index

Author/Creator: Steve Achelis of Equis International

Data components required: Advances (A), Declines (D), New Highs (H), New Lows (L), Up Volume (UV), Down Volume (DV).

Description: The Composite Tape Index shows market strength and direction. Because the CTI displays market strength (momentum), it tends to be a trend following indicator. The indicator can be used to anticipate market moves, but it is best not to "fight the tape" (a phrase Martin Zweig coined years ago). Once the Composite Tape Index forms a trend, it tends to stay in that trend for some time. And once the trend is broken, it is usually broken for good and a new trend is then established. Because the CTI is a composite of several different momentum indicators, it is not as subject to false readings and whipsaws as often as a single indicator.

Interpretation: The basic analysis of the Composite Tape Index requires determining the current trend and deciding when the trend has changed. One method of determining the trend is to wait for the indicator to enter the overbought/oversold zones and then rise/fall from these levels. Buy signals are given when the indicator falls below -15 and then rises above -15, or any time the indicator rises above +15. Likewise, sell signals are generated when the indicator rises above +15 and then falls below +15, or any time the indicator falls below -15. Another system that works wells is to buy when CTI rises above zero and sell when it falls below zero. Chart 9-14 shows the medium term composite tape index.

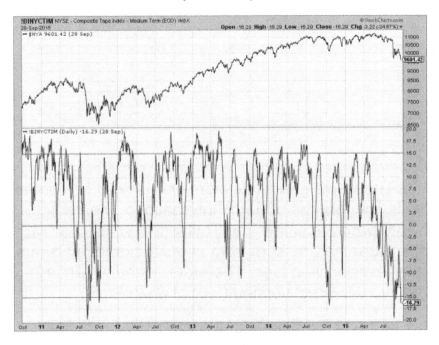

Chart 9-14

The short term composite index uses faster parameters and is shown in chart 9-15. In general terms, the parameters for the short term version are about 20% less than the medium term tape index. The overbought and oversold levels that seem to work well are +10 and -10. The analysis and use of the short term composite is the same as the medium term composite.

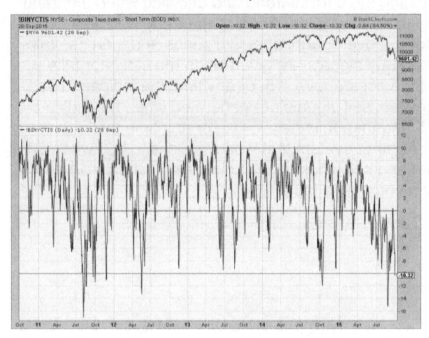

Chart 9-15

Author Comments: These are great indicators and I know they come from Steven Achelis, the founder of Equis International. Years ago, Steve had a software program called The Technician which was MS-DOS based and I'm sure the pressure from users to come out with a MS-Windows based version was high. Therefore, it has essentially been incorporated into the latest version (9.0) of MetaStock.

I prefer to use this indicator for signals that occur when it crosses above and below the zero line. They seem to work better and avoid the often-times subjective nature of overbought and oversold.

If there is a short and medium term version, why not a long term version? For this, I just doubled the value of the default parameters of the medium version to get the chart below. Here is how I would use this version: It does a great job of identifying tops and bottoms using +30 for overbought and -20 for oversold. It also seems to be good using the zero-line crossover. One can begin to leg in on the oversold crossing from below to above the -20 line, then take more positions after crossing the zero line. Selling can be done the same way. Partially exit positions when it comes from above to below the +30 line, then exit all when it drops below the zero line. Chart 9-16 is my version of the long term composite tape indicator.

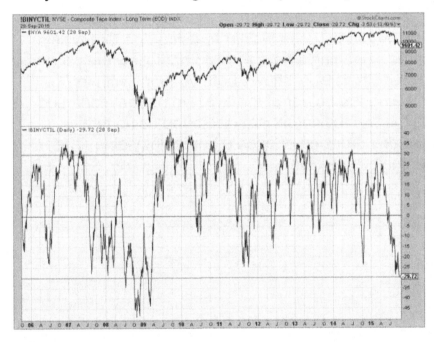

Chart 9-16

StockCharts.com's Symbols: !BINYCTIS, !BINYCTIM, !BINYCTIL

References:

MetaStock Professional 9.0, Equis International, Salt Lake City, UT.

Dysart Positive Negative Volume

Author/Creator: Paul Dysart

Data components required: Advances (A), Declines (D) Volume (V).

Description: Paul Dysart used a similar concept to Granville's On Balance Volume with his Positive and Negative Issues Traded Indexes. The positive version was the summation of advances minus declines only on days when the total volume of trading increases over that of the previous day. The negative version is similar in that it uses the advance decline difference when the volume decreases.

Interpretation: This would be used similar to using Joe Granville's On Balance Volume. Spotting where they do not follow the price will lead to market turns. Chart 9-17 shows both versions with the negative version being the bolder of the two. Do not get confused with this chart as the two indicators are displayed using totally different scales so any crossing of each other is not viable. The darker line is the positive version.

Chart 9-17

Author Comments: There is very little written about these indicators. They are take-offs of Dysart's original Negative Volume Index.

Formula: If the close today is greater than the close yesterday, use up volume. If not, use down volume. Then accumulate the numbers.

StockCharts.com's Symbols: !BINYDNI, !BINYDPI

References:

Merrill, Arthur, "Negative Volume Divergence Index." <u>Stocks & Commodities</u>, Volume 8, October 1990, pp. 396-397.

Peterson, Dennis, "Market Breadth: Volume." <u>Stocks & Commodities</u>, Volume 19, February 2001, pp. 57-60.

Eliades New TRIN

Author/Creator: Peter Eliades

Data components required: Advances (A), Declines (D), Up Volume (UV), Down Volume (DV).

Description: The Eliades New TRIN calculation is a 10-day moving average of down volume, divided by a 10-day moving average of up volume, further divided by a 10-day moving average of the Arms Index (TRIN).

Interpretation: When the indicator crosses below .8, and then moves back above .8, a sell signal is generated. Chart 9-18 shows Eliades New TRIN.

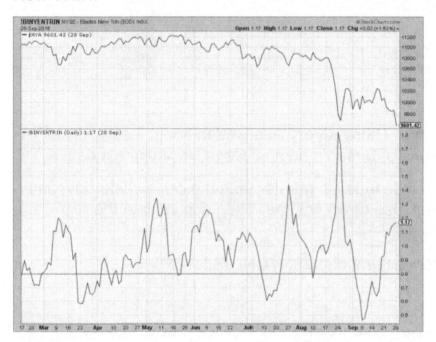

Chart 9-18

Author Comments: Once again, inverting the chart of this indicator will make it more intuitive, but does not add anything to the interpretation. However, my seventh grade algebra says that this is essentially just the ratio of declines and advances. The act of smoothing the components keeps this somewhat different than the decline advance ratio in that the levels are a little different; however, the lines are close to the same. Since Peter Eliades has made significant contributions to technical analysis, I suspect his interpretation would be better than mine.

Formula: (DV / AV) / ((A / D) / (UV / DV))

StockCharts.com's Symbol: !BINYENTRIN

References:

Swenlin, Carl, www.decisionpoint.com.

Eliades, Peter, www.stockmarketcycles.com.

Haller Theory

Author/Creator: Gilbert Haller

Data components required: Advances (A), Declines (D), New Highs (H), New Lows (L).

Description: The Haller Theory for determining market tops and bottoms is more than just a breadth-based method. It involves the yield on the Dow Jones Industrial Average in addition to weekly advance decline line data and weekly new high and new low data. There are essentially two types of buy signals, one which is an opportunity to buy during an identifiable trend and the other is during a selling climax. The sell signals are basically the opposite.

Interpretation:

Trend Buy Signal

1. The advance decline line must turn up by 2400 points.

2. The new high new low difference must equal a net +80 new highs.

3. There can be no Trend Buy until there has been a Trend Sell Signal.

Trend Sell Signal

1. The yield on the Dow Jones Industrial Average must be less than 5%.

2. The advance decline line must turn down by 2400 points.

3. The new high new low difference must equal a net -80 new lows.

4. There can be no Trend Sell Signal until there has been a Trend Buy Signal.

Bottom Buy Signals.

1. Buy the start of the fourth week after the net new lows equals -750.

2. If there is a week in which there are more new lows that the week that gave the first signal, start the 4-week timing over.

3. If there is not Bottom Buy Signal, buy at the next Trend Buy Signal.

Top Sell Signals

1. The yield on the Dow Jones Industrial Average was less than 4% at one time during the bull move.

2. The bull move had to last for at least a year.

3. The advance decline line must have failed, which is a move that drops below a previous low with each leg being at least two weeks in length.

4. The initial peak of the advance decline line is the high for the line.

5. The advance decline line must rise for three weeks to make a third peak.

6. The advance decline line then must drop by over 300 points.

7. The net number of new highs must be less than the that of the final peak than earlier.

8. Volume must also be lower on the final peak than previously based upon a 6 week moving average.

Author Comments: Haller's self-published book is an interesting read. The concept he developed is fairly simple insofar at the data relationship and effective, but not conducive for a chart with an indicator or trading system. I spent quite a bit of time on creating an indicator that would reflect this system, even to the point of pairing it down to using only the breadth data. I like the idea of using trend signals along with climactic buy and sell signals. He claimed that from 1942 to 1964 there were no bad signals, however, not mention of drawdown or other risk-based analysis was offered. You can also sense his deep understanding of the difficulty of timing market tops based upon the complex methodology given in the Top Sell Signals. Finally, keep in mind this was all done over 40 years ago with columnar pad and not even a calculator, let alone a computer. Chart 9-19 shows portions of the Haller Theory. I used 200 for the Trend limits on the high low component because at the time of this indicator's development, the total of weekly new highs plus new lows plus 1000 is more than double now. The dotted upward spikes that reach +3 are the Bottom Buy Signals. The dotted downward spikes that reach -1 are the Trend Sell Signals. The solid line that reaches +1 are the Trend Buy Signals. The Top Sell Signals could not be reproduced because of the subjectivity of his rules.

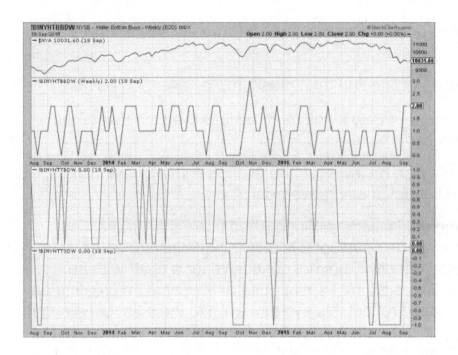

Chart 9-19

StockCharts.com's Symbols: !BINYHTBBDW, !BINYHTTBDW, !BINYHTTSDW

References:

Haller, Gilbert. <u>The Haller Theory of Stock Market Trends</u>. West Palm Beach: Gilbert Haller, 1965.

Hindenburg Omen

Also known as: New High New Low Sell Signal

Author/Creator: James R. Miekka.

Data components required: New Highs (H), New Lows (L), Advances (A), Declines (D), Total Issues (TI), Market Index (MKT).

Description: This indication of market tops was created by James R. Miekka and dubbed "the Hindenburg Omen" by Kennedy Gammage of the Richland Report. You'll recognize Kennedy as the former provider of the McClellan Oscillator and Summation Index numbers on FNN and now, CNBC television.

The remaining material on this indicator was written by the late James R. Miekka, creator of the Hindenburg Omen:

The Hindenburg Omen is a sell signal that occurs when NYSE new highs and new lows each exceed 2.8% of advances plus declines on the same day. In addition, the NYSE index must be above the value it had 50 trading days (ten weeks) ago. Once the signal has occurred, it is valid for 30 trading days. Any additional signals given during the 30-day period should be ignored. During the 30 days, the signal is activated whenever the McClellan Oscillator (MCO) is negative, but deactivated whenever the MCO is positive. The signal starting point was originally calculated to be when NH and NL equaled or exceeded 2.4% of total issues traded, but was later simplified to 2.8% of advances plus declines. This signal was developed as an improvement upon the Split Market Sell Signal developed by Gerald Appel. Appel's signal used a fixed number of new highs and new lows (45 of each), which was not indexed for increasing numbers of shares trades, and his signal did not require validation by the MCO being negative.

Interpretation: This signal generally occurs after a rising market when the number of new lows is rising rapidly, but when new highs are still quite numerous. The large number of highs and lows suggests that the market is indecisive and probably at a turning point. Of course, a similar scenario can occur during a falling market when new lows are numerous but new highs begin to rise rapidly. The latter condition would suggest that such market indecision could be a buy signal in a falling market. This has not been studied, at least not by James Miekka, other than to note that the sell signal is not reliable when NYSE is below its ten-weeks-ago value. To utilize the Hindenburg Omen signal, Miekka suggests the following:

1. Go short the market whenever the McClellan Oscillator is negative during the 30 trading days after a valid signal has been given.

2. Exit the market for 30 days whenever the signal is given, or at least be wary of any new stock or stock index purchases while the signal is valid and especially if it is activated by a negative MCO.

By exiting the market when a signal was given on September 23, 1987, you would have avoided the crash of 1987.

Author Comments: Jim Miekka has provided a significant indicator of market danger. An indicator developed from a logical point of view is usually one that will serve you well. This one does just that. In chart 9-20 I have tried to recreate this indicator as closely to Miekka's parameters as I can. Any difference between the chart signals and Jim's actual are a fault with my programming.

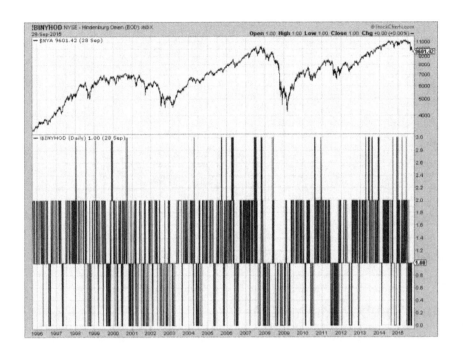

Chart 9-20

While it is not the purpose of this book to discern performance of these breadth indicators, Jim provided this for me and I want to deviate from that purpose just this once. The following table gives a history of the Hindenburg Omen from 1993 to 2004, using the old NYSE as the index. To convert to new NYSE, multiply the points by 10.78.

Date Signal Given	NYSE New Highs	NYSE New Lows	NH or NL* as % of A + D	McClellan Oscillator at start	# of days short**	G/L in old NYSE Points
02/22/93	177	61	3.1	-43	20	-0.80
03/15/94	93	80	3.7	-5	22	+9.68
10/28/94	89	114	3.9	+22	22	+18.55
10/10/96	66	68	2.9	-117	15	-6.56
11/26/97	128	91	3.2	+24	12	+6.21
07/09/98	120	96	3.3	+109	20	+38.64
01/29/99	96	91	3.0	-48	23	+9.69
04/08/99	97	122	3.2	+37	3	-0.97
10/29/99	117	90	2.9	+161	14	+12.57
12/20/99	90	291	2.9	-38	11	-14.22
06/30/00	104	98	3.1	+9	13	-14.32
09/18/00	90	111	3.1	-118	30	+18.77
12/22/00	206	96	3.3	+79	0	+0
10/01/02	92	152	2.8	+5	12	-23.34
04/13/04	114	111	3.3	-174	26	+24.08
					NET	+77.98

* New Highs or New Lows, whichever is smaller.

** Short only when the McClellan Oscillator is negative for 30 days after signal is given.

StockCharts.com's Symbol: !BINYHOD

References:

Gammage, Kennedy, 2004, The Richland Report, LaJolla, CA.

Miekka, James R., The Sudbury Bull and Bear Report, St. Petersburg, FL.

Market Thrust

Author/Creator: Tushar Chande

Data components required: Advances (A), Declines (D), Up Volume (UV), Down Volume (DV).

Description: Tushar Chande offers this as a way to overcome some of the perceived limitations in the Arms Index. The advantages of this indicator are that it subdivided the product of advances and up volume, and the declines and down volume. This helps identify a strong up or down day. It also shows the net balance between bullish and bearish activity using relative volume flows, and it presents consistent information.

Interpretation: This indicator, as shown in chart 9-21, is basically used to spot large moves in the market. Using the product of advances and up volume will generate significant up moves in this indicator if volume is flowing into the advances and many stocks are advancing. Likewise, the down moves are signaled by the product of declines and down volume.

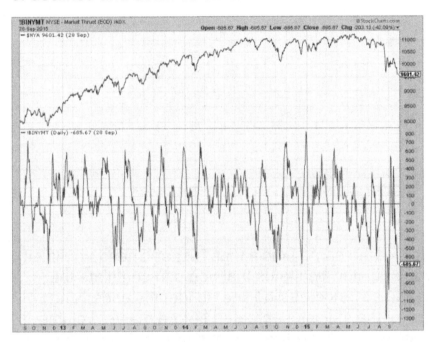

Chart 9-21

Chande further refines his concept to create a Thrust Oscillator. This is the Market Thrust concept put into a dimensionless ratio and shown in chart 9-22. He states that this may be considered a volume-weighted advance decline ratio variation.

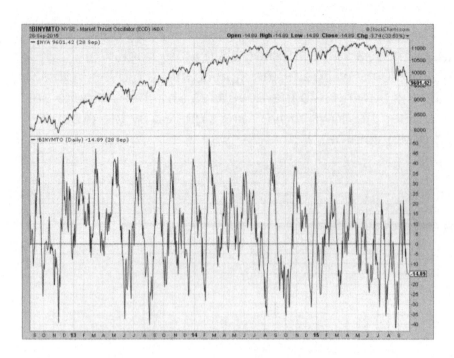

Chart 9-22

Author Comments: In the same article that Tushar Chande outlines his Market Thrust indicator, he states that you can cumulate the daily values (like the advance decline line) to identify underlying trends. Like many of the indicators created before market volume increased, the change to decimalization, and the addition of many interest sensitive stocks to the NY exchange, this summation index does not seem to add much to the picture. Any interpretation must be kept within a short period of data to remove the above mentioned affects. In a later article Tushar Chande shows many charts to give weight to his Market Thrust Summation indicator over the more common Advance Decline Line. The argument is convincing, as I have always liked a volume component to price based indicators. That is what I did with the McClellan Oscillator and Summation Index. Chart 9-23 shows the cumulative Market Thrust indicator.

Chart 9-23

In his book, "The New Technical Trader," Chande points out that the Arms Index is bounded between 0 and 1 for up days, but unbounded beyond 1 on down days. This, he states, is why smoothing the Arms Index makes it difficult to use. If you think about it, he has a good point. Weak market action can produce an Arms Index reading of 3, 4, and higher, and, in fact, has done so many times. However, the strongest breadth day cannot ever get to 0 on the Arms Index. In other words, the scaling is skewed. This is not so with his Thrust Oscillator, which helps identify strong up and down days equally.

Chande offers a couple of trading strategies in his book with Stanly Kroll. One is the take a 5-day simple moving average of his Thrust Oscillator and overlay a 5-day exponential average on it for trading signals. This is somewhat like Stochastics %K and its 3-day smoothing for %D. A longer term strategy would be to plot a 50-day simple moving average of the Thrust Oscillator and using its crossing of that smoothed value for signals.

Stuart Meibuhr, suggested in a later article to use Chande's Thrust Oscillator in a similar manner as Richard Arms used his Open Arms indicator. Additionally, Meibuhr said that Chande's Thrust Oscillator, when it went below -0.30, and smoothed by 21 days was very good at pointing out market bottoms. This was looking at the 21 day and 55-day average of the Thrust Oscillator. Chart 9-24 is a plot which shows the two averages and the difference between them. I took the concept a simple step further by smoothing the difference with a 5-day average. One can easily justify trading using the crossing of the zero line.

Chart 9-24

Formula: ((A * UV) – (D * DV)) / ((A * UV) + (D * DV))

StockCharts.com's Symbols: !BINYMT, !BINYMTO, !BINYMTO2155, !BINYMTS

References:

Chande, Tushar S. and Kroll, Stanley. The New Technical Trader. John Wiley & Sons, 1994.

Chande, Tushar S., "Market Thrust," Stocks & Commodities, Volume 10, August 1992, pp. 347-350.

Chande, Tushar S., "The Cumulative Market Thrust Line," Stocks & Commodities, Volume 11, December 1993, pp. 506-511.

Meibuhr, Stuart, "Oex and the Thrust Oscillator." Stocks & Commodities, March 1993, pp. 127-132.

Rusin, Jack, "An issue/volume-weighted long-term Arms index," Stocks & Commodities, Volume 9, October 1991, pp. 419-421.

Rusin, Jack, "The Internal Dynamics of Trin," Stocks & Commodities, Volume 10, January 1992, pp. 22-25.

McClellan Oscillator with Volume

Author/Creator: Greg Morris

Data components required: Advances (A), Declines (D), Up Volume (UV), Down Volume (DV).

Description: This is the McClellan Oscillator with a volume component calculated into the formula. Instead of using just advances (A), I have used advances times up volume (A * UV). Similarly, instead of using just declines (D), I have used (declines times down volume (D * DV). The formula is identical to the original McClellan Oscillator other than that.

Interpretation: The interpretation is exactly the same as that used for the McClellan Oscillator. This is somewhat of a combination of the McClellan Oscillator and the McClellan Oscillator that using volume – this one uses both the advance decline data enhanced with volume and is shown in chart 9-25.

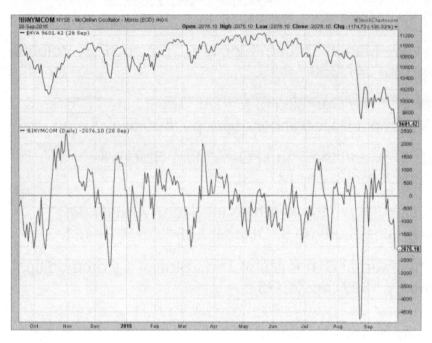

Chart 9-25

Author Comments: I have always preferred the influence of volume on most price-based indicators. This seems to generate some great signals for picking market bottoms, similar to the volume only oscillator that the McClellans use. However, this one seems to identify market tops quite well using the extreme oscillator readings. Whenever this indicator peaks and reverses, a top, even if just a trading decline, is occurring. I would imagine that smoothing this oscillator to dampen it and using an exponential smoothing overlay to give signals would work well. Chart 9-26 smooths the volume-based oscillator by a 10 period exponential average and also by a 3 period exponential average. You can see that the use of the zero-line crossing from below to above is good for buy signals and the crossing of the 10 period smooth (bolder line) below the 3 period smooth is good for sell signals.

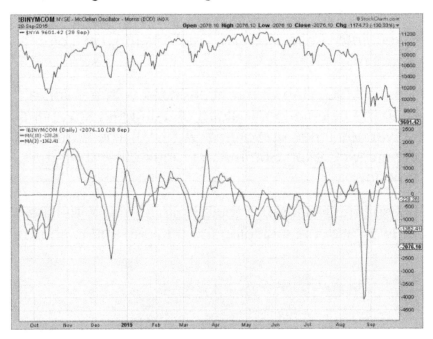

Chart 9-26

Formula: Previous Value + ((Today's 19 exp average of (A*UV – D*DV) – (Today's 39 exp average of (A*UV – D*DV))

StockCharts.com's Symbol: !BINYMCOM

References:

McClellan, Sherman and Marian. <u>Patterns for Profit</u>. Lakewood, WA : McClellan Financial Publications, Inc., 1976. This book was originally published by Trade Levels in 1970.

McClellan Family Interview, "It's All In the Family: Sherman, Marian, and Tom McClellan." <u>Stocks and Commodities</u>, Volume 12, June

1994, pp. 264-273.

McClellan Summation Index with Volume

Author/Creator: Greg Morris

Data components required: Advances (A), Declines (D), Up Volume (UV), Down Volume (DV).

Description: This is the McClellan Summation Index with a volume component added to the calculation. Instead of using just advances (A), I have used advances times up volume (A * UV). The formula is identical to the original McClellan Summation Index other than the added volume component.

Interpretation: This summation index should be interpreted just the same as the other two versions, including the original, and is shown in chart 9-27.

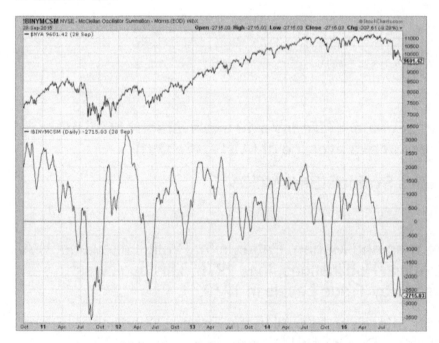

Chart 9-27

Author Comments: I have always preferred the influence of volume on price-based indicators. Like the original McClellan Summation Index, the direction and the level of this indicator are important.

Formula: This is the accumulation of the McClellan Oscillator that uses both advances and declines, and up volume and down volume.

StockCharts.com's Symbol: !BINYMCSM

References:

McClellan, Sherman and Marian. <u>Patterns for Profit</u>. Lakewood, WA: McClellan Financial Publications, Inc., 1976. This book was originally published by Trade Levels in 1970.

McClellan Family Interview, "It's All In the Family: Sherman, Marian, and Tom McClellan." <u>Stocks and Commodities</u>, Volume 12, June 1994, pp. 264-273.

Meyers Systems

Author/Creator: Dennis Meyers

Data components required: Advances (A), Declines (D), Up Volume (UV), Down Volume (DV) New Highs (H), New Lows (L).

Description: These are relative strength systems based up new highs, new lows, a market index, and combinations of up volume and down volume, or advances and declines.

Interpretation: Meyers, a Ph.D in applied mathematics in engineering wrote four articles in Stocks & Commodities magazine describing market systems using various combinations of breadth data. The market index used was the Dow Jones Industrial Average, however all his testing was done on the Standard and Poors 500 Index.

The Advance-Decline, New-High, New-Low Market System

Thus one used weekly data and looked at the advance decline line relative to the market along with the relative strength of the new highs and new lows. With these three indicators he identified thresholds for buying and selling.

A/D Volume, New-High, New-Low System

With this one, Meyers moved to using daily breadth data instead of weekly. This is similar to the first one, but instead of using the advances and declines, he used up volume and down volume. The volume was calculated in a ratio similar to what the McClellan's and the Carl Swenlin use, $(UV - DV) / (UV + DV)$. Like the first system he calculated the relative strength of the volume to the market in addition to using the same new high and new low indicators.

A Daily A-D New-High, New Low Market System

Almost a year after publishing his first system, this one uses the same breadth components, but for daily data. Meyers also smoothed some of the raw data in this system.

The Turbo A/D, NH, NL Market System

Meyers came out with this system after discovering a problem he denoted as a lockout condition. This is common in internally normalized equations as strong moves will lock a normalized indicator at its extremes with very little fluctuation.

Author Comments: Everyone who has an interest in designing breadth-based systems needs to read the four articles by Dennis Meyers. He did not uncover anything earth shattering, but his approach to the full understanding of the markets and these components is good. Meyers addresses the downfalls of blind optimization which would serve as a good primer for anyone undertaking the task of creating a system. The systems did not do well after the market top in 2000, which is not surprising since the data used to test the four trading systems did not contain a significant bear market. My thanks to Dennis for sharing the details on these systems with me.

References:

Meyers, Dennis, "The Advance Decline, New High, New Low Market System." Stocks & Commodities, Volume 14, February 1996, pp. 69-75.

Meyers, Dennis, "A/D Volume, New High, New Low System." Stocks & Commodities, Volume 14, July 1996, pp. 302-310.

Meyers, Dennis, "A Daily A-D New High New Low Market System." Stocks & Commodities, Volume 15, January 1997, pp. 11-19.

Meyers, Dennis, "The Turbo A/D, NH, NL Market System." Stocks & Commodities, Volume 15, August 1997, pp. 337-346.

Moving Balance Indicator

Creator: Humphrey E. D. Lloyd

Data required: Advances (A), Declines (D), Up Volume (UV), Down Volume (DV)

Description: Dr. Humphrey Lloyd developed the Moving Balance Indicator (MBI) in the mid-1970s. He wanted to find an indicator that would identify extremes in overbought and oversold areas. He came up with an indicator that contained three distinct components. The three components were: The A-D component, The Up Volume component, and the Trader's Index (TRIN) component.

The A-D component: This is the 10-day simple moving average of the advancing issues divided by the 10-day simple moving average of the declining issues. The difference was then multiplied by 10.

The Up Volume component: This is the 10-day simple moving average of Up Volume. This component was used to help identify really strong up moves. As time progressed and market volume increased, he changed this to moderate its affect on the MBI. This change was to make Up Volume a percentage of active volume (Up Volume plus Down Volume), and divide it by 3.

The Traders' Index component: This is the advances divided by the declines, then divided by the up volume divided by the down volume (see formula for better understanding). This is also known as the Arms Index. Since TRIN is an inverse indicator, Dr. Lloyd used a "look up" table to assign values for various levels of TRIN to reverse its value and give it a better component weight equal in magnitude to the other two components.

The Moving Balance Indicator is then completed by adding the three components together and dividing by 1.5. This was done to give it values in the 20 to 100 range so it could be used with other popular indicators such as Welles Wilder's Relative Strength Index (RSI).

Interpretation: Dr. Lloyd laid out several methods of determining buy and sell signals using actual MBI values. Volume on the various exchanges has increased so much since he developed this indicator that those actual numbers are no longer valid. However, the concept he used was good and is as follows:

Buy Signals

1. The MBI has to penetrate a particular level.

2. A valid break of a trendline which consists of at least 3 peaks.

3. A positive divergence between the MBI and the market.

He further stated that it was rare to find all three signals at once, but if you did, it was probably a very good trade. A good trade was also expected with any two signals.

Sell Signals:

This was much more difficult to define. He used a number of different methods but finally resorted to using MBI primarily for entry (buy) signals, and using MBI in combination with other indicators for sell signals. Chart 9-28 shows the Moving Balance Indicator using Dr. Lloyd's signals.

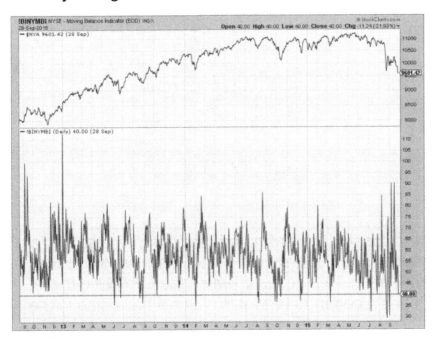

Chart 9-28

Joseph T. Stewart, in his book, "Dynamic Stock Option Trading," used MBI, but further smoothed it using a simple 5 day moving average of MBI. You can see in chart 9-29 that if you also include a longer moving average you can generate some good buy signals. In chart 9-29 a 17 day moving average was used. Notice that it is not a good system for trending markets, but only good for oscillating markets.

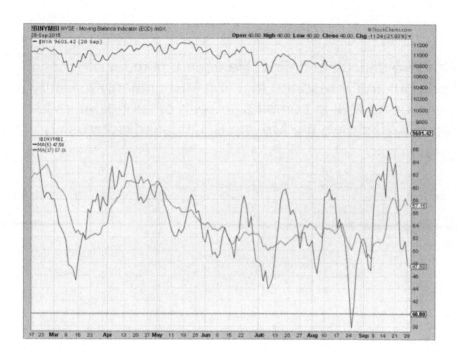

Chart 9-29

Author Comments: Joseph Stewart noted that the MBI also has a cyclic interpretation to it, so you should get in sync with that cycle. He states there are often 10-20 days in which the MBI will decline. Watch to see if it has it gotten to a level in which it has rising in the past.

When I first read about Dr. Lloyd's new indicator in the very early 1980s, I programmed it into my Apple II computer using N-Squared Computing's Market Analyzer software. I dealt with the TRIN look up table issue by inverting TRIN and including a multiplier of 10. This seemed to generate similar results as the original MBI. Like Dr. Lloyd, I found that using MBI for entry signals was better. Of course this goes with most indicators because of the nature of market bottoms being quick and decisive and market tops being long drawn out distributions that are much more difficult to define. I used to use a value of 57 for determining a buy signal on MBI. This was when

MBI crossed from below to above 57. However, in more recent times because of changing market conditions, a buy signal using an MBI value of 40 seems to work well. In chart 9-30, instead of showing where MBI was below 40, I drew vertical lines at good market bottoms so you could see that MBI was coincident or leading as an indicator of market bottoms. Humphrey has been a good friend and confidant for many years.

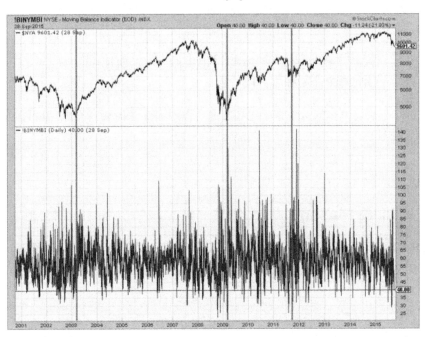

Chart 9-30

Joseph Stewart points out a phenomenon during bullish moves that one needs to be aware of. That is the act of the moving balance index to slip into an overbought situation during strong upward moves accompanied by heavy volume. His warning is to not be fooled by the action of the indicator and use other tools to help identify the top. This is sound advice from Stewart, but it applies to any oscillator during the type of upward thrust he is talking about.

Formula: (((((10dayMA A) / (10dayMA D)) * 10) + ((10dayMA (((UV) / (UV + DV))) / 3) + (1/((A / D) / (UV / DV)) * 10)) / 1.5

StockCharts.com's Symbol: !BINYMBI

References:

Lloyd, Humphrey E. D. <u>The Moving Balance System, A New Technique for Stock and Option Trading</u>. Brightwaters, N.Y., Windsor Books, 1976

Lloyd, Humphrey E. D., <u>The RSL Market Timing System</u>. Brightwaters, N.Y.: Windsor Books, 1991.

Stewart, Joseph T. <u>Dynamic Stock Options Trading</u>. New York: John Wiley and Sons, 1981.

Technical Index

Author/Creator: William Mason

Data components required: Advances (A), Declines (D), Up Volume (UV), Down Volume (DV), New Highs (H), New Lows (L), Total Issues (TI), Volume (V).

Description: The Technical Index is created by taking the net difference of the advances and declines, up and down volume, and new highs and new lows; expressing them as a percentage of their respective base, combining them to get a new value; and accumulating this value similar to the advance decline line. Mason said that the reason for using percentages is that no single parameter will dominate.

Interpretation: Like most accumulated breadth indicators that look at differences, the disparity between them and their base index is what is looked for. The diversions will usually happen near market tops and bottoms as shown in chart 9-31.

Chart 9-31

Author Comments: I really like the concept of composite indicators, and as you might expect, especially like it when the components are those of breadth. This indicator could be viewed as the all-encompassing breath line. Like most breadth indicators, look for divergence with the market. One can also use a rate of change of the Technical Index. Chart 9-32 is a 21-day rate of change of William Mason's Technical Index. Above the zero line is generally good for the market.

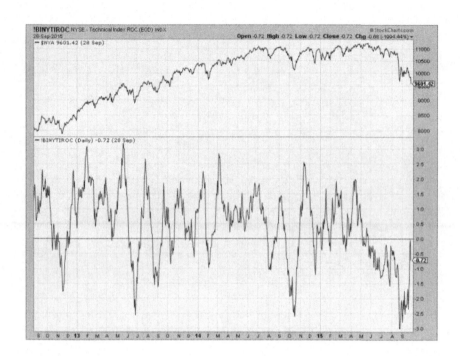

Chart 9-32

Formula: Previous Value + Today's (((A – D) / TI) + ((UV – DV) / V) + ((H – L) / TI))

StockCharts.com's Symbol: !BINYTI, !BINYTIROC

References:

Mason, William, "Technical Index Measures Market Breadth." <u>Stocks & Commodities</u>, Volume 7, January, 1989, pp. 9-12.

Titanic Syndrome

Author/Creator: Bill Omaha, with modifications by Dennis Myers

Data components required: Advances (A), Declines (D), Up Volume (UV), Down Volume (DV), New Highs (H), New Lows (L).

Description: Bill Omaha first wrote about his idea in Stocks & Commodities, November, 1988. He coined the name after looking at a series of market tops in the mid-1960s and stating that, like the Titanic, it was full speed ahead presumably unprotected against disaster.

Interpretation: When the Dow Jones Industrial Average hits a new high for the year, and in the time frame of seven days before or after that date, the number of new lows on the New York Stock Exchange exceeds the new highs. This excess of new lows is the iceberg that Omaha refers to.

Bill Omaha also adds that in addition to the new high, one could also use the signal whenever the Dow Jones Industrial Average rallies over 400 points. At the time of his writing, the Dow Industrials were at 2150, so a 400-point rally was about 18.5%. Incidentally, the Titanic Syndrome appeared on August 25, 1987; the Dow Industrials hit an all-time high at 2746.45, and six days later the new lows outnumbered the new highs on September 2, 1987. On October 21, 1987 (less than 3 months later), it was at 1951.76, at drop of almost 29%. Chart 9-3 shows the Titanic Syndrome in its original form.

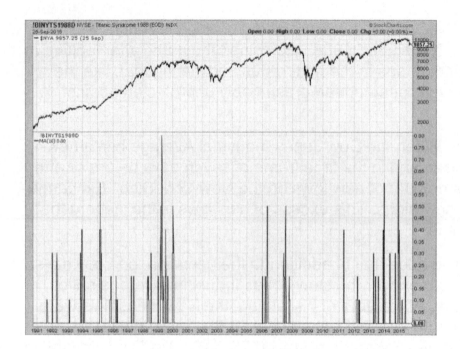

Chart 9-33

In 1991, Bill Omaha provided an upgraded version of his Titanic Syndrome in the Equis Monitor, a publication by Equis International, the creators of MetaStock.. Here he included many of the confirmation indications that he only mentioned three years before. This time he offered buy and sell criteria.

Sell Criteria

1. The DJIA makes a new 52-week high.

and

2. Seven days, either before or after that new high, the NYSE new lows are greater than the new highs.

and

3a. After the new high in the DJIA, the declining issues are greater than 1000 for two consecutive days and one of those days shows an

314

advance/decline ratio less than 0.25.

or

3b. After the new high in the DJIA, four out of seven days have the declines greater than 1000.

Buy Criteria:

1. A 10% drop in the DJIA from the new high.

and

2. After the 10% drop, the advances are greater than 1000 for two consecutive days and one of those days has the advance/decline ratio greater than 4.0.

and

3. After the 10% drop, the advance/decline ratio is greater than 9.0 (a) or less than 0.11 (b).

or

4. After the 10% drop, four out of seven days have advances greater than 1000.

A sell signal reverses to a buy signal if the yearly new high in the DJIA (the new high that generated the sell signal), is penetrated on the upside by 2%. Dennis Meyers, a frequent contributor to Stocks & Commodities magazine, further refined Omaha's Titanic Syndrome in 1995 by added additional components. Meyers removed the buy criteria that after a 10% drop in the DJIA, the advance/decline ratio is less than 0.11 (Buy Criteria 3(b)). Meyers also realized that the advance and decline issue using 1000 as a criterion had to be increased. Meyers applied what most have had to do lately, and that is to use a ratio of advances and declines – a dimensionless variable. He applied this logic throughout the Titanic

Syndrome. Finally, he added the one breadth component that was always missing, volume. He used an up volume down volume ratio of 9 to 1, just like Martin Zweig used in his book, Winning on Wall Street.

Author Comments: This is good stuff, someone has an original thought on an indicator and then modifies it publicly, only to be modified further by someone else later on. This is how good indicators are created. I also like indicators that use most of the major components of breadth. This one does. However, creating formulae to represent the full impact of the indicator was next to impossible since it was beyond the formula language I was using. The charts showing the Titanic Syndrome should be viewed as an attempt to reflect the concept.

StockCharts.com's Symbol: !BINYTS1988D

References:

Omaha, Bill, "Patterns that Detect Stock Market Reversals," Stocks & Commodities, Volume 6, November 1988, ppp.416-421.

Omaha, Bill, "How to Avoid Sinking with the Titanic," Equis Monitor, June/July 1991.

Meyers, Dennis, "Making the Titanic Fly." Stocks & Commodities, Volume 13, May 1995, 189-195.

Zweig, Martin E. Winning on Wall Street. New York: Warner Books, 1986.

Trend Exhaustion Index

Author/Creator: Clifford L. Creel

Data components required: Advances (A), New Highs (H).

Description: This is a 10-day exponential average of the New Highs divided by the Advances.

Interpretation: Creel states that during a bull market many stocks are making new highs and thus a large proportion of advancing stocks each day are also making new highs. This results in a high value for TEI. As the market tops, there is generally a shift to more conservative blue chip stocks. While the top plays out, with occasional rallies, the results will generate advances, but not new highs. This will cause the TEI to decline. The Trend Exhaustion Index is shown in chart 9-34.

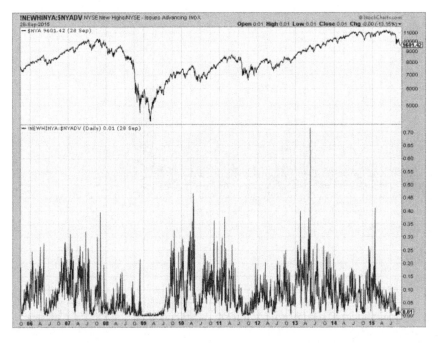

Chart 9-34

Author Comments: Using new highs and advances is an unusual twist to using breath as most breadth indicators stick with like pairs, such as advances and declines, new highs and new lows, etc. Chart 9-35 is a plot of new lows and declines using a similar formula as the trend exhaustion index. A good name might be trend explosion index. It seems, visually, that whenever this indicator rises above 0.15 a market bottom has been put into place. If anything, the Trend Exhaustion Index and Trend Explosion Index will assist you in warning of a change in market direction.

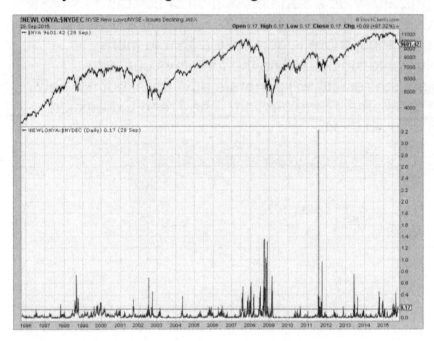

Chart 9-35

Formula: (H / A)

References:

Creel, Clifford L., "Trend Exhaustion Index." <u>Stocks & Commodities</u>, Volume 9, January, 1991, pp. 9-11.

CH 10 - The McClellan Indicators

This chapter consists of contributions from Sherman McClellan, Tom McClellan, and James Miekka. It is the author's opinion that the McClellan indicators, and in particular, the McClellan Summation Index, is the single best breadth indicator available. If you had to pick just one, this would be it. This chapter elaborates on its creation, its concept, its modifications, and its usefulness. An important concept in using and understanding the McClellan Summation Index is also in chapter 12, Conclusions. Also, don't forget the traditional coverage of the McClellan Oscillator and Summation Index in chapters 4, 8, and 9.

Tom and Sherman McClellan use a lot of different breadth indicators in their analysis, including those discussed here, plus variations based on them. Tom McClellan shares a few of them with us:

One interesting permutation of using the A-D and Volume numbers is to draw comparisons about their strength. This is not easy to do, because they are in different units, but when we employ the Summation Index calculations to this data it makes such comparisons possible.

We use "ratio-adjusted" values for both the daily A-D and UV-DV breadth:

$$\frac{(A-D)}{(A+D)} \times 1000 \qquad \frac{(UV-DV)}{(UV+DV)} \times 1000$$

The reason for multiplying these ratios by 1000 is to put the result back up into the realm of real numbers. Dealing with tiny decimal numbers can be difficult mentally, and also makes for funny scaling on a chart.

We then calculate a Ratio-Adjusted McClellan Oscillator (RAMO) for each, and from those Oscillator values we can calculate Ratio-Adjusted Summation Indices (RASIs) for each. If the volume numbers are persistently stronger than the A-D numbers, then the Volume RASI will rise faster than the A-D RASI.

If we calculate the difference between the Volume RASI and the A-D RASI, we can get a sort of a relative strength line for the volume versus the A-D numbers, as shown in chart 10-1.

Chart 10-1

When this indicator is moving upward, it indicates that the Volume breadth numbers are acting stronger than the A-D breadth numbers, and those conditions are usually associated with rising prices. It can also show extreme conditions when it moves outside of the +/-500 area. Notice that during 2000, the NYSE Comp was making higher highs while this indicator was making a series of lower highs, indicating that the volume numbers were no longer showing as much strength as they had been, and foreshadowing the weakness in the general market that was to appear later on.

The RASI values for A-D and UV-DV have value on their own, in terms of being able to tell us when an up move has the strength to

320

continue into a longer term uptrend, or when it is instead a failing effort. Chart 10-2 shows the NYSE's RASI for A-D data.

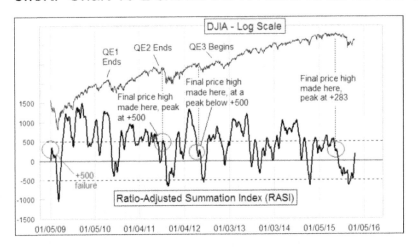

Chart 10-2

Notice that when the RASI goes above +500, it says that there is more upward movement yet to come. The higher it goes above +500, the stronger that message. The term we use for this is "escape velocity", a title borrowed from the field of rocketry where it is used to describe a rocket having enough speed built up to be able to escape a planet's gravitational field.

Getting above +500 does not mean that the market cannot undergo a normal periodic correction, and even take the RASI back down to an oversold reading. But going above +500 does say that we should expect a higher price high on the subsequent move. When an up move fails to exceed +500, that says there are problems with the market being able to find sufficient liquidity to continue. Notice in Chart 10-2 that the final highs for important uptrends tend to end with a RASI peak below +500 (the 2010 peak was a notable exception).

This idea of the RASI showing strength for a continuation of the up move is similar to the principle of the McClellan A-D Oscillator going up above the +150 level, as discussed in Chapter 4 under McClellan Oscillator.

The RASI+500 principle also works on the Volume RASI.

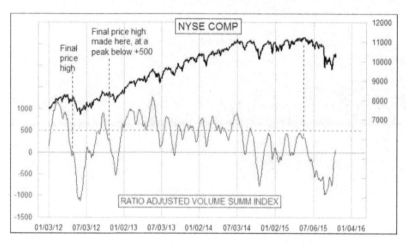

Chart 10-3

Most of the work we do continues to be on the NYSE A-D and UV-DV data. We have looked at some other permutations, and some of them have value. Back in 1968, when Sherman and Marian McClellan first started doing the work that led to the McClellan Oscillator and Summation Index, there were only two exchanges: the NYSE and the American Stock Exchange (AMEX). For a while, we kept breadth data on the AMEX, but its role as a rather distinct exchange for certain unusual types of listings has made that endeavor less useful. The AMEX was eventually bought by the Intercontinental Exchange (ICE) the same parent company of the NYSE, and the AMEX is now known as NYSE MKT.

The Nasdaq market was created in 1971 as the "National Association of Securities Dealers Automated Quotation (NASDAQ) system, and later turned that acronym into its name. Breadth data did not become available until 1972. Because the listing standards on the Nasdaq have generally been softer than for companies wanting to list on the NYSE, the Nasdaq A-D data have a strong downward bias. As a trivia question, we like to ask other technical analysts, "When was the last time that the Nasdaq A-D Line made a new all-time high?" This is a trick question, because it has never made a new all-time high. It started going down right from the beginning of the data in 1972, and has never made it back up that high.

Chart 10-4

So if you ever see a chart showing a supposed divergence between a higher Nasdaq Comp price high but a lower Nasdaq A-D Line high, you should understand that it is a fairly common occurrence, and it does not carry the same bearish meaning that such a divergence has for the NYSE's A-D Line.

Knowing that the overall Nasdaq A-D Line had a bearish bias, we wondered about the behavior of the leading stocks in that market, which are organized into the Nasdaq 100 Index (NDX). So back in 1999, we undertook to build our own database on the stocks which comprise that index, in order to see what the A-D and other data looked like. This was before a lot of data providers started to build their own versions of these subset breadth data.

One difficulty was that accurate data on index component changes was hard to come by. The Nasdaq publishes some records on that, but sadly did not go back as far as we would have liked. We could only construct what we considered to be a full and accurate listing of component changes and price & volume data back to 1993, and we have approximated values for years prior to then. Here in Chart 10-5 is what the Nasdaq 100 A-D Line looks like:

Chart 10-5

You can see that it does not have the same degree of a bearish bias as the overall Nasdaq A-D Line. There are some notable divergences, such as the weakness going into the 2000 top, and also throughout the 2003-07 bull market.

In the process of gathering that data, we also tabulated daily volume for the component stocks, which gave us the ability to create our own Up-Down Volume Line, shown in Chart 10-6.

Chart 10-6

This is a case of the breadth data looking too much like the price data, and thereby taking away most of the value of the exercise. The whole point of looking at breadth data is to see the market in a different way from what the price indices are showing. So creating an UV-DV Line that looks almost identical to the Nasdaq 100 Index does not give us much opportunity to see a different message.

But that does not mean the NDX UV-DV data are without value. Since we have the overall Nasdaq market UV-DV data from the Wall Street Journal, and since we calculate the data for the stocks in the Nasdaq 100 Index, if we find the difference between them then we have a view on what's happening among the rest of the Nasdaq stocks which did not make the varsity team.

All we had to do was subtract the NDX volume statistics from the composite Nasdaq Up and Down Volume numbers. It turns out that these "ex-NDX" volume numbers are a lot less noisy, and they offer us good insights about the health of the small cap market.

Chart 10-7 shows this ex-NDX Nasdaq Volume Line compared to the Russell 2000 Index, which is a small-cap stock benchmark. The two correlate quite nicely with each other, at least most of the time.

The insights come from the rare instances when they diverge from one another. In these instances, it is usually this ex-NDX Nasdaq Volume Line which tells the true story about the strength of the market.

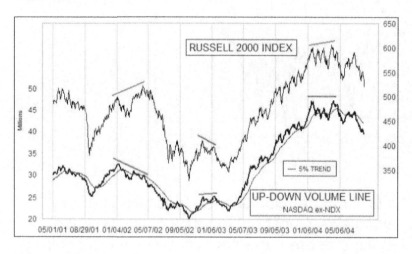

Chart 10-7

In cases when the Russell 2000 Index makes higher highs and this Volume Line fails to confirm, the result is a big decline in the Russell 2000. Prolonged strength in this Volume Line, like we saw in early 2003, tends to foretell continuing strength for the small cap market.

We later had to make one additional adjustment to these data, because the Nasdaq moved its big ETF, QQQ, back from trading on the AMEX to instead trade on the Nasdaq. It did not seem right to us to have the volume data for the QQQ contributing to Up or Down Volume, so we excised that data as well. Here in Chart 10-8 is a more current view:

Chart 10-8

When the Russell 2000 makes a penetration of its 5% Trend which is unconfirmed by this Up-Down Volume Line, it can be an important message of failure for that penetration.

Looking at the "Common Only" A-D Data

It has long been a criticism of the A-D data on the NYSE that the list of "stocks" is contaminated by so called "interest sensitive" issues which are traded like stocks on the NYSE. These include preferred stocks, rights, warrants, bond-related closed end funds (CEFs), and other specialty items which one would not categorize as common stocks.

Interestingly, this same criticism has been around for 50+ years. Back in the 1960s, when analysts were first starting to use the A-D data in earnest, critics claimed that it was contaminated by interest sensitive stocks of utilities and insurance companies.

We have been keeping data on common stocks in a couple of different ways, and we find that this argument is largely without merit.

From the 1980s to the early 2000s, the NYSE published A-D data on what it called "common only" stocks. But the NYSE's methodology was not what it should have been; they just filtered for issues whose symbols had 3 letters or less. That got rid of the preferred stocks and other issues with symbol suffixes, but still allowed in the bond CEFs.

Starting on Feb. 9, 2005, the NYSE changed its procedures for tabulating the "common only" stocks, eliminating what they called "derivatives", including the bond CEFs. The NYSE also reformulated the NYSE Composite Index ($NYA) to include only real common stocks, and furthermore to only include one class of common stock for each listed company. So if a company had "B" or "C" shares, it did not get additional votes.

It was around that same time we decided to start our own project to more thoroughly examine this hypothesis that the bond CEFs were contaminating the overall data, and that the proper data to watch were the "common only". Using data on all NYSE-listed issues, we built our own database of A-D and UV-DV data, and broken down into several subcategories including common only, bond CEFs, ETFs (which the NYSE moved to NYSE MKT in late 2007), preferred stocks, foreign stocks, and "specialty" which is where were put all of the other odds and ends.

Keeping up with this effort has become more difficult, because the NYSE no longer publishes its list of the components of the NYSE Composite Index (which are the common only stocks). So we have been left to make our own decisions when new issues join the NYSE list to determine what category they should be in.

We understand that the staff at StockCharts.com has undertaken a similar effort to derive the common only A-D data. You can see those in the symbol catalog; just search on the word _common_.

One of the first findings from our study is that we do not see as many of the same types of classic A-D Line divergences versus prices when looking at the Common Only A-D Line. Here in Chart 10-9 is an example of what we mean:

Chart 10-9

By contrast, the Bond CEF A-D Line may actually be a better indication of liquidity conditions than anything else. Chart 10-10 below takes a look at the 2007 stock market top, which saw the SP500 finally make its highest top in October 2007. The Common Only A-D Line and the composite (all issues) A-D Line had seen a peak in June 2007, so there was a classic A-D Line divergence by the time the final price high arrived.

But the Bond CEF A-D Line had peaked even earlier, back in May 2007, giving even more advanced warning about the drying up of the liquidity pool. And as the final price high was being made in October 2007, once again the Bond CEF A-D Line was looking weaker than the Common Only version.

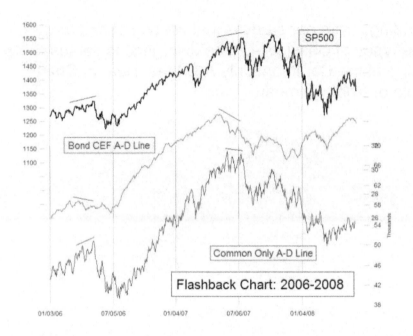

Chart 10-10

Turning to a more recent example, Chart 10-11 shows a comparison just between the SP500 and the Bond CEF A-D Line for 2014-15.

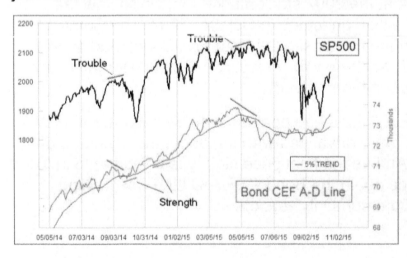

Chart 10-11

When there is a disagreement between the Bond CEF A-D Line and the SP500, it is worth paying attention to the message from the Bond CEF A-D Line. The point to take from this is that the hypothesis about bond CEFs contaminating the data is off base. If anything, they are making the overall A-D data better for their inclusion, as strange as that may be to believe.

Thoughts on the Continuing Validity of the A-D Line

While the criticisms over the supposed "contamination" of the A-D will no doubt continue forever (because some people cannot handle the truth), we would urge everyone to take it as it is and learn to benefit from its messages. What many technicians, and most fundamentalists, do not understand is that the A-D Line is still the best indication of liquidity out there. Every issue that gets a vote in the daily A-D statistics represents a war between the bulls and the bears, and so reviewing the overall battlefield statistics gives us a useful review of how the war is going.

This liquidity concept is often lost on analysts who focus on earnings projections, dividend yields, book value, and other fundamental factors. In truth, there are only two fundamental factors which matter when it comes to the subject of where the overall market is going: (1) How much money is there? and (2) How willing is that money to be invested in stocks? The first of these explains why liquidity matters, and the second explains why sentiment indicators matter, since investors who are already bullish cannot get more bullish.

To see how the A-D Line matters in the real world, take a look at the comparison in chart 10-12. The ratio-adjusted NYSE A-D Line is on top, and the bottom line shows after-tax corporate profits as a percentage of GDP. What this illustrates is that when liquidity is strong, thereby driving up the A-D Line, it also helps companies achieve relatively greater profitability. Perhaps even more important, we can see what the A-D data are doing every day in real time, whereas we have to wait for the corporate profits and GDP data to get tabulated and reported, and then later to get revised. This is why it is important for even the fundamentalists to follow what the A-D Line is doing.

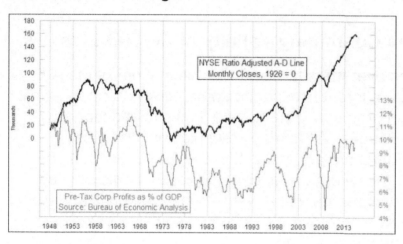

Chart 10-12

The Relationship between an Exponential Oscillator and its Summation Index

by James R. Miekka and Richard G. Miekka

The McClellan Oscillator and Summation Index

The purpose of this article is to show that there is a simple, direct mathematical relationship between the McClellan Oscillator and its Summation Index, and to derive that mathematical relationship. The second part shows the relationship using a simpler algebraic step-by-step format.

The McClellan Oscillator (MCO) and its Summation Index (MCOSI) are standard tools of technical analysis of stocks and stock indexes, which are included in most technical analysis computer programs and listings of tools/indicators.

The MCO is the difference between two exponential moving averages (EMAs) or "trends" of the (daily) difference between the number of advancing and the number of declining issues on one of the stock indexes (NYSE, NASDAQ, etc.), but most commonly the NYSE. The two EMAs are called the fast and slow trends or indexes. Specifically, Sherman and Marian McClellan have chosen the 19-day (10%) EMA minus the 39-day (5%) EMA as the value of MCO. The MCOSI is the sum of all consecutive values of the MCO, starting (by convention) at a value of +1000 when both exponential moving averages are zero.

Early in 1991 James Miekka determined that the MCOSI could be calculated directly from the fast and slow trends of the MCO. Prior to that time, it was generally assumed that the Summation Index was dependent only on the history of the Oscillator and was not mathematically related to the then-current values of the fast (10%) and slow (5%) trends. James disclosed his equation to Sherman McClellan shortly after its derivation, and it was soon published in Technical Analysis of Stock and Commodities[1] as part of an interview between the magazine and Sherman McClellan, and dubbed the "Miekka method" for calculating MCOSI. Since then, the formula has been widely used, but its mathematical derivation has never been published. This article will show how the relationship between the MCO and the MCOSI was derived.

Let us begin with a review of the mathematical expressions for the McClellan Oscillator, its fast and slow trends, and its Summation Index.

The MCO is given by the expression:

Equation 1: $MCO_n = F_n - S_n$

Where F is the faster, or 10% trend (EMA), S is the slower, or 5% trend (EMA), and the subscript n denotes the nth value of MCO and its trends. In turn, F and S are defined by the equations:

Equation 2: $F_n = F_{n-1}(0.9) + \Delta_n(0.1)$, and

Equation 3: $S_n = S_{n-1}(0.95) + \Delta_n(0.05)$,

Where Δ_n is the new (current) value of daily advancing minus declining issues on the New York Stock Exchange, and the subscript n-1 denotes the preceding (yesterday's) value of S or F.

Note that Δ can be positive or negative, so S, F, and MCO can also be positive or negative.

The McClellan Oscillator Summation Index (MCOSI), which is the sum of all oscillator values beginning at some convenient starting point or zero point, can be expressed mathematically as:

Equation 4:

$$MCOSI_n = \sum_{i=0}^{n} MCO_i$$

where the subscript i refers to the ith value of the Oscillator.

In more generalized terms let us express the multiplier (0.1) for the faster trend by the letter P, and the multiplier (0.05) for the slower trend as Q, because we may not always want to use 0.1 and 0.05 as the multipliers. Thus:

Equation 2a: $F_n = F_{n-1}(1-P) + \Delta_n(P)$, and

Equation 3a: $S_n = S_{n-1}(1-Q) + \Delta_n(Q)$,

The 10% trend of the MCO is nominally a 19-day EMA and the 5% trend is nominally a 39-day EMA, where the number of days in each trend is given by the formula

Equation 5: $P = 2/(D_P+1)$, and in the case of the McClellan Oscillator, $P = 2/(19+1) = 0.1$

Equation 5a: $Q = 2/(D_Q+1)$, and in the case of the McClellan Oscillator, $Q = 2/(39+1) = 0.05$

Where D_P and D_Q are the nominal durations (days) of the faster and slower trends using the multipliers P and Q. About 86.5% of the values of F and S are contributed by their changes in the last D_P and D_Q days, respectively.

Let us now examine a short sequence of days with ☐ chosen in such a way that we can observe the relationships among F, S, MCO, and MCOSI, and in particular the relationship between MCO and MCOSI.

Although the sequence chosen is short, and the values of ☐ were chosen to illustrate certain factors, the same behavior would be observed for very long sequences of ☐ .

From the data, one can make the following observations;

1.   If MCOSI is positive and MCO is 0 then if the next ☐ is 0, MCO becomes negative (days 7 & 8).

2.   If MCOSI is negative and MCO is 0, then if the next ☐ is 0, MCO becomes positive (days 15 & 16).

3.   If one repeatedly enters the value of 0 for ☐ , one returns to the starting values for F, S, MCO, and MCOSI, which in our case are all equal to zero (days 153 & 154).

Thus, one can see that some direct mathematical relationship must exist between MCO and MCOSI, since MCOSI can never drift off into values unrelated to the then-current F, S, and MCO.

The Neutral Point Concept

We observed that if MCO = 0, then if the next □ = 0, MCO rises if MCOSI is negative, and falls if MCOSI is positive. What value would MCO need to have in order that it would not change if □ = 0? Let us calculate, in general, how to arrive at such a value for MCO, starting from any random MCO. To do this we will determine the □ required to move the MCO to a new value from which, if the following □ = 0, then MCO will be unchanged. Let us call this the "neutral point" and use the subscript "NP" to designate the mathematical functions that relate to the neutral point. The following equation must be satisfied in order to arrive at the neutral point:

Equation 6:

MCO_{NP}= [F (1- P) + □ $_{NP}$ P] – [S (1-Q) + □ $_{NP}$ Q] = {[F (1- P) + □ $_{NP}$ P] (1- P) + □ P}–{[S (1-Q) + □ $_{NP}$ Q] (1- Q) + □ Q}

Where □ on the right hand side of the equation is zero, so the equation simplifies to:

MCO_{NP}= [F (1- P) + □ $_{NP}$ P] – [S (1-Q) + □ $_{NP}$ Q] = {[F (1- P) + □ $_{NP}$ P] (1- P)} –{[S (1-Q) + □ $_{NP}$ Q] (1- Q)}

Where: F and S are values of the fast and slow EMA trends at any random point, □ $_{NP}$ is the □ required to move MCO to its neutral point, and MCO_{NP} is the "neutral point" value of the MCO.

Solving for □ $_{NP}$ in terms of F, S, P and Q yields the equation:

Equation 7:   □ $_{NP}$ = FP(1- P) - SQ(1-Q)

$$(Q^2 - P^2)$$

Substituting equation 7 into (the right hand side of) equation 6 yields the following formula for MCO_{NP}:

Equation 8: $Osc_{NP} = MCO_{NP} = F(1-P) - S(1-Q) + \underline{(FP^2 - FPQ)(1-P) - (SQ^2 - SPQ)(1-Q)}$

$$(Q^2 - P^2)$$

In the case of the standard MCO where $P = 0.10$ and $Q = 0.05$, this equation reduces to:

Equation 9: $MCO_{NP} = \dfrac{9F - 19S}{30}$

While routinely calculating MCO, MCOSI, and MCO_{NP}, one of us (James) noted that a), when MCOSI was positive, MCO_{NP} was negative, b), when MCOSI was negative, MCO_{NP} was positive, and when MCOSI was zero (or + 1000 in the case of the standard MCOSI), MCO_{NP} was also zero, leading to the suggestion that an inverse mathematical relation existed between MCOSI and MCO_{NP}.

Finally, if one multiplies MCO_{NP} by -30, one gets exactly MCOSI. The formula for the MCOSI using the conventional values of $X_F = 0.10$ and $X_S = 0.05$ thus becomes:

Equation 10: $MCOSI = (-30)\dfrac{(9F-19S)}{30} = 19S - 9F$

And, if one adjusts for the fact that, by convention, the published MCOSI is normally increased by a constant of 1000:

Equation 10a: MCOSI = 1000 + 19S – 9F, or

Equation 10b: MCOSI = 1000 + MCO + 20S – 10F

Equations 10a and 10b are the commonly published forms of the "Miekka method" for calculating the McClellan Summation Index.

Acknowledgement: The authors wish to thank Suzanne Schulz of Greely Colorado, Richard A. Fotland of Franklin, MA, and James and Edward Hanson of Maynard, MA for their helpful suggestions in clarifying the text and nomenclature and correcting some wrongly transposed equations.

A Step-by-Step Process

The derivation of the mathematical relationship between MCO and MCOSI was straightforward, but contained rather complex algebraic formulas. Here is another way of calculating the neutral point Oscillator and Summation Index consists of a six step process as follows:

Step 1: Add the McClellan Oscillator to its 10% trend (=MCO + 10%)

Step 2: Divide by 3 (= [MCO + 10%]/3)

Step 3: Subtract above from MCO (= MCO - [MCO + 10%]/3)

Step 4: Multiply by -30 (= -30*{MCO - [MCO + 10%]/3})

Step 5: Add 1000 (= 1000 -30*{MCO - [MCO + 10%]/3})

Step 6: Add MCO (MCOSI = 1000 + MCO -30*{MCO - [MCO + 10%]/3} = 1000 + 19* (5%) -9* (10%)

The logic of the above is as follows:

Step 1: Calculate the value advances minus declines (A-D) that would keep the Oscillator unchanged (i.e., that would make tomorrow's Oscillator the same as today's Oscillator):

$$(A-D)nc = 2*(10\%) - (5\%) = MCO + (10\%)$$

Where (A-D)nc is the "no change" value of advances minus declines needed to keep the Oscillator unchanged, and (10%) and (5%) are the ten percent and five percent trends, respectively.

Step 2: If we happen to be at MCOSI = +1000, and if the MCO is at, say, +100, then to keep it unchanged, A-D would have to be +300. Or, if the Oscillator were at +150, then A-D would have to be +450 to keep MCO unchanged. In each case, the Oscillator value would be given by the formula:

$$MCO\ nc@neut. = (A-D)nc/3.$$

Where MCO nc@neut is the value MCO would have if MCOSI were at its neutral or zero point of +1000

So, for the moment, let's pretend that the Summation Index is at +1000. If this is true, then MCOnc is given by the formula above.

Step 2: Divide (A-D)nc by 3, or

$$MCO\ nc@neut = (A-D)nc/3 = (MCO + 10\%)/3$$

Step 3: But since MCOSI is not really at +1000, we must make an adjustment to find MCOnc for our real-world case. This is accomplished by subtracting MCOnc@neut from The current value for MCO:

Step 3 Subtract MCOnc@neut from MCO, or

$$MCOnp = MCO - (MCO + 10\%)/3$$

Where MCOnp is the value MCO that will be unchanged if the next (A-D) is zero.

Step 4: When routinely calculating the daily values of MCOnp and MCOSI, James noted that there is an inverse relationship between the two, and that the factor is -30.

Step 4: Multiply MCOnp by -30

Step 5: By convention, we add 1000 to the "natural" value of the Summation Index.

Step 5: Add 1000

Step 6: The number obtained in step 5 turns out to be yesterday's MCOSI, so we need to add MCO to get today's MCOSI.

Step 6: add MCO

The final formula becomes:

$$MCOSI = 1000 + MCO -30*[MCO - (MCO + 10\%)/3]$$
$$= 1000 + MCO -30(MCO) + 10(MCO) + 10(10\%)$$
$$= 1000 -19(MCO) +10(10\%)$$
$$= 1000 - 19(10\%) + 19(5\%) + 10 (10\%)$$
$$= 1000 + 19(5\%) - 9(10\%)$$

The final formula is the same as the formula obtained using alternate algebra earlier in this article.

Jim Miekka actually uses the first MCOSI formula in the above series in his own calculations of the Summation Index, which he does in his head.

Of course, the real value of the Miekka formula is that when it is used, the MCOSI becomes self-correcting, so any errors is adding up all the values of MCO are eliminated. A drift in MCOSI will almost always occur in the "add-up" method, even if there are no mistakes in the MCO values, unless the values contain a very large number of significant figures.

The second part of the MCOSI derivation explains the relation between any oscillator that is the difference between two exponential moving averages and its summation index. The summation index (SI) can be calculated from the following formula:

$$SI = C + Osc + S/Q - F/P$$

Where: SI is the summation index, C is an arbitrary constant, if used, Osc is the Oscillator, calculated as the difference between a faster trend (F) and a slower trend (S), P is the multiplying factor for the fast trend, calculated as $2/(N + 1)$, where N is the number of units (typically days) on which the fast trend is based. In the case of the McClellan Oscillator, $P = 2/(19+1) = 0.1$

Q is the multiplying factor for the slow trend, calculated as $2/(N + 1)$, where N is the number of units (typically days) on which the slow trend is based. In the case of the McClellan Oscillator, $Q = 2/(39+1) = 0.05$.

McClellan Summation Index Buy Signal

by James R. Miekka

The McClellan Summation Index Buy Signal occurs when the normalized NYSE McClellan Summation Index (MCOSI) rises above +1500. The signal remains in effect until the normalized Summation Index drops below +1500. To normalize the MCOSI, the 5% and 10% components of the McClellan Oscillator (MCO) are calculated from "normalized" values for advances minus declines, $(A-D)_{norm}$, calculated by the formula: $(A-D)_{norm} = (A-D)* (2000/ \text{ current total issues traded})$. The reason for normalizing to 2000 total issues is historical. The original work was done when there were, in fact, about 2000 issues traded on the NYSE each day. The purpose of the normalization is to compensate for the increasing number of issues traded on the NYSE over time.   For instance, if the total number of issues traded is at 3500 per day, the regular (not normalized) MCOSI will be at about +1875 when the normalized MCOSI is at +1500.

The higher the Summation Index, the greater the tendency for the market to rise. This can be defined mathematically by noting that for every 1000 point increase in the Summation Index, it takes 100 additional advances minus declines to keep the Summation Index at that level (*i.e.*, to keep the McClellan Oscillator at zero). By convention, the Summation Index is classified as neutral at +1000. Thus, at a MCOSI of +2000, there must be 100 more advances than declines each day, or 500 per week, to keep MCOSI constant. Using the estimate of Michael Burke, of Investors Intelligence, that there are 600 NYSE advances minus declines for each 1% increase in the market, this would equate to the market changes vs. MCOSI values tabulated below in Table 10-2.

Table 10-2

McClellan Summation Index (MCOSI) level	Number of daily Advances minus Declines needed to keep MCO at zero	% Change per week of stock market if MCOSI stays constant (MCO averages zero)
+5000	+400	+3.33
+4000	+300	+2.50
+3000	+200	+1.67
+2000	+100	+0.83
+1000	0	+0.00
+0	-100	-0.83
-1000	-200	-1.67
-2000	-300	-2.50
-3000	-400	-3.33

If MCOSI is high and steady, but the market is falling (or rising at a rate less than the listed values), this means that there is a positive divergence between the A-D breadth and the market, and indicates that higher prices are to come. Conversely, if the market is rising faster than the tabulated values would indicate, this is a sign of negative divergence and the market is likely to turn down, since the divergence acts as a leading indicator.

The Miekka Formula, which gives the mathematical relation between the MCOSI and the components of the MCO, arose from a study to determine the number of advances minus declines needed to hold the MCO constant at different Summation Index levels.

Information about the McClellans and James R. Miekka

McClellan Financial Publications, Inc.

P.O. Box 39779

Lakewood, WA 98496-3779

(253) 581-4889

(253) 581-8194 fax

tom@mcoscillator.com

www.mcoscillator.com

The McClellan Market Report

Our twice monthly newsletter. The cost is $195.00 per year. Every issue contains our unique analysis of market trends as described by the large set of technical tools we follow, including the McClellan Oscillator and Summation Index. We also provide our proprietary Timing Model dates of forecasted future turning points for stocks, bonds, and gold. Our Bottom Line appears on the first page of every issue and sums up our expectations for the market during the weeks that follow.

http://www.mcoscillator.com/user/041015.pdf The Daily Edition

Market followers who need access to more frequent information about market movements enjoy reading our Daily Edition. It is published every day the market trades, and goes out in the evening via PDF attachment to an email. Each Edition contains a large table of data including McClellan Oscillator calculations for the NYSE and Nasdaq, and even for the 100 stocks in the Nasdaq 100 Index. We also provide calculations of Price Oscillators and important support/resistance levels for the major stock market averages, gold, and T-Bonds. Active mutual fund traders appreciate our "Current Opinions" sections. We give our current take, either bullish, bearish, or neutral on stocks, bonds, and gold.

Chart In Focus

A free weekly article on a single topic, designed to help everyone learn more about technical analysis and about the tools we use.

James R. Miekka

Jim's Father, Richard provided me with Jim's Obituary. I spoke with Jim on the phone many times; what a tragic loss. He shared his work with me without concern.

James Richard (Jim) Miekka who was blind, was walking on the side of a road on the morning of August 19, 2014 with his guide dog, Zoey, when he was struck by an SUV. He was pronounced dead at the scene. So ended a fascinating career that spanned 54 years and encompassed periods of both glory and tragedy.

James was born in Massachusetts on July 21, 1960. He had a rather ordinary childhood that was punctuated with glimpses of special abilities. He started to talk at 8 months, and began to read when he was three. At the age of 8, his teacher accused him of cheating on an arithmetic exam because he wrote down the answers without showing any calculations. When his mother was called it to discuss his wayward behavior, mom asked that he be brought into the conference room to demonstrate his ability to do the calculations mentally. The interrogators were asked to pick any two 3-digit numbers and to write them on a blackboard. Jim stood at the blackboard and correctly wrote the answer without making any other notations, absolving himself of the cheating accusation.

Jim became intensely focused on any subject that caught his fancy. After the usual absorptions with dinosaurs, plants (especially cactus plants), and planets, he became enthralled with bicycles, and eventually made two transcontinental round trips from Massachusetts to California by bicycle when he was 16, then again when 20. He was also very proud of getting a speeding ticket (vehicle model Schwinn) for going 55 MPH drafting behind a truck.

In college, Jim earned a BS degree in Environmental Science with a minor in education and then became employed as a high school science and math teacher in Brawley, California. James lost his eyesight in 1986 following an explosion from a chemical experiment. He and his brother were trying to find a better way to extract minerals from rock, but the chemicals caused an explosion that damaged his hands and eyes. He ultimately was blinded by complications during an ensuing eye operation. "The last thing I saw was the eye chart going into surgery," he told WSJ journalist Steven Russolillo in 2010.

As he recuperated, James began listening to television shows that focused on investing. He became interested in technical analysis while following Kennedy Gammage on FNN. He then started actively trading stocks, and began writing a financial newsletter under contract from a local financial adviser. He met and became a close correspondent with Gammage who had derived some of his own indicators from the work of Sherman and Marian McClellan, creators of the McClellan Oscillator and its associated Summation Index. Eventually Jim began selling his newsletter, which he named the Sudbury Bull and Bear Report, to a number of interested investors and financial advisors. His greatest reason for the SBB report, though, was to help organize his own thoughts for personal investing. Since Jim was blind, he dictated the weekly updates to his father, Richard, who acted as secretary/editor for the newsletter.

The McClellan Oscillator (MCO) and its Summation Index (MCOSI), calculated from the daily stock advance and decline values (A-D) for the NYSE, were prominently featured in Jim's newsletter, and he spent time on his long walks with his guide dog thinking about ways to improve on the existing formulas. Eventually, after noting that the Oscillator changed by differing amounts for a given A-D value at high vs. low Summation Index values, Jim started calculating a "neutral point", which was the theoretical A-D value that would leave the Oscillator unchanged the following day. After some time he noted that the neutral point behaved inversely to the Summation Index, and found that the multiplier to convert between the neutral point and the Summation Index was -30.

It turns out that nobody had previously noted that there was a simple direct mathematical relationship between the MCO and the MCOSI, so when Jim published the formula, it was quickly tested and then adopted by virtually everybody using those indicators. It is now known as the Miekka Formula.

Jim made numerous modifications to the published mathematical indicator formulas of other technicians, some of which he published in his newsletter, and some of which he had not disclosed at the time of his death. He found that, on average, short term indicators remained valid for more years than did longer term indicators, so studied stringing together groups of short term indicators to create investment systems. Some of these worked well for a time, but most faded as stock market indexes and investment vehicles changed (evolved) over time. The necessity to create timely new predictors/indicators was an incentive for Jim to continue the newsletter. Because he could not see, Jim seldom used charts or graphs, but concentrated on formulas.

His most famous indicator was the Hindenburg Omen, a modified and restricted version of an indicator earlier published by Martin Zweig, then tweaked by Gerald Appel. The Omen (activated when NYSE daily new highs and new lows each exceed a threshold level and also meets several other criteria) has shown up within 60 days before every major stock market plunge, but has given so many false alarms that it is usually ignored by investors (but makes many nervous nonetheless). Jim sought ways to reduce the false alarms, such as restricting the types of stocks in the signal, but never found a magic fix.

Jim's favorite hobby was target shooting with pistols and rifles. As with everything he pursued, Jim immersed himself wholeheartedly in this leisure time activity, and developed the ability to score in the 90's (perfect score 100) shooting at standard NRA rifle targets from a distance of 100 yards, and occasionally at 200 yards. To accomplish this feat, Jim designed, with some sighted help, a custom apparatus that converted light into sound, and allowed him to "hear" his targets. Now this scope is being studied by Michigan State University as an aid for the blind. Jim with his shooting apparatus can be seen in action on You Tube by Googling "blind marksman."

Jim was active in charitable activities. He spent time as an unpaid tutor at a local high school, and he raised more than $3,000 for the Florida-based organization Blind Americans by walking 130 miles from its headquarters in Hernando to St. Petersburg. He used a global positioning system and Zoey, his guide dog, and completed the walk in a week and a half.

As an advocate for the blind he was vice president of Blind Americans in Hernando Florida, once walking 130 miles from his home in Homosassa to Saint Petersburg to raise funds for the organization. Channel 9 TV documented his effort. At other times Jim's activities have appeared in The Tampa Bay Times, The

TAMPA tribune, The Bangor Times, Der Spiegel in Germany, and BBC in England and on CNBC television, but his most important legacy came from the way he lived his day to day to day life replacing fear with faith and despair with hope with a message that others can do it too.

James is survived by his girlfriend Susan Tate, parents, Richard and Jeanette Miekka, a brother, Frederick Miekka, and a sister, Cynthia Bordas.

Printed in Great Britain
by Amazon

44088976R00203

*Fetishes, Florentine Girdles, and Other Explorations
Into the Sexual Imagination*